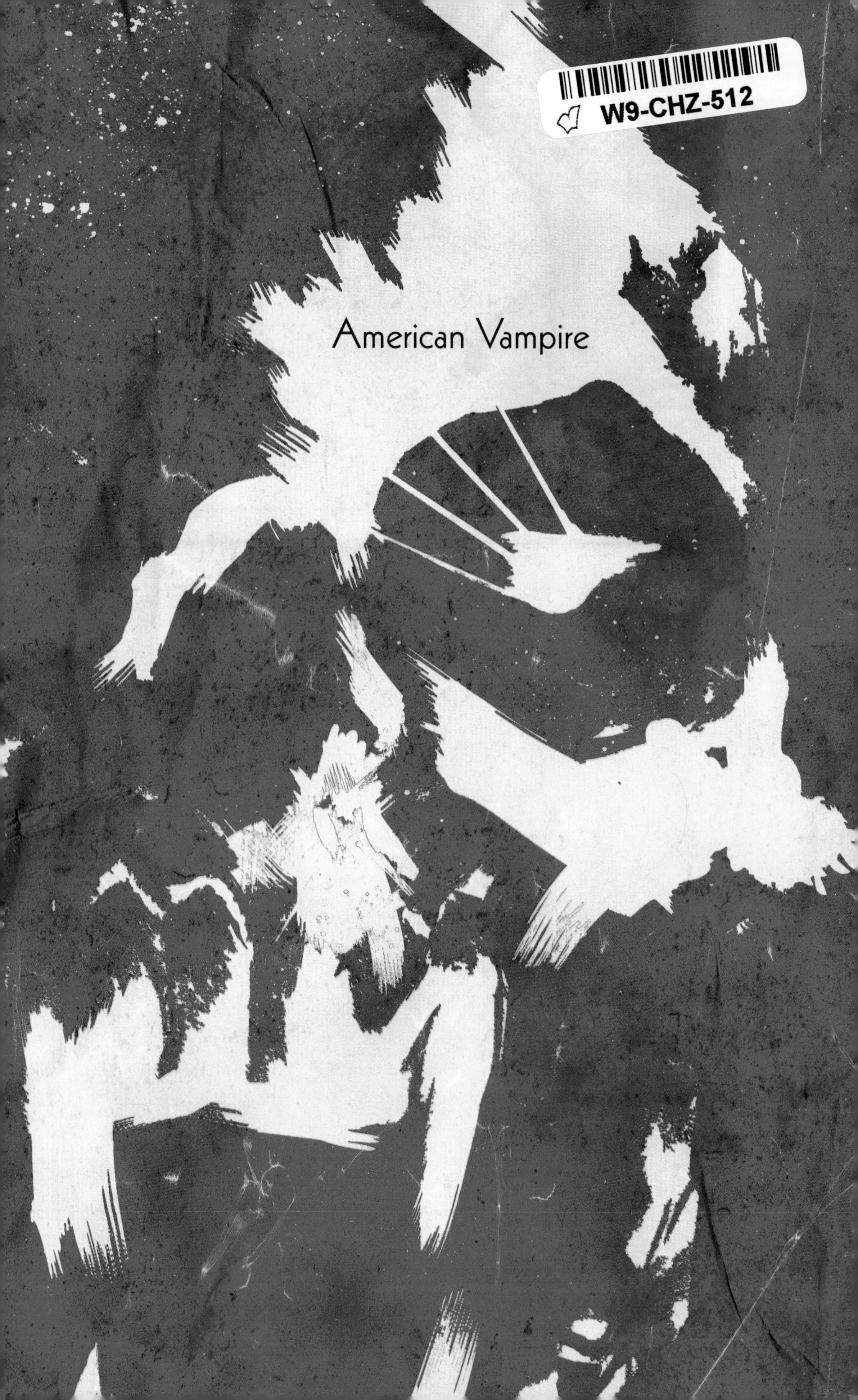
American Vampire

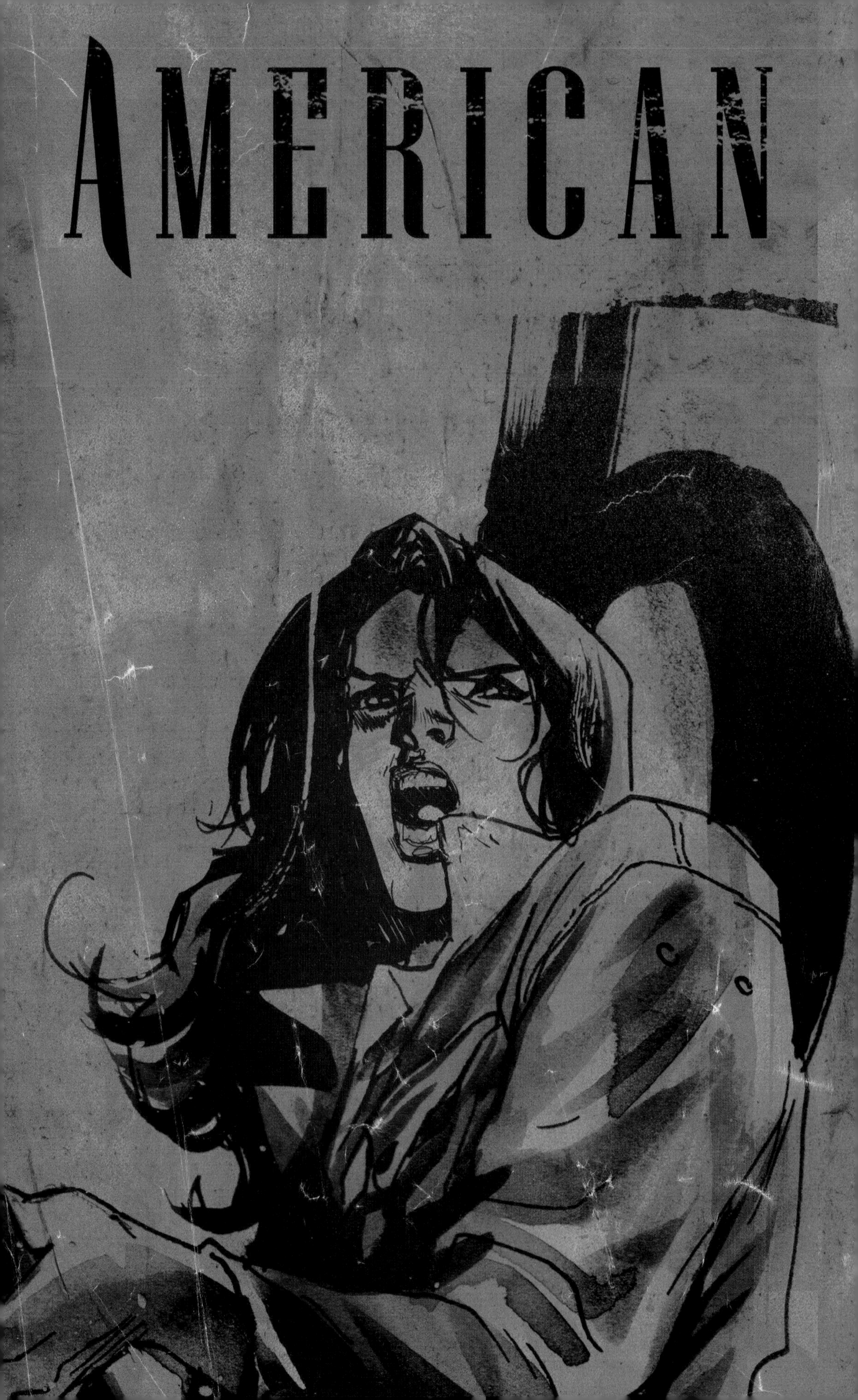
AMERICAN

VAMPIRE

VOLUME EIGHT

Scott Snyder Writer

Rafael Albuquerque Artist

Dave McCaig Colorist

Steve Wands Letterer

Rafael Albuquerque
Cover Artist

American Vampire created by
Scott Snyder and
Rafael Albuquerque

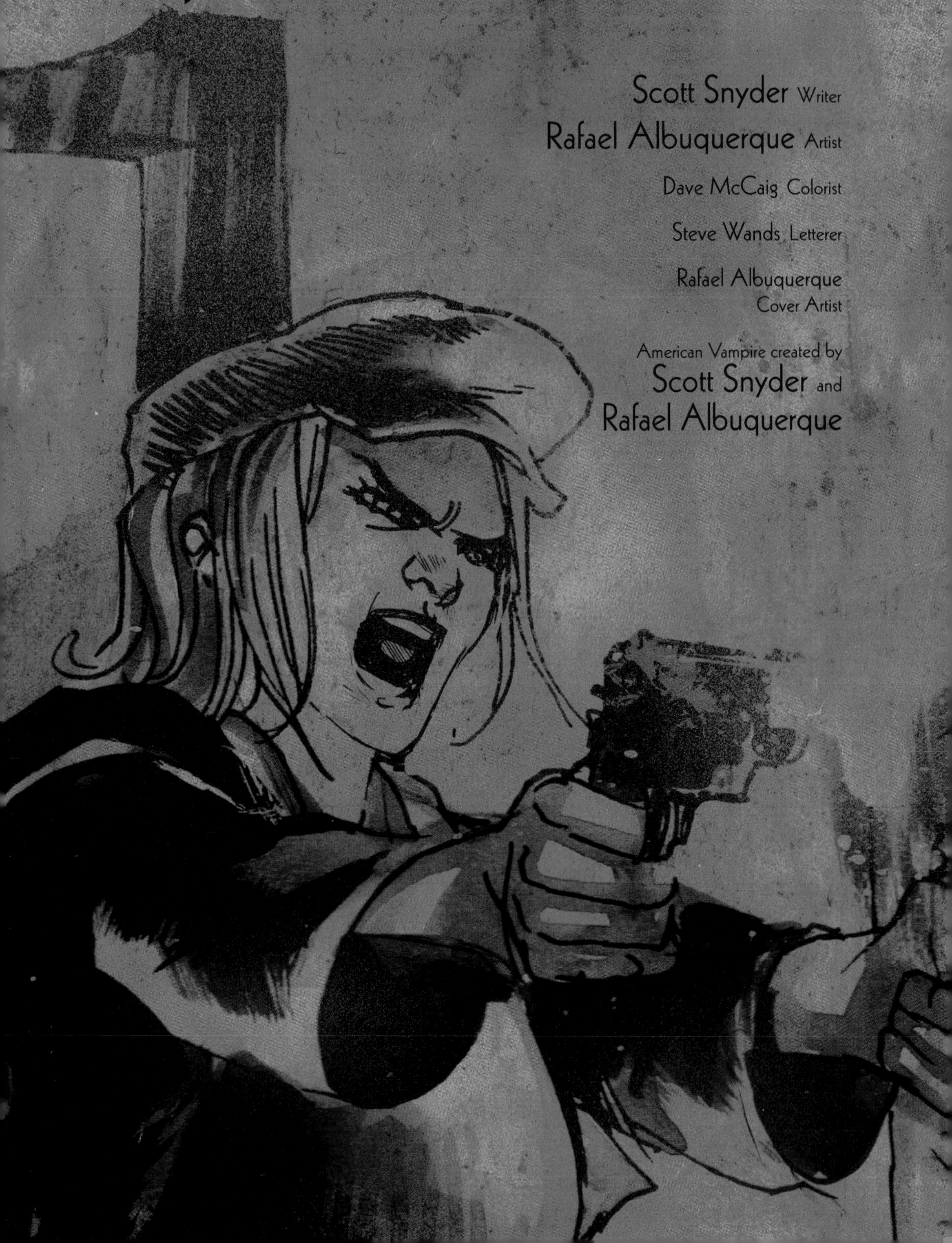

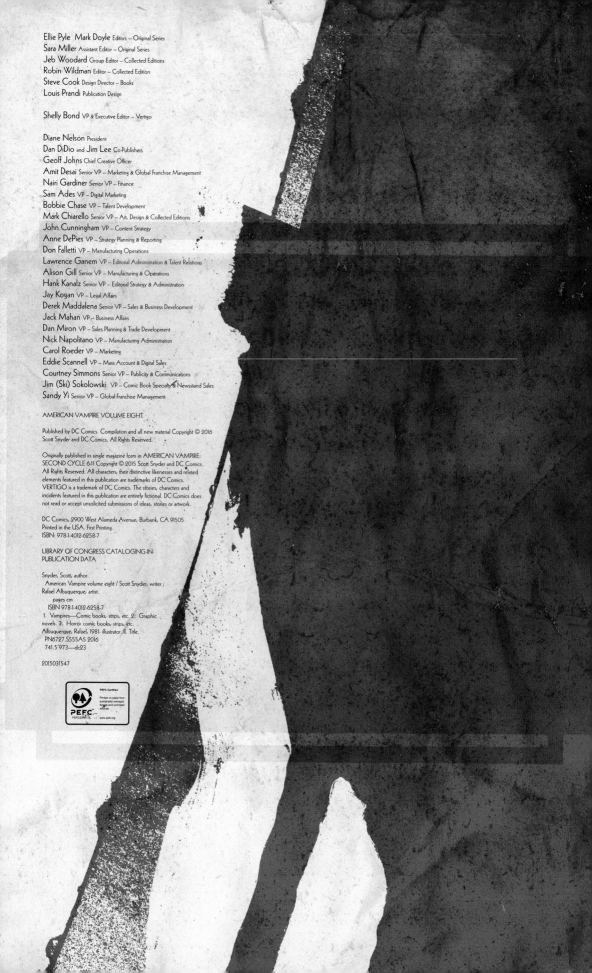

Ellie Pyle Mark Doyle Editors – Original Series
Sara Miller Assistant Editor – Original Series
Jeb Woodard Group Editor – Collected Editions
Robin Wildman Editor – Collected Edition
Steve Cook Design Director – Books
Louis Prandi Publication Design

Shelly Bond VP & Executive Editor – Vertigo

Diane Nelson President
Dan DiDio and Jim Lee Co-Publishers
Geoff Johns Chief Creative Officer
Amit Desai Senior VP – Marketing & Global Franchise Management
Nairi Gardiner Senior VP – Finance
Sam Ades VP – Digital Marketing
Bobbie Chase VP – Talent Development
Mark Chiarello Senior VP – Art, Design & Collected Editions
John Cunningham VP – Content Strategy
Anne DePies VP – Strategy Planning & Reporting
Don Falletti VP – Manufacturing Operations
Lawrence Ganem VP – Editorial Administration & Talent Relations
Alison Gill Senior VP – Manufacturing & Operations
Hank Kanalz Senior VP – Editorial Strategy & Administration
Jay Kogan VP – Legal Affairs
Derek Maddalena Senior VP – Sales & Business Development
Jack Mahan VP – Business Affairs
Dan Miron VP – Sales Planning & Trade Development
Nick Napolitano VP – Manufacturing Administration
Carol Roeder VP – Marketing
Eddie Scannell VP – Mass Account & Digital Sales
Courtney Simmons Senior VP – Publicity & Communications
Jim (Ski) Sokolowski VP – Comic Book Specialty & Newsstand Sales
Sandy Yi Senior VP – Global Franchise Management

AMERICAN VAMPIRE VOLUME EIGHT

DC Comics, 2900 West Alameda Avenue, Burbank, CA 91505
Printed in the USA. First Printing.
ISBN: 978-1-4012-6258-7

LIBRARY OF CONGRESS CATALOGING-IN-
PUBLICATION DATA

Snyder, Scott, author.
  American Vampire volume eight / Scott Snyder, writer ;
Rafael Albuquerque, artist.
    pages cm
  ISBN 978-1-4012-6258-7
  1. Vampires—Comic books, strips, etc. 2. Graphic
novels. 3. Horror comic books, strips, etc.
Albuquerque, Rafael, 1981- illustrator. II. Title.
  PN6727.S555A5 2016
  741.5'973—dc23

2015031547

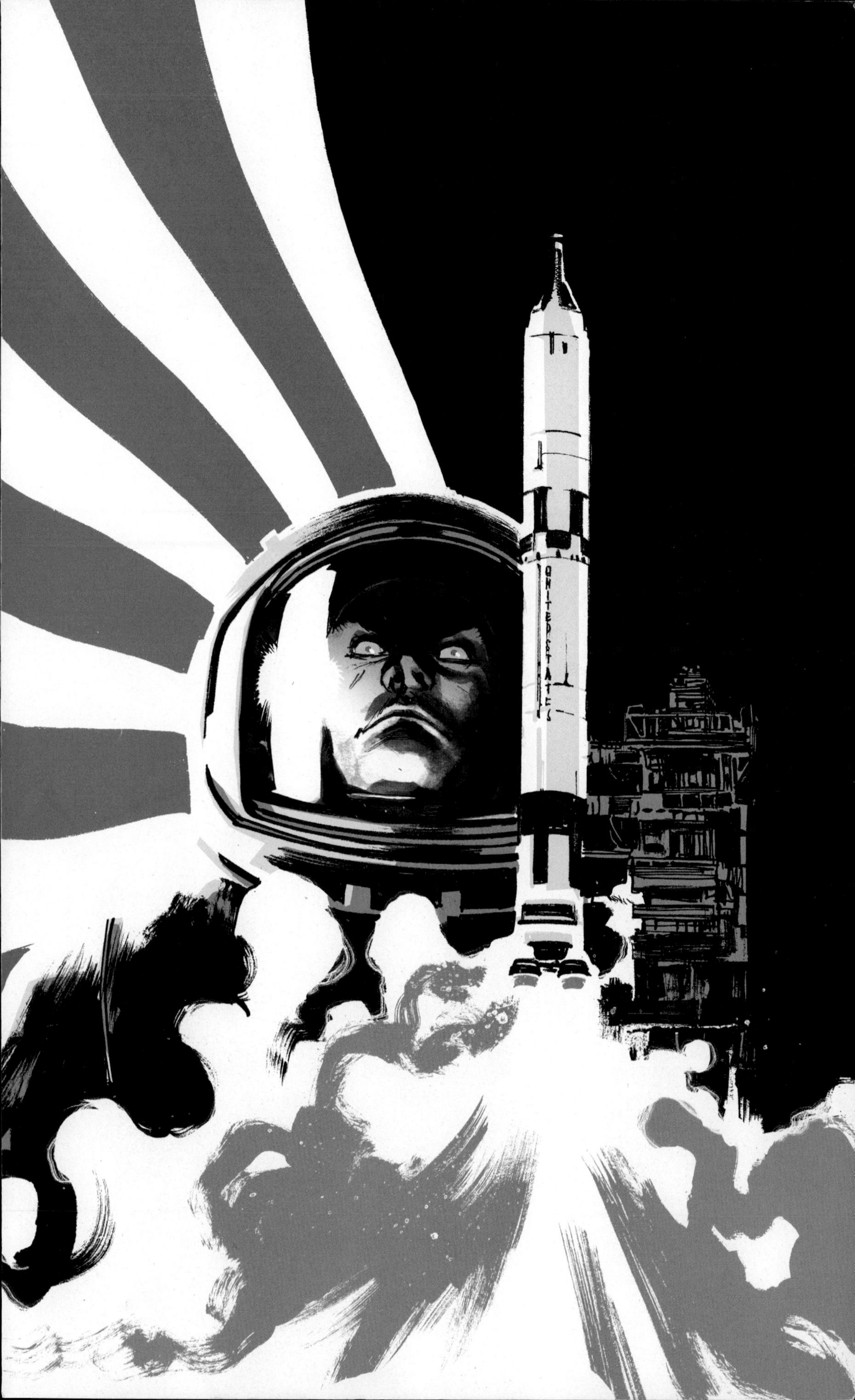
UNITED STATES

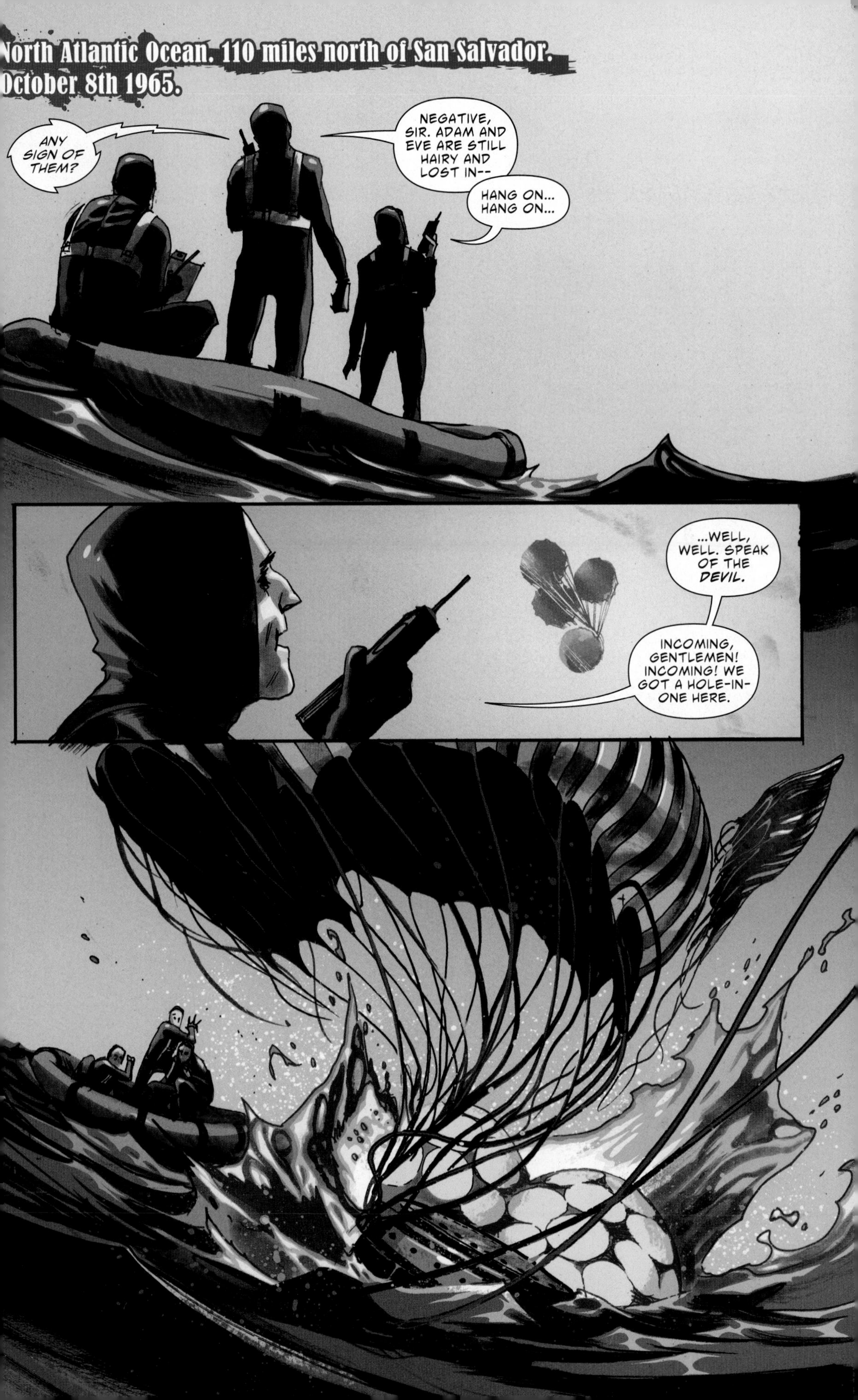
North Atlantic Ocean. 110 miles north of San Salvador.
October 8th 1965.
ANY SIGN OF THEM?
NEGATIVE, SIR. ADAM AND EVE ARE STILL HAIRY AND LOST IN--
HANG ON... HANG ON...
...WELL, WELL. SPEAK OF THE DEVIL.
INCOMING, GENTLEMEN! INCOMING! WE GOT A HOLE-IN-ONE HERE.

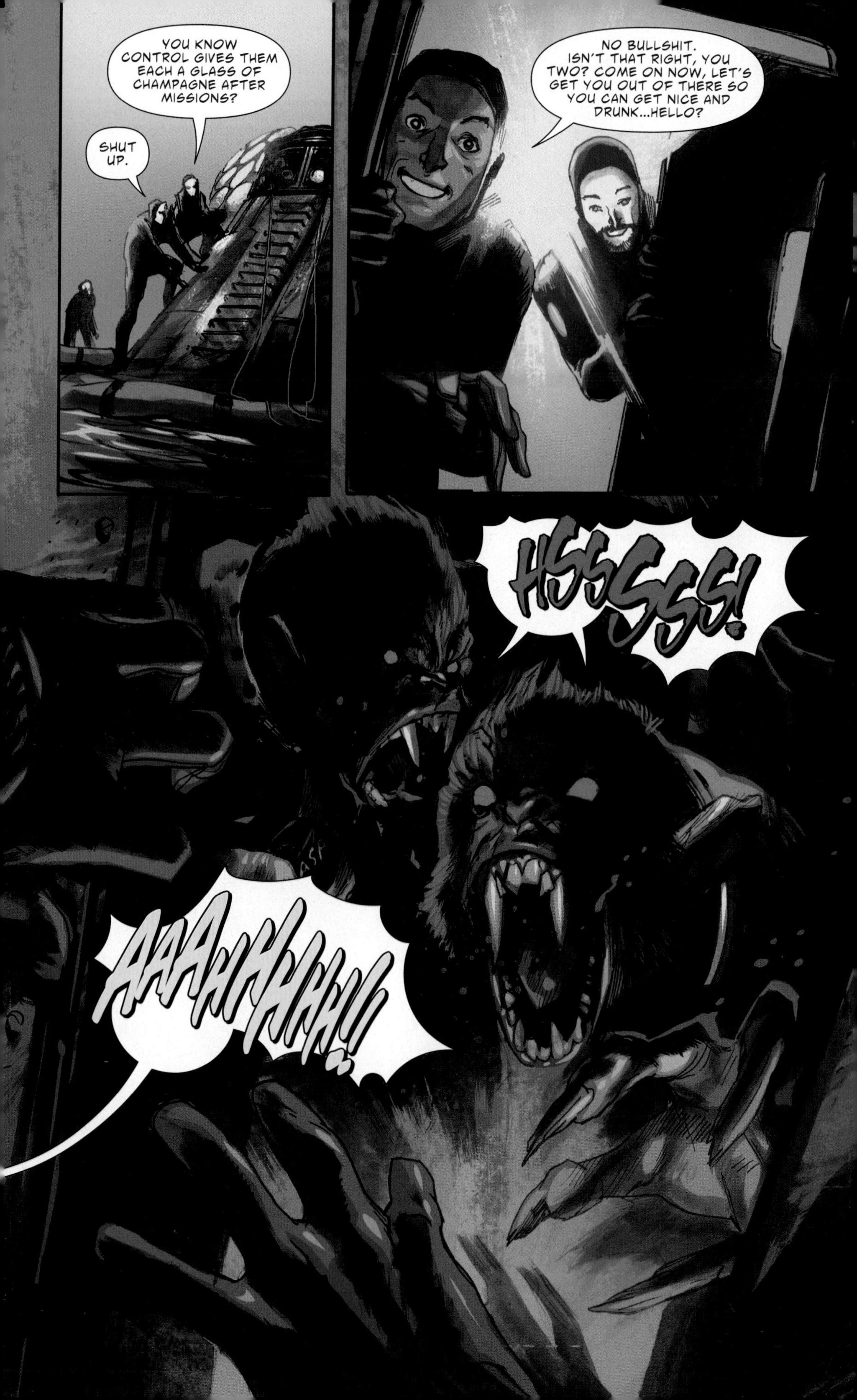
YOU KNOW CONTROL GIVES THEM EACH A GLASS OF CHAMPAGNE AFTER MISSIONS?
SHUT UP.
NO BULLSHIT. ISN'T THAT RIGHT, YOU TWO? COME ON NOW, LET'S GET YOU OUT OF THERE SO YOU CAN GET NICE AND DRUNK...HELLO?
HSSSSS!
AAAHHHHH!!

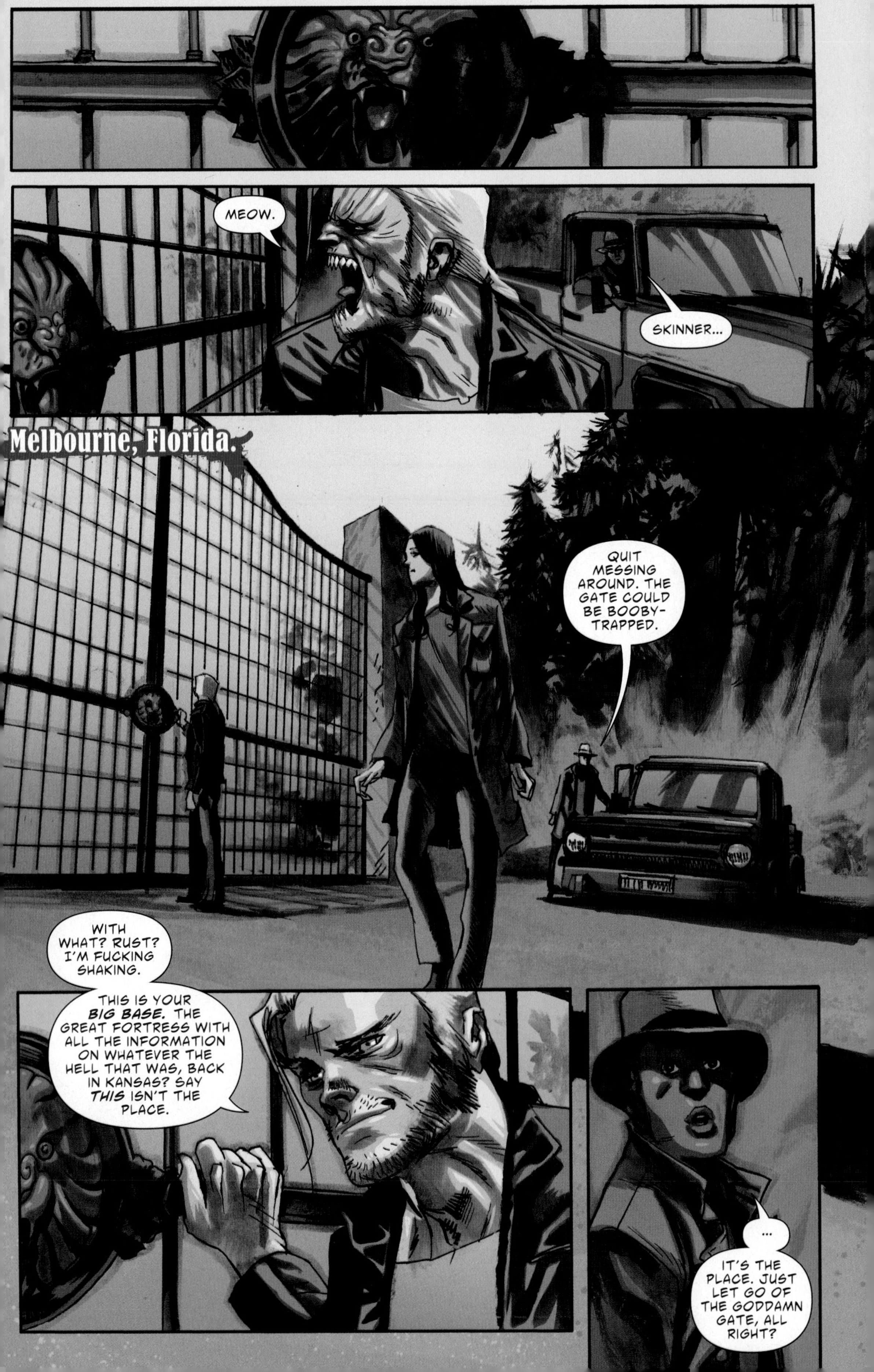

MEOW.
SKINNER...
Melbourne, Florida.
QUIT MESSING AROUND. THE GATE COULD BE BOOBY-TRAPPED.
WITH WHAT? RUST? I'M FUCKING SHAKING.
THIS IS YOUR *BIG BASE.* THE GREAT FORTRESS WITH ALL THE INFORMATION ON WHATEVER THE HELL THAT WAS, BACK IN KANSAS? SAY *THIS* ISN'T THE PLACE.
...
IT'S THE PLACE. JUST LET GO OF THE GODDAMN GATE, ALL RIGHT?

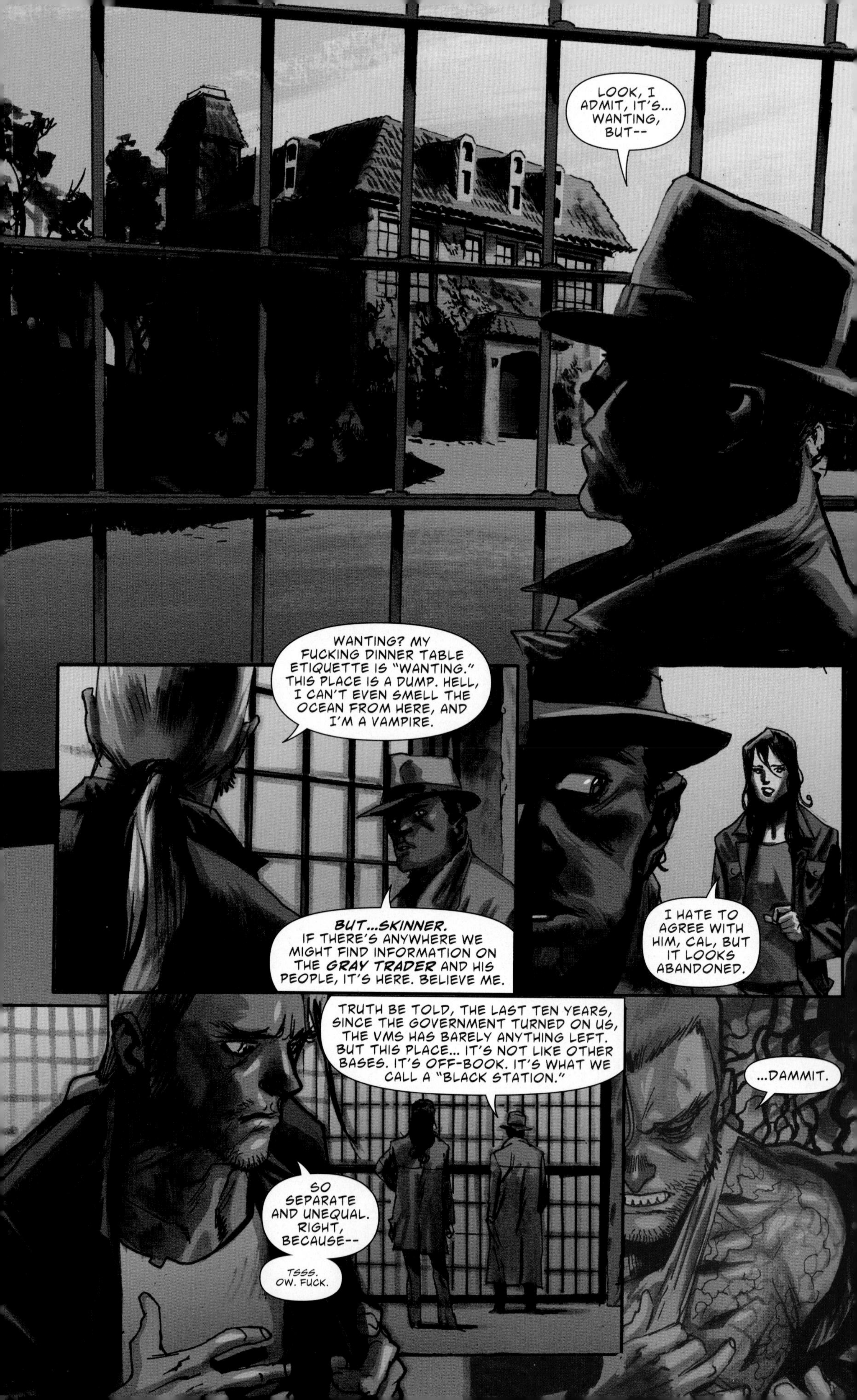
LOOK, I ADMIT, IT'S... WANTING, BUT--
WANTING? MY FUCKING DINNER TABLE ETIQUETTE IS "WANTING." THIS PLACE IS A DUMP. HELL, I CAN'T EVEN SMELL THE OCEAN FROM HERE, AND I'M A VAMPIRE.
BUT...SKINNER. IF THERE'S ANYWHERE WE MIGHT FIND INFORMATION ON THE GRAY TRADER AND HIS PEOPLE, IT'S HERE. BELIEVE ME.
I HATE TO AGREE WITH HIM, CAL, BUT IT LOOKS ABANDONED.
TRUTH BE TOLD, THE LAST TEN YEARS, SINCE THE GOVERNMENT TURNED ON US, THE VMS HAS BARELY ANYTHING LEFT. BUT THIS PLACE... IT'S NOT LIKE OTHER BASES. IT'S OFF-BOOK. IT'S WHAT WE CALL A "BLACK STATION."
...DAMMIT.
SO SEPARATE AND UNEQUAL. RIGHT, BECAUSE--
TSSS. OW. FUCK.

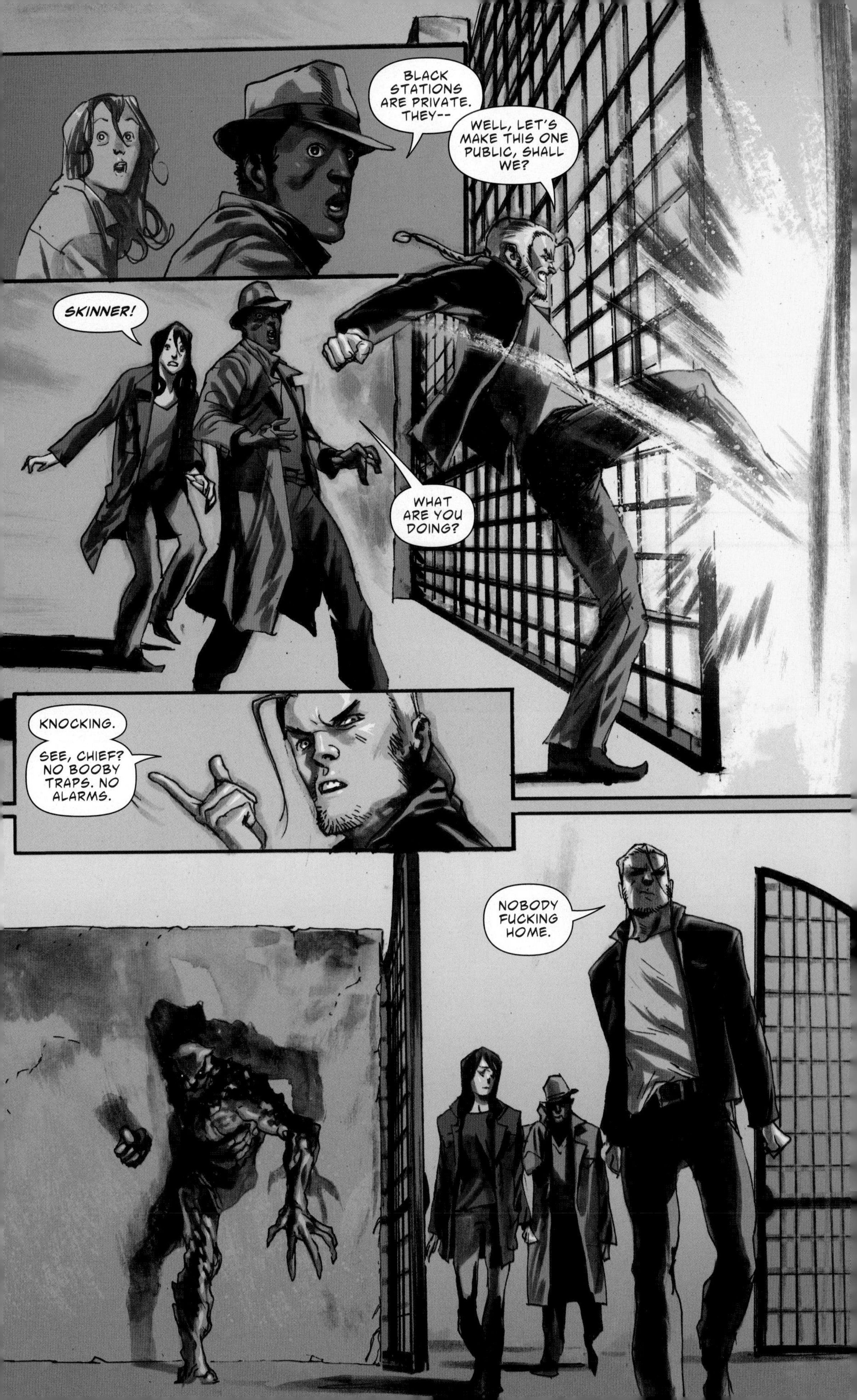
BLACK STATIONS ARE PRIVATE. THEY--
WELL, LET'S MAKE THIS ONE PUBLIC, SHALL WE?
SKINNER!
WHAT ARE YOU DOING?
KNOCKING.
SEE, CHIEF? NO BOOBY TRAPS. NO ALARMS.
NOBODY FUCKING HOME.

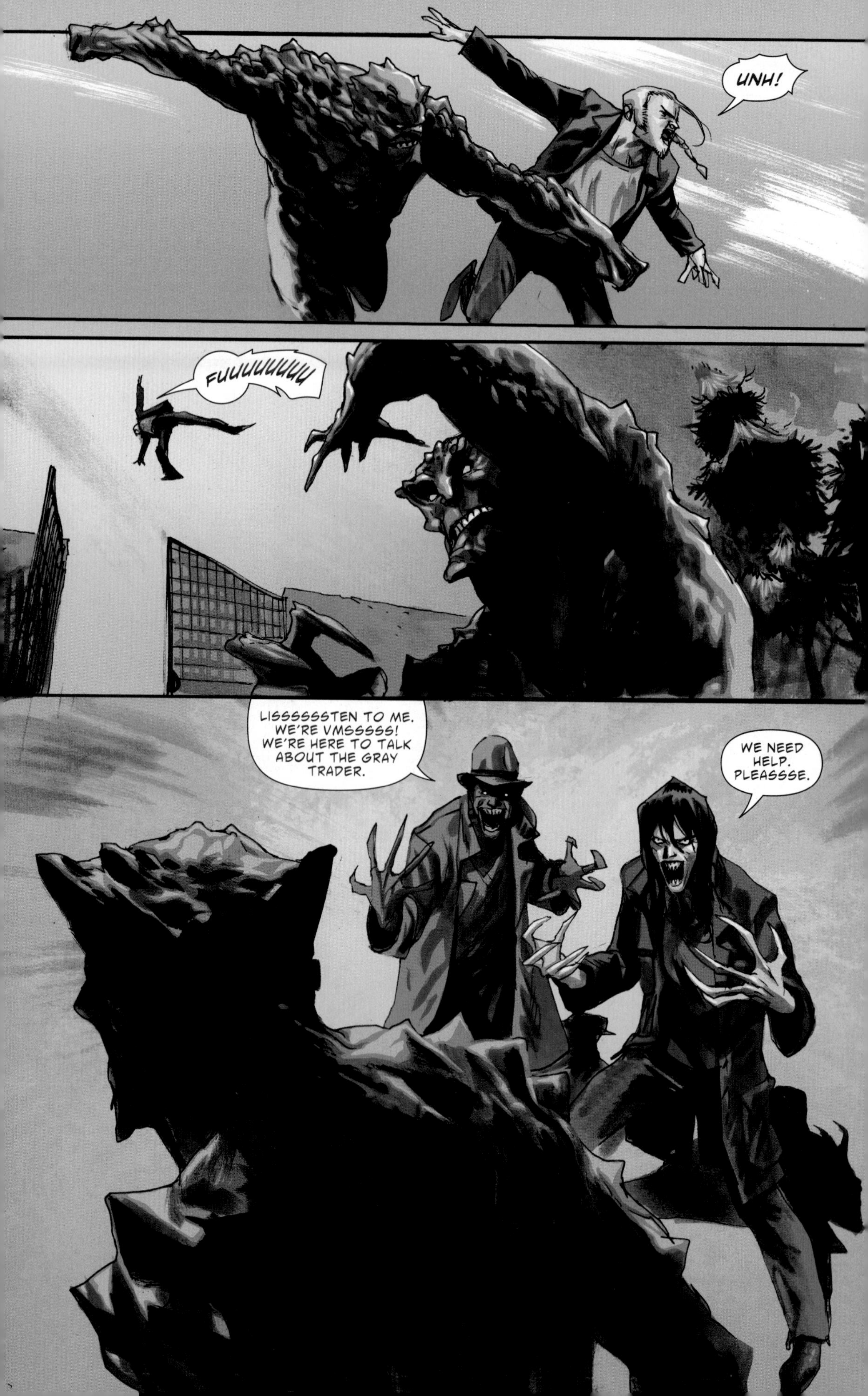
UNH!
FUUUUUUUU
LISSSSSSTEN TO ME. WE'RE VMSSSSS! WE'RE HERE TO TALK ABOUT THE GRAY TRADER.
WE NEED HELP. PLEASSSE.

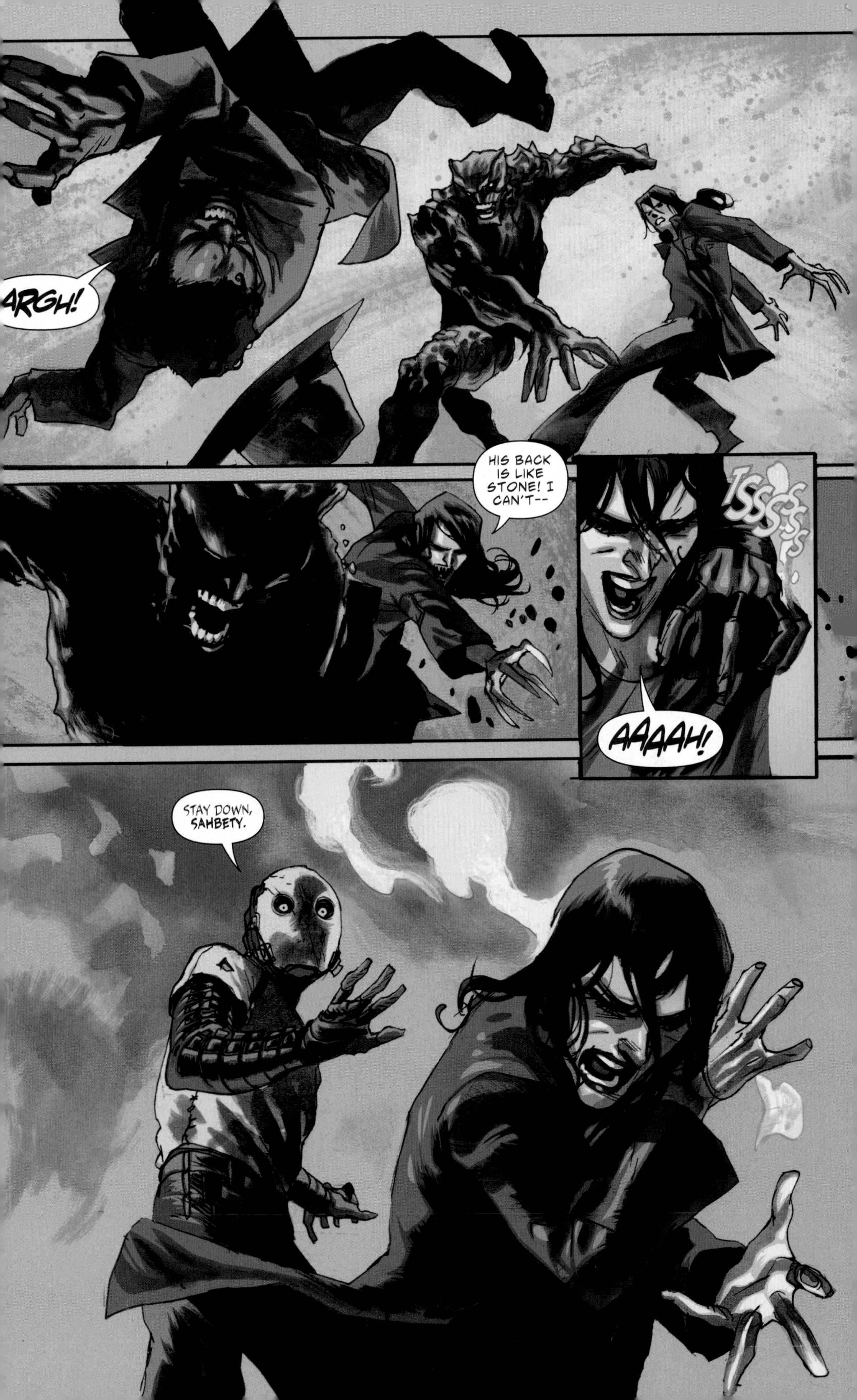
ARGH!
HIS BACK IS LIKE STONE! I CAN'T--
TSSSSSS
AAAAH!
STAY DOWN, SAHBETY.

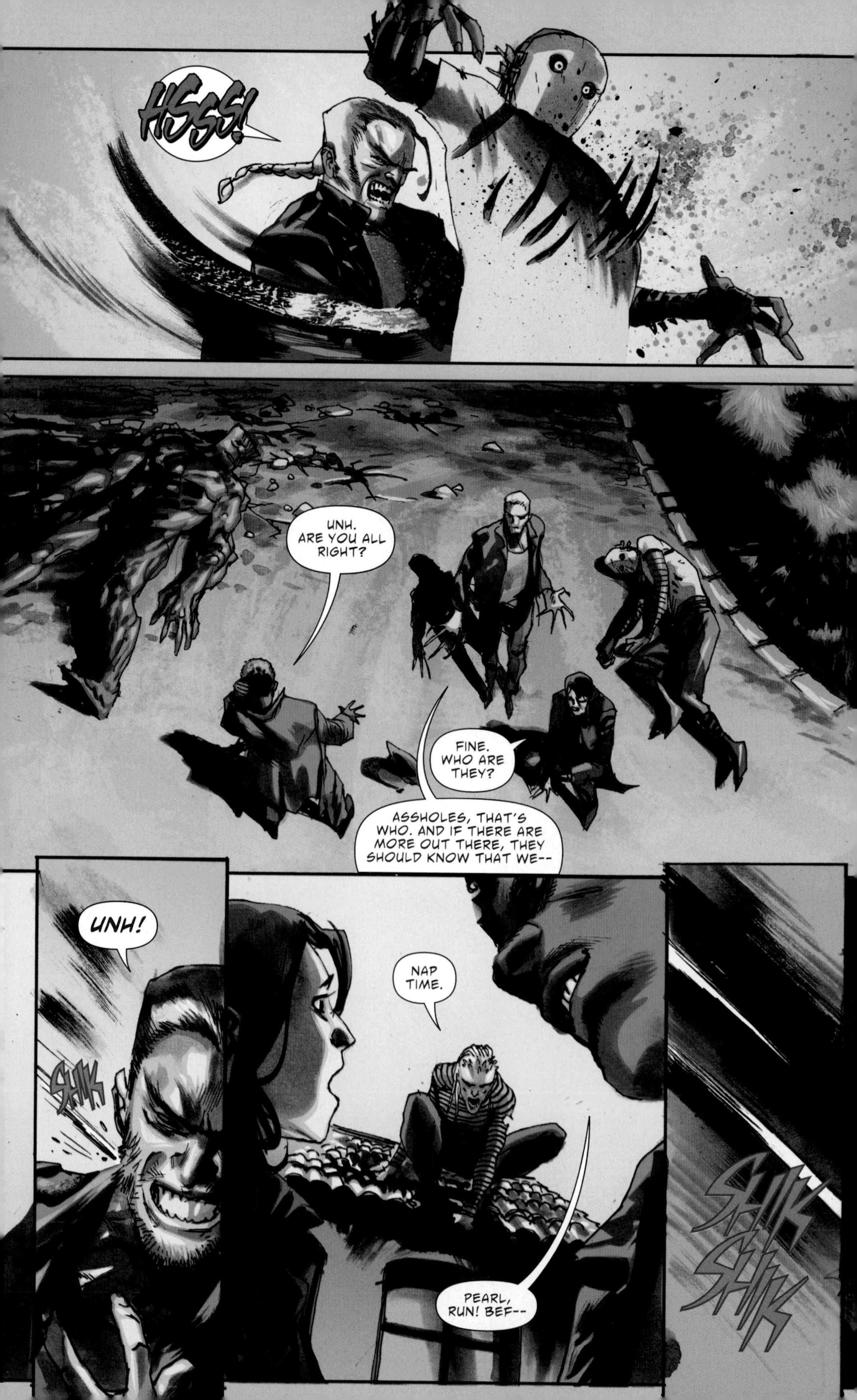
HSSS!
UNH. ARE YOU ALL RIGHT?
FINE. WHO ARE THEY?
ASSHOLES, THAT'S WHO. AND IF THERE ARE MORE OUT THERE, THEY SHOULD KNOW THAT WE--
UNH!
SHIK
NAP TIME.
PEARL, RUN! BEF--
SHIK
SHIK
SHIK

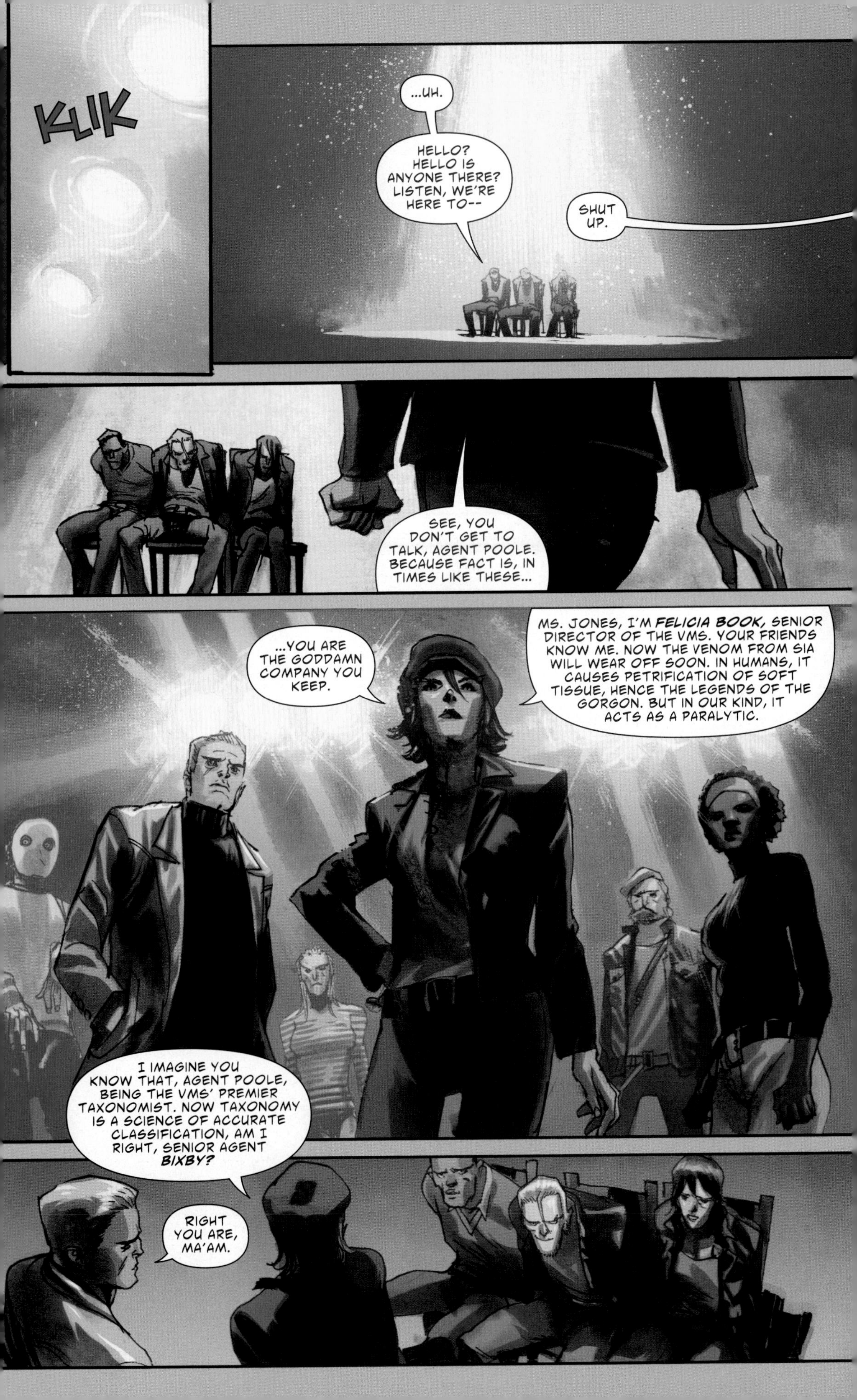
KLIK
...UH.
HELLO? HELLO IS ANYONE THERE? LISTEN, WE'RE HERE TO--
SHUT UP.
SEE, YOU DON'T GET TO TALK, AGENT POOLE. BECAUSE FACT IS, IN TIMES LIKE THESE...
...YOU ARE THE GODDAMN COMPANY YOU KEEP.
MS. JONES, I'M FELICIA BOOK, SENIOR DIRECTOR OF THE VMS. YOUR FRIENDS KNOW ME. NOW THE VENOM FROM SIA WILL WEAR OFF SOON. IN HUMANS, IT CAUSES PETRIFICATION OF SOFT TISSUE, HENCE THE LEGENDS OF THE GORGON. BUT IN OUR KIND, IT ACTS AS A PARALYTIC.
I IMAGINE YOU KNOW THAT, AGENT POOLE, BEING THE VMS' PREMIER TAXONOMIST. NOW TAXONOMY IS A SCIENCE OF ACCURATE CLASSIFICATION, AM I RIGHT, SENIOR AGENT BIXBY?
RIGHT YOU ARE, MA'AM.

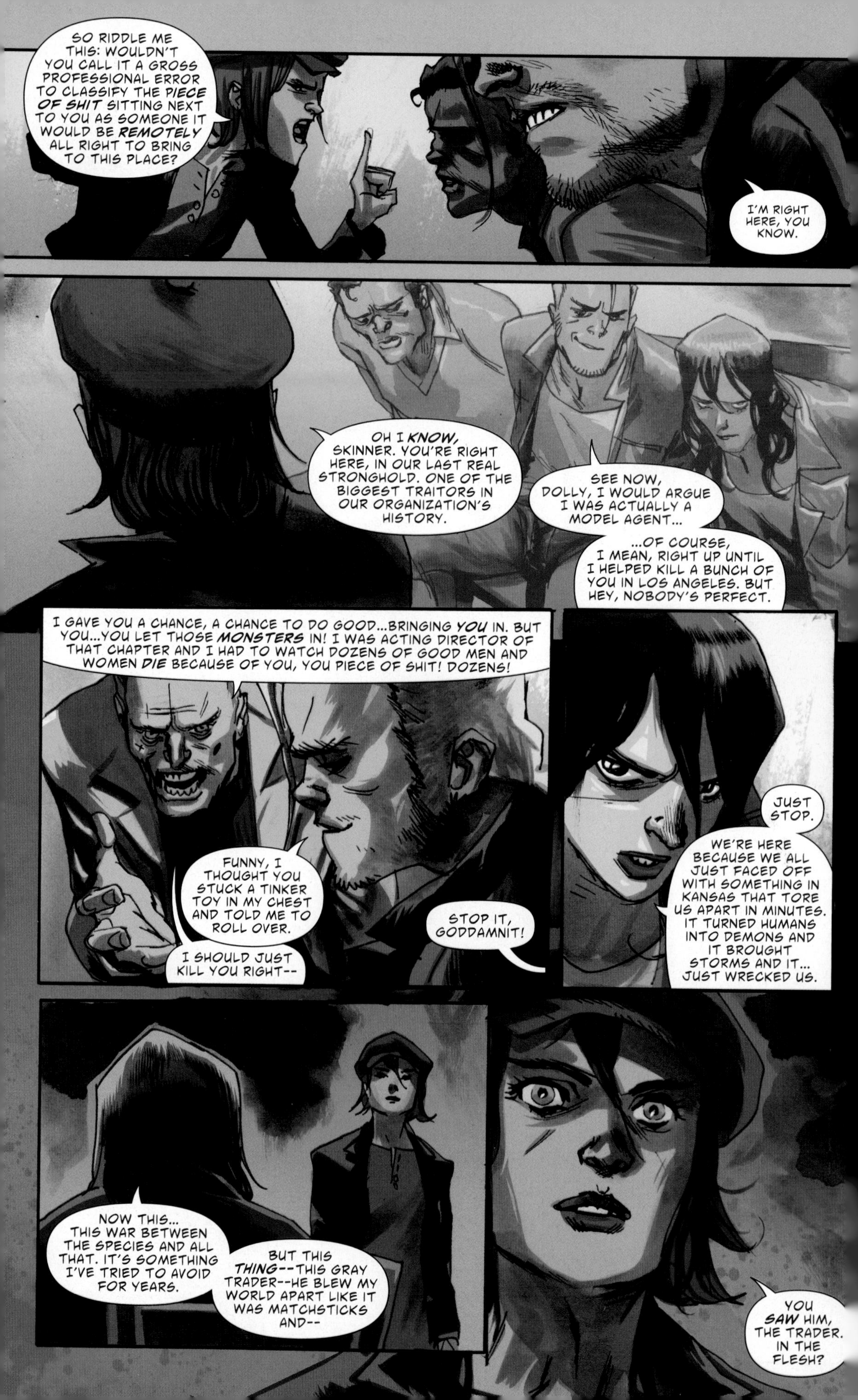

SO RIDDLE ME THIS: WOULDN'T YOU CALL IT A GROSS PROFESSIONAL ERROR TO CLASSIFY THE PIECE OF SHIT SITTING NEXT TO YOU AS SOMEONE IT WOULD BE REMOTELY ALL RIGHT TO BRING TO THIS PLACE?
I'M RIGHT HERE, YOU KNOW.
OH I KNOW, SKINNER. YOU'RE RIGHT HERE, IN OUR LAST REAL STRONGHOLD. ONE OF THE BIGGEST TRAITORS IN OUR ORGANIZATION'S HISTORY.
SEE NOW, DOLLY, I WOULD ARGUE I WAS ACTUALLY A MODEL AGENT...
...OF COURSE, I MEAN, RIGHT UP UNTIL I HELPED KILL A BUNCH OF YOU IN LOS ANGELES. BUT HEY, NOBODY'S PERFECT.
I GAVE YOU A CHANCE, A CHANCE TO DO GOOD...BRINGING YOU IN. BUT YOU...YOU LET THOSE MONSTERS IN! I WAS ACTING DIRECTOR OF THAT CHAPTER AND I HAD TO WATCH DOZENS OF GOOD MEN AND WOMEN DIE BECAUSE OF YOU, YOU PIECE OF SHIT! DOZENS!
FUNNY, I THOUGHT YOU STUCK A TINKER TOY IN MY CHEST AND TOLD ME TO ROLL OVER.
I SHOULD JUST KILL YOU RIGHT--
STOP IT, GODDAMNIT!
JUST STOP.
WE'RE HERE BECAUSE WE ALL JUST FACED OFF WITH SOMETHING IN KANSAS THAT TORE US APART IN MINUTES. IT TURNED HUMANS INTO DEMONS AND IT BROUGHT STORMS AND IT... JUST WRECKED US.
NOW THIS... THIS WAR BETWEEN THE SPECIES AND ALL THAT. IT'S SOMETHING I'VE TRIED TO AVOID FOR YEARS.
BUT THIS THING--THIS GRAY TRADER--HE BLEW MY WORLD APART LIKE IT WAS MATCHSTICKS AND--
YOU SAW HIM, THE TRADER. IN THE FLESH?

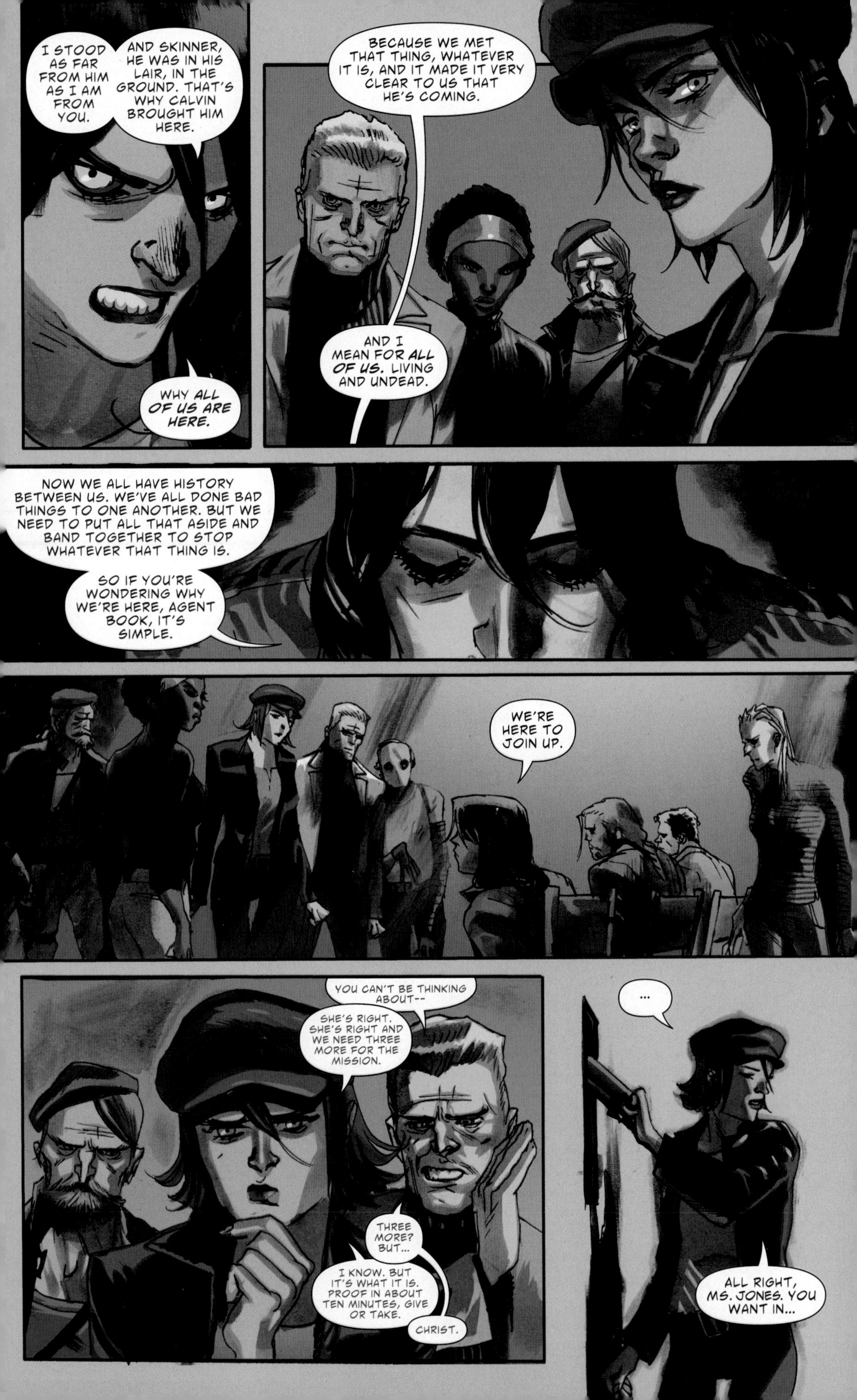
I STOOD AS FAR FROM HIM AS I AM FROM YOU.
AND SKINNER, HE WAS IN HIS LAIR, IN THE GROUND. THAT'S WHY CALVIN BROUGHT HIM HERE.
WHY ALL OF US ARE HERE.
BECAUSE WE MET THAT THING, WHATEVER IT IS, AND IT MADE IT VERY CLEAR TO US THAT HE'S COMING.
AND I MEAN FOR ALL OF US. LIVING AND UNDEAD.
NOW WE ALL HAVE HISTORY BETWEEN US. WE'VE ALL DONE BAD THINGS TO ONE ANOTHER. BUT WE NEED TO PUT ALL THAT ASIDE AND BAND TOGETHER TO STOP WHATEVER THAT THING IS.
SO IF YOU'RE WONDERING WHY WE'RE HERE, AGENT BOOK, IT'S SIMPLE.
WE'RE HERE TO JOIN UP.
YOU CAN'T BE THINKING ABOUT--
SHE'S RIGHT. SHE'S RIGHT AND WE NEED THREE MORE FOR THE MISSION.
THREE MORE? BUT...
I KNOW. BUT IT'S WHAT IT IS. PROOF IN ABOUT TEN MINUTES, GIVE OR TAKE.
CHRIST.
...
ALL RIGHT, MS. JONES. YOU WANT IN...

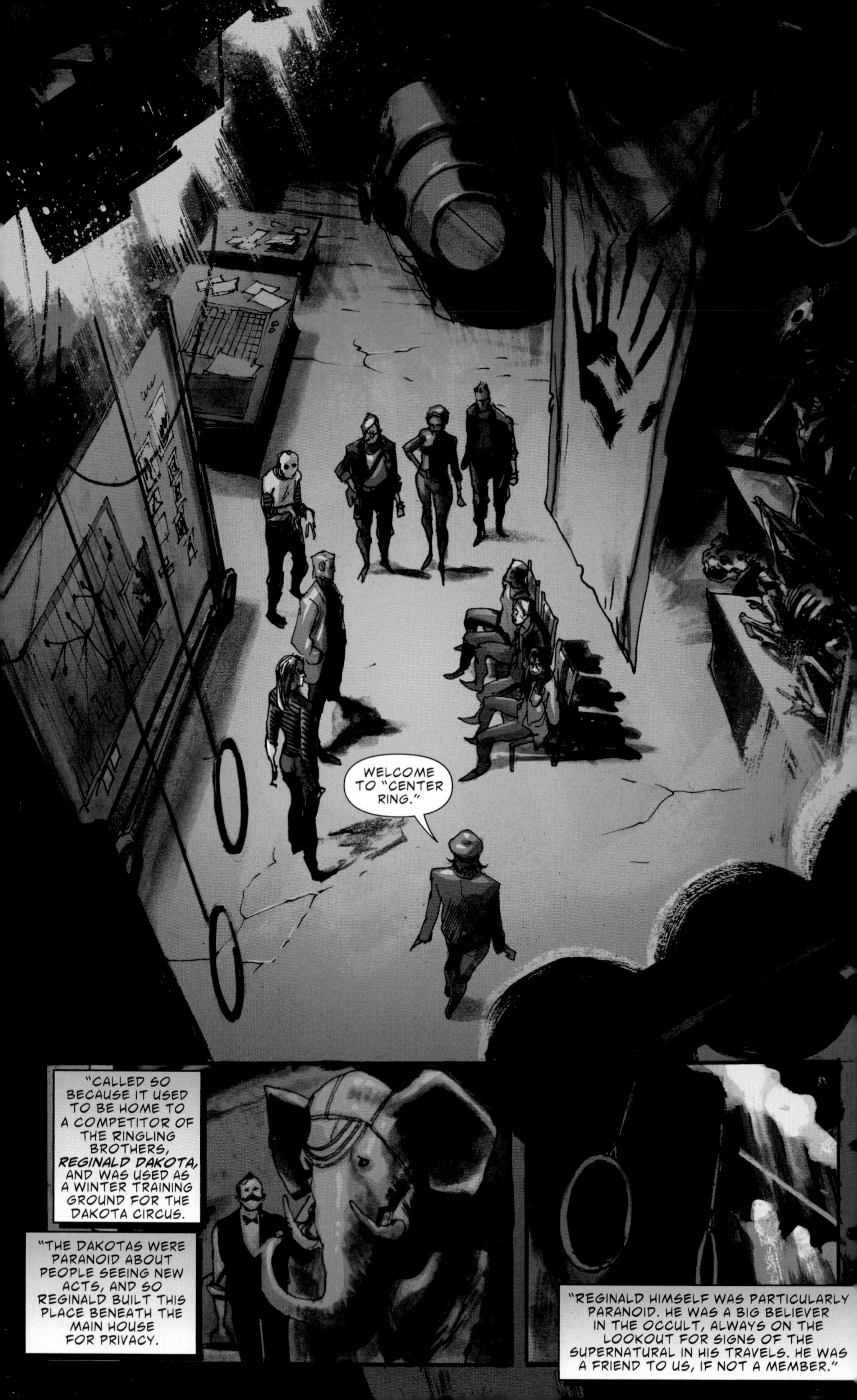
WELCOME TO "CENTER RING."
"CALLED SO BECAUSE IT USED TO BE HOME TO A COMPETITOR OF THE RINGLING BROTHERS, REGINALD DAKOTA, AND WAS USED AS A WINTER TRAINING GROUND FOR THE DAKOTA CIRCUS.
"THE DAKOTAS WERE PARANOID ABOUT PEOPLE SEEING NEW ACTS, AND SO REGINALD BUILT THIS PLACE BENEATH THE MAIN HOUSE FOR PRIVACY.
"REGINALD HIMSELF WAS PARTICULARLY PARANOID. HE WAS A BIG BELIEVER IN THE OCCULT, ALWAYS ON THE LOOKOUT FOR SIGNS OF THE SUPERNATURAL IN HIS TRAVELS. HE WAS A FRIEND TO US, IF NOT A MEMBER."

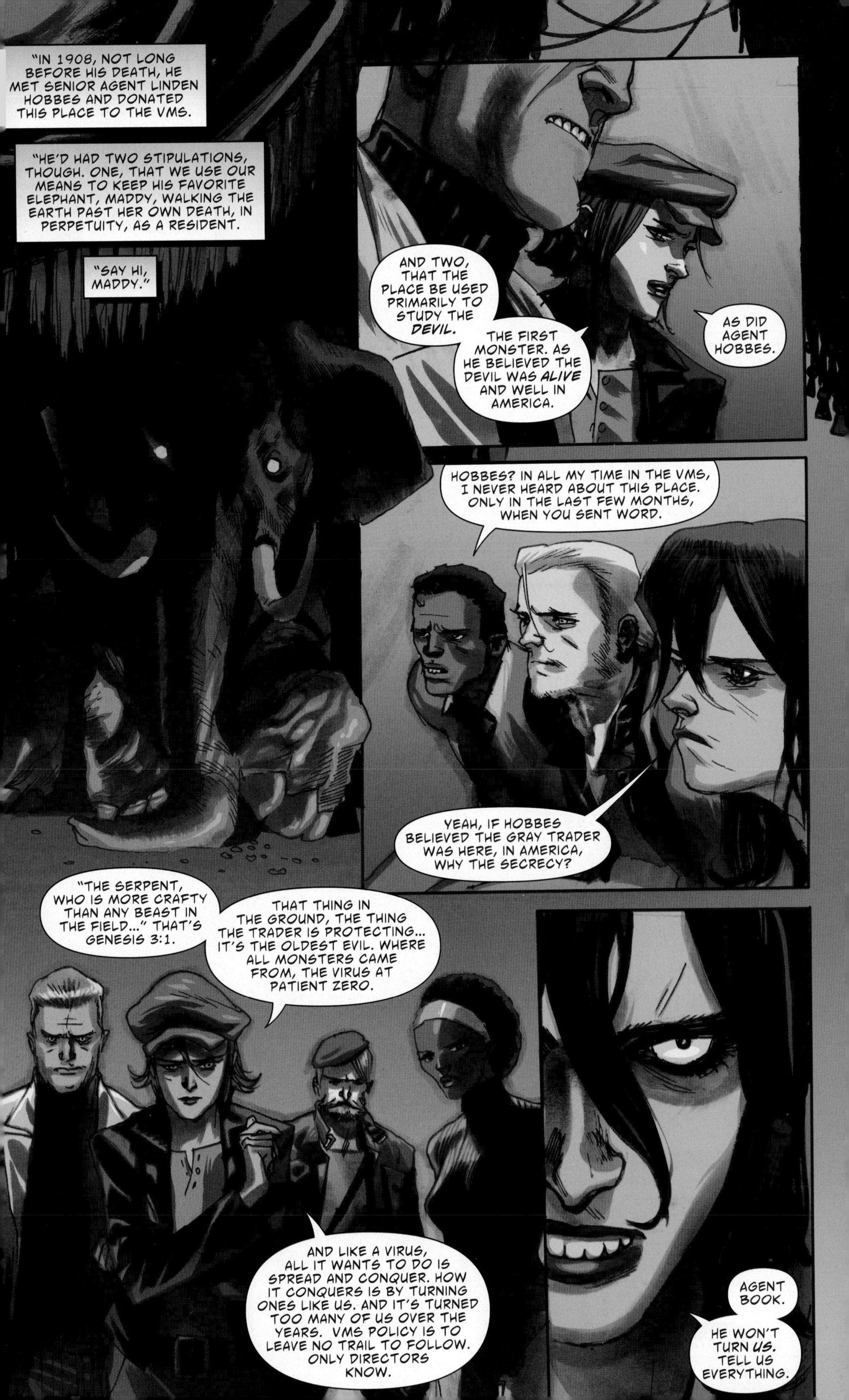
"IN 1908, NOT LONG BEFORE HIS DEATH, HE MET SENIOR AGENT LINDEN HOBBES AND DONATED THIS PLACE TO THE VMS.
"HE'D HAD TWO STIPULATIONS, THOUGH. ONE, THAT WE USE OUR MEANS TO KEEP HIS FAVORITE ELEPHANT, MADDY, WALKING THE EARTH PAST HER OWN DEATH, IN PERPETUITY, AS A RESIDENT.
"SAY HI, MADDY."
AND TWO, THAT THE PLACE BE USED PRIMARILY TO STUDY THE *DEVIL.*
THE FIRST MONSTER. AS HE BELIEVED THE DEVIL WAS *ALIVE* AND WELL IN AMERICA.
AS DID AGENT HOBBES.
HOBBES? IN ALL MY TIME IN THE VMS, I NEVER HEARD ABOUT THIS PLACE. ONLY IN THE LAST FEW MONTHS, WHEN YOU SENT WORD.
YEAH, IF HOBBES BELIEVED THE GRAY TRADER WAS HERE, IN AMERICA, WHY THE SECRECY?
"THE SERPENT, WHO IS MORE CRAFTY THAN ANY BEAST IN THE FIELD..." THAT'S GENESIS 3:1.
THAT THING IN THE GROUND, THE THING THE TRADER IS PROTECTING... IT'S THE OLDEST EVIL. WHERE ALL MONSTERS CAME FROM, THE VIRUS AT PATIENT ZERO.
AND LIKE A VIRUS, ALL IT WANTS TO DO IS SPREAD AND CONQUER. HOW IT CONQUERS IS BY TURNING ONES LIKE US. AND IT'S TURNED TOO MANY OF US OVER THE YEARS. VMS POLICY IS TO LEAVE NO TRAIL TO FOLLOW. ONLY DIRECTORS KNOW.
AGENT BOOK.
HE WON'T TURN *US.* TELL US EVERYTHING.

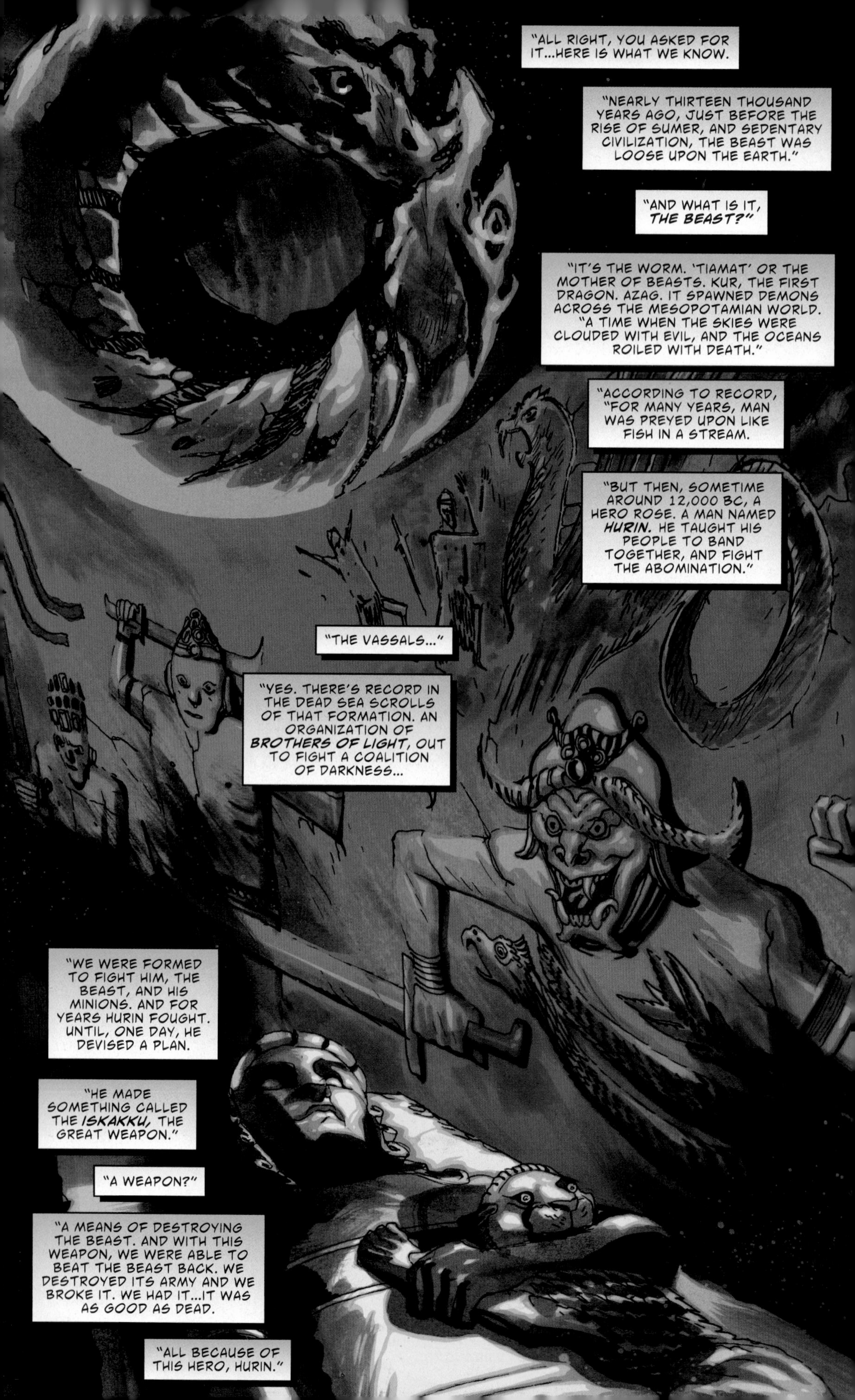
"ALL RIGHT, YOU ASKED FOR IT...HERE IS WHAT WE KNOW.
"NEARLY THIRTEEN THOUSAND YEARS AGO, JUST BEFORE THE RISE OF SUMER, AND SEDENTARY CIVILIZATION, THE BEAST WAS LOOSE UPON THE EARTH."
"AND WHAT IS IT, *THE BEAST?*"
"IT'S THE WORM. 'TIAMAT' OR THE MOTHER OF BEASTS. KUR, THE FIRST DRAGON. AZAG. IT SPAWNED DEMONS ACROSS THE MESOPOTAMIAN WORLD. "A TIME WHEN THE SKIES WERE CLOUDED WITH EVIL, AND THE OCEANS ROILED WITH DEATH."
"ACCORDING TO RECORD, "FOR MANY YEARS, MAN WAS PREYED UPON LIKE FISH IN A STREAM.
"BUT THEN, SOMETIME AROUND 12,000 BC, A HERO ROSE. A MAN NAMED ***HURIN.*** HE TAUGHT HIS PEOPLE TO BAND TOGETHER, AND FIGHT THE ABOMINATION."
"THE VASSALS..."
"YES. THERE'S RECORD IN THE DEAD SEA SCROLLS OF THAT FORMATION. AN ORGANIZATION OF ***BROTHERS OF LIGHT,*** OUT TO FIGHT A COALITION OF DARKNESS...
"WE WERE FORMED TO FIGHT HIM, THE BEAST, AND HIS MINIONS. AND FOR YEARS HURIN FOUGHT. UNTIL, ONE DAY, HE DEVISED A PLAN.
"HE MADE SOMETHING CALLED THE ***ISKAKKU,*** THE GREAT WEAPON."
"A WEAPON?"
"A MEANS OF DESTROYING THE BEAST. AND WITH THIS WEAPON, WE WERE ABLE TO BEAT THE BEAST BACK. WE DESTROYED ITS ARMY AND WE BROKE IT. WE HAD IT...IT WAS AS GOOD AS DEAD.
"ALL BECAUSE OF THIS HERO, HURIN."

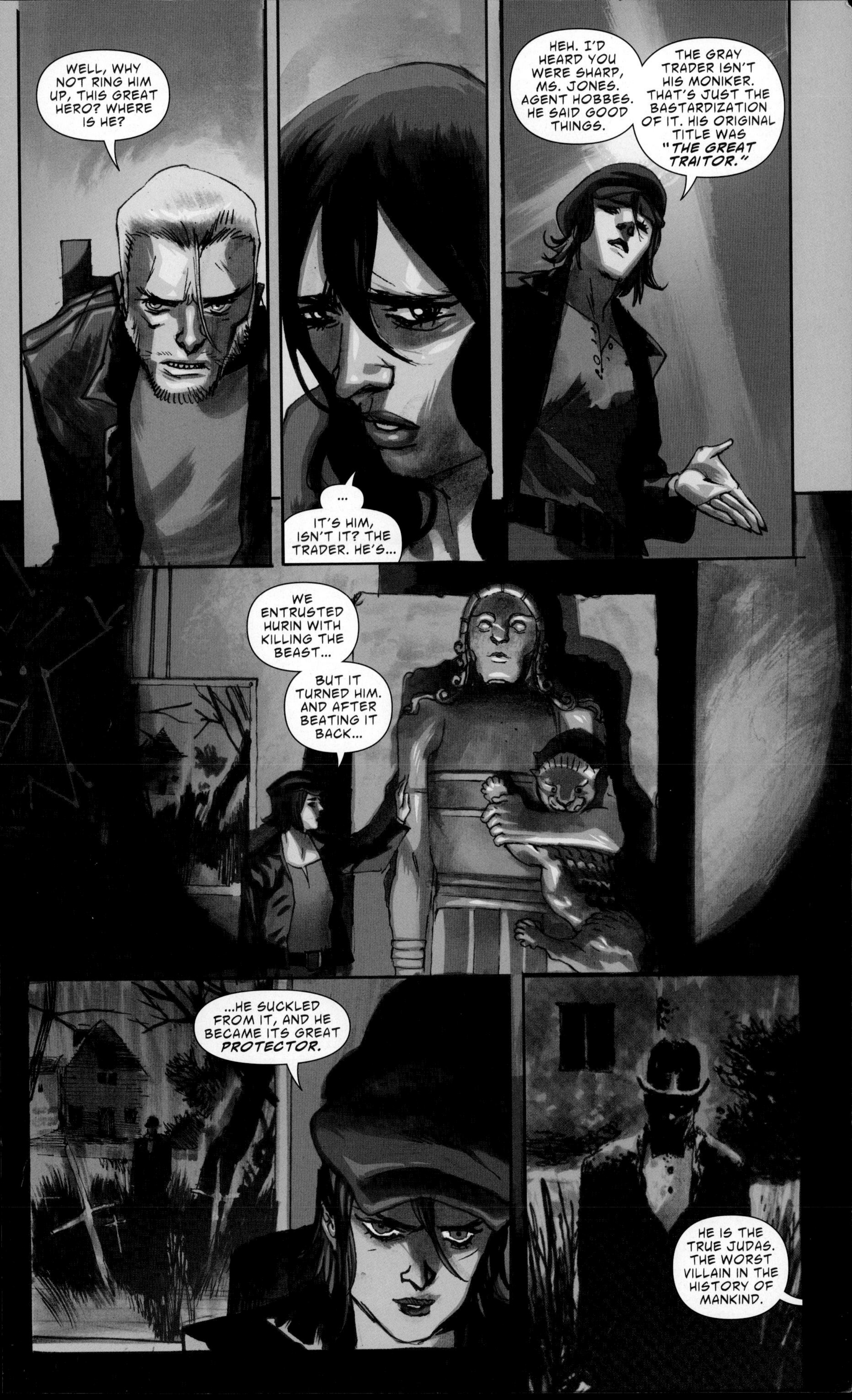
WELL, WHY NOT RING HIM UP, THIS GREAT HERO? WHERE IS HE?
...
IT'S HIM, ISN'T IT? THE TRADER. HE'S...
HEH. I'D HEARD YOU WERE SHARP, MS. JONES. AGENT HOBBES. HE SAID GOOD THINGS.
THE GRAY TRADER ISN'T HIS MONIKER. THAT'S JUST THE BASTARDIZATION OF IT. HIS ORIGINAL TITLE WAS "THE GREAT TRAITOR."
WE ENTRUSTED HURIN WITH KILLING THE BEAST...
BUT IT TURNED HIM. AND AFTER BEATING IT BACK...
...HE SUCKLED FROM IT, AND HE BECAME ITS GREAT PROTECTOR.
HE IS THE TRUE JUDAS. THE WORST VILLAIN IN THE HISTORY OF MANKIND.

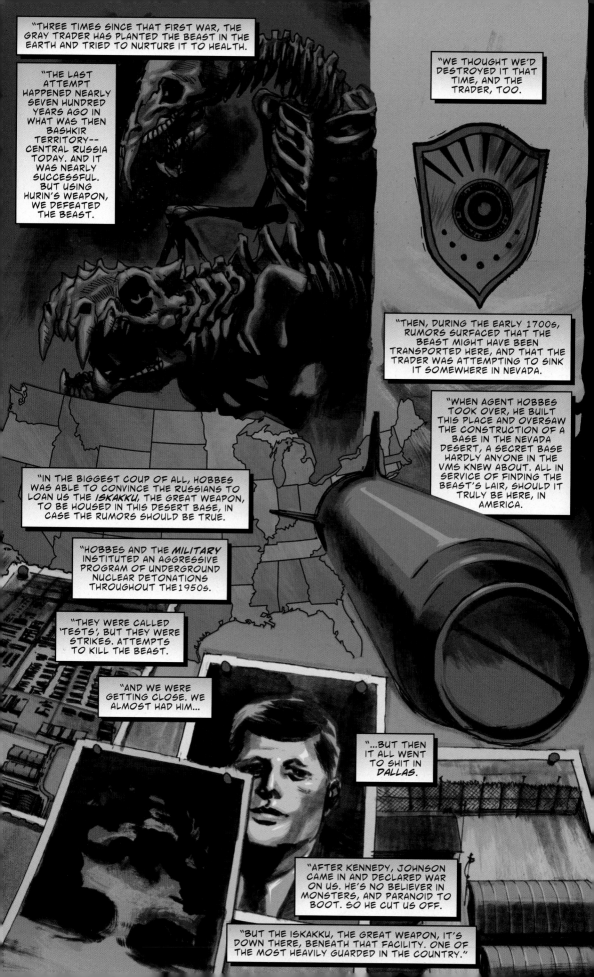

"THREE TIMES SINCE THAT FIRST WAR, THE GRAY TRADER HAS PLANTED THE BEAST IN THE EARTH AND TRIED TO NURTURE IT TO HEALTH.

"THE LAST ATTEMPT HAPPENED NEARLY SEVEN HUNDRED YEARS AGO IN WHAT WAS THEN BASHKIR TERRITORY-- CENTRAL RUSSIA TODAY. AND IT WAS NEARLY SUCCESSFUL. BUT USING HURIN'S WEAPON, WE DEFEATED THE BEAST.

"WE THOUGHT WE'D DESTROYED IT THAT TIME, AND THE TRADER, TOO.

"THEN, DURING THE EARLY 1700s, RUMORS SURFACED THAT THE BEAST MIGHT HAVE BEEN TRANSPORTED HERE, AND THAT THE TRADER WAS ATTEMPTING TO SINK IT SOMEWHERE IN NEVADA.

"WHEN AGENT HOBBES TOOK OVER, HE BUILT THIS PLACE AND OVERSAW THE CONSTRUCTION OF A BASE IN THE NEVADA DESERT, A SECRET BASE HARDLY ANYONE IN THE VMS KNEW ABOUT. ALL IN SERVICE OF FINDING THE BEAST'S LAIR, SHOULD IT TRULY BE HERE, IN AMERICA.

"IN THE BIGGEST COUP OF ALL, HOBBES WAS ABLE TO CONVINCE THE RUSSIANS TO LOAN US THE *ISKAKKU*, THE GREAT WEAPON, TO BE HOUSED IN THIS DESERT BASE, IN CASE THE RUMORS SHOULD BE TRUE.

"HOBBES AND THE *MILITARY* INSTITUTED AN AGGRESSIVE PROGRAM OF UNDERGROUND NUCLEAR DETONATIONS THROUGHOUT THE 1950s.

"THEY WERE CALLED 'TESTS', BUT THEY WERE STRIKES. ATTEMPTS TO KILL THE BEAST.

"AND WE WERE GETTING CLOSE. WE ALMOST HAD HIM...

"...BUT THEN IT ALL WENT TO SHIT IN *DALLAS*.

"AFTER KENNEDY, JOHNSON CAME IN AND DECLARED WAR ON US. HE'S NO BELIEVER IN MONSTERS, AND PARANOID TO BOOT. SO HE CUT US OFF.

"BUT THE ISKAKKU, THE GREAT WEAPON, IT'S DOWN THERE, BENEATH THAT FACILITY. ONE OF THE MOST HEAVILY GUARDED IN THE COUNTRY."

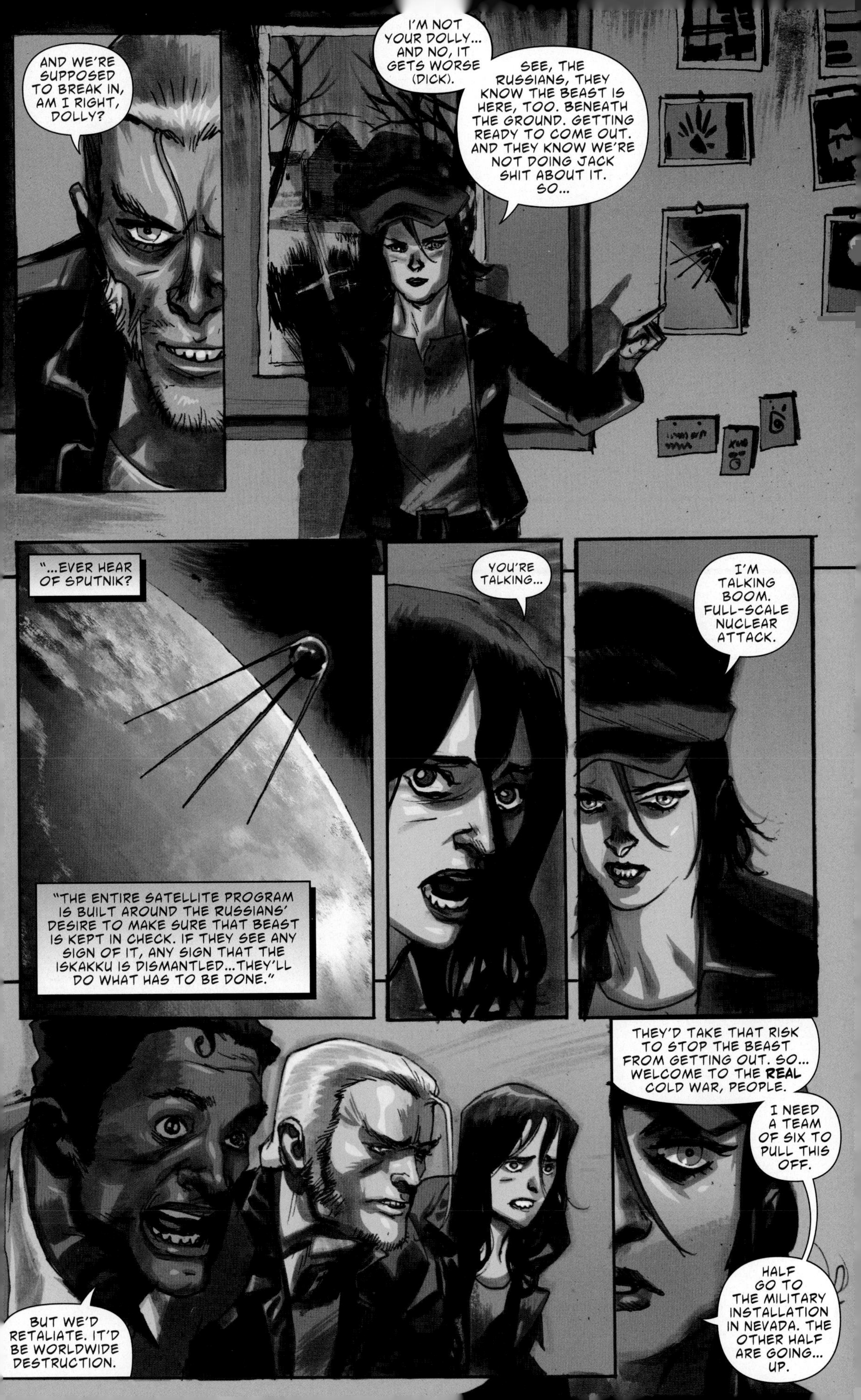
AND WE'RE SUPPOSED TO BREAK IN, AM I RIGHT, DOLLY?
I'M NOT YOUR DOLLY... AND NO, IT GETS WORSE (DICK).
SEE, THE RUSSIANS, THEY KNOW THE BEAST IS HERE, TOO. BENEATH THE GROUND. GETTING READY TO COME OUT. AND THEY KNOW WE'RE NOT DOING JACK SHIT ABOUT IT. SO...
"...EVER HEAR OF SPUTNIK?
"THE ENTIRE SATELLITE PROGRAM IS BUILT AROUND THE RUSSIANS' DESIRE TO MAKE SURE THAT BEAST IS KEPT IN CHECK. IF THEY SEE ANY SIGN OF IT, ANY SIGN THAT THE ISKAKKU IS DISMANTLED...THEY'LL DO WHAT HAS TO BE DONE."
YOU'RE TALKING...
I'M TALKING BOOM. FULL-SCALE NUCLEAR ATTACK.
BUT WE'D RETALIATE. IT'D BE WORLDWIDE DESTRUCTION.
THEY'D TAKE THAT RISK TO STOP THE BEAST FROM GETTING OUT. SO... WELCOME TO THE **REAL** COLD WAR, PEOPLE.
I NEED A TEAM OF SIX TO PULL THIS OFF.
HALF GO TO THE MILITARY INSTALLATION IN NEVADA. THE OTHER HALF ARE GOING... UP.

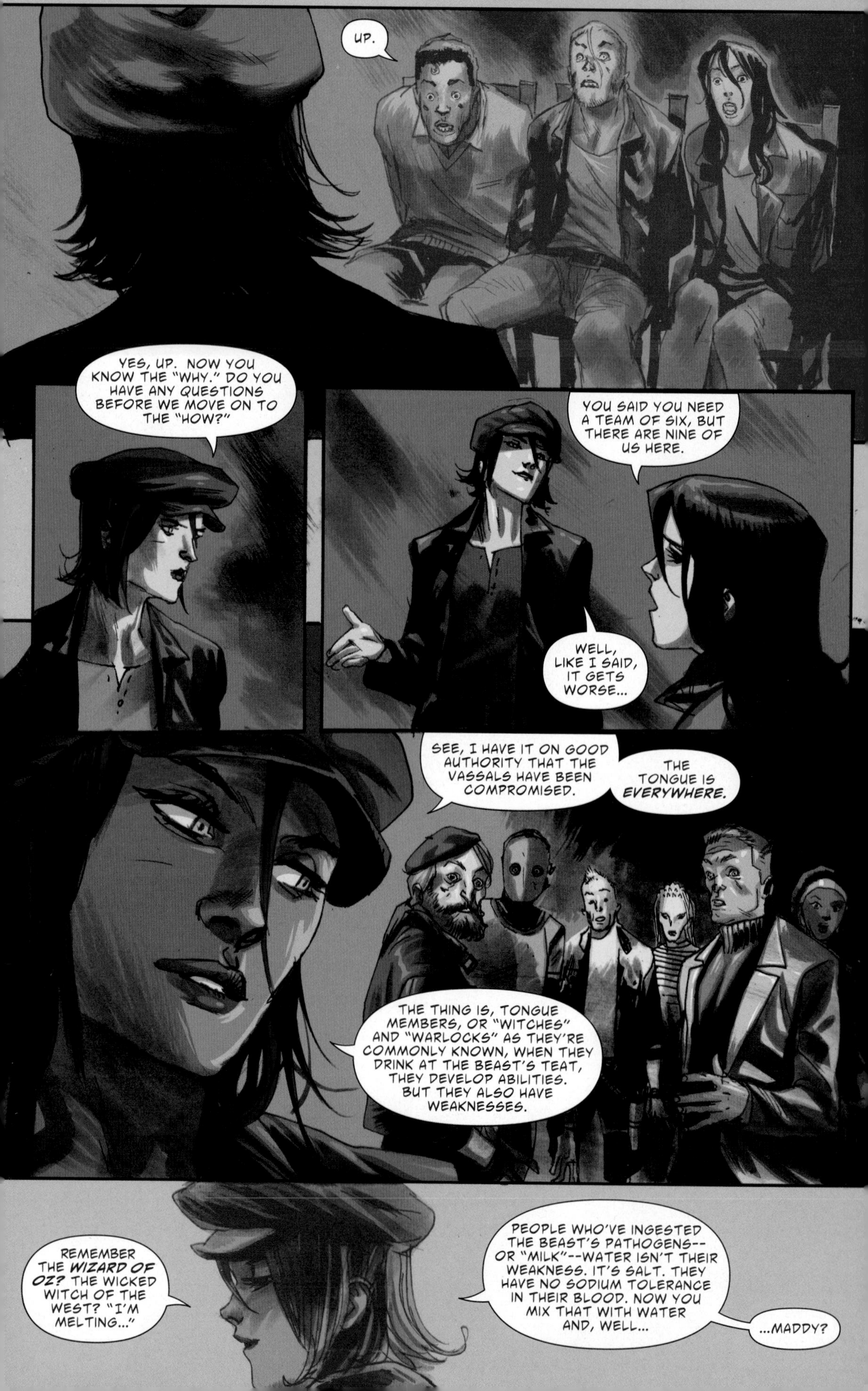
UP.
YES, UP. NOW YOU KNOW THE "WHY." DO YOU HAVE ANY QUESTIONS BEFORE WE MOVE ON TO THE "HOW?"
YOU SAID YOU NEED A TEAM OF SIX, BUT THERE ARE NINE OF US HERE.
WELL, LIKE I SAID, IT GETS WORSE...
SEE, I HAVE IT ON GOOD AUTHORITY THAT THE VASSALS HAVE BEEN COMPROMISED.
THE TONGUE IS *EVERYWHERE.*
THE THING IS, TONGUE MEMBERS, OR "WITCHES" AND "WARLOCKS" AS THEY'RE COMMONLY KNOWN, WHEN THEY DRINK AT THE BEAST'S TEAT, THEY DEVELOP ABILITIES. BUT THEY ALSO HAVE WEAKNESSES.
REMEMBER THE *WIZARD OF OZ?* THE WICKED WITCH OF THE WEST? "I'M MELTING..."
PEOPLE WHO'VE INGESTED THE BEAST'S PATHOGENS-- OR "MILK"--WATER ISN'T THEIR WEAKNESS. IT'S SALT. THEY HAVE NO SODIUM TOLERANCE IN THEIR BLOOD. NOW YOU MIX THAT WITH WATER AND, WELL...
...MADDY?

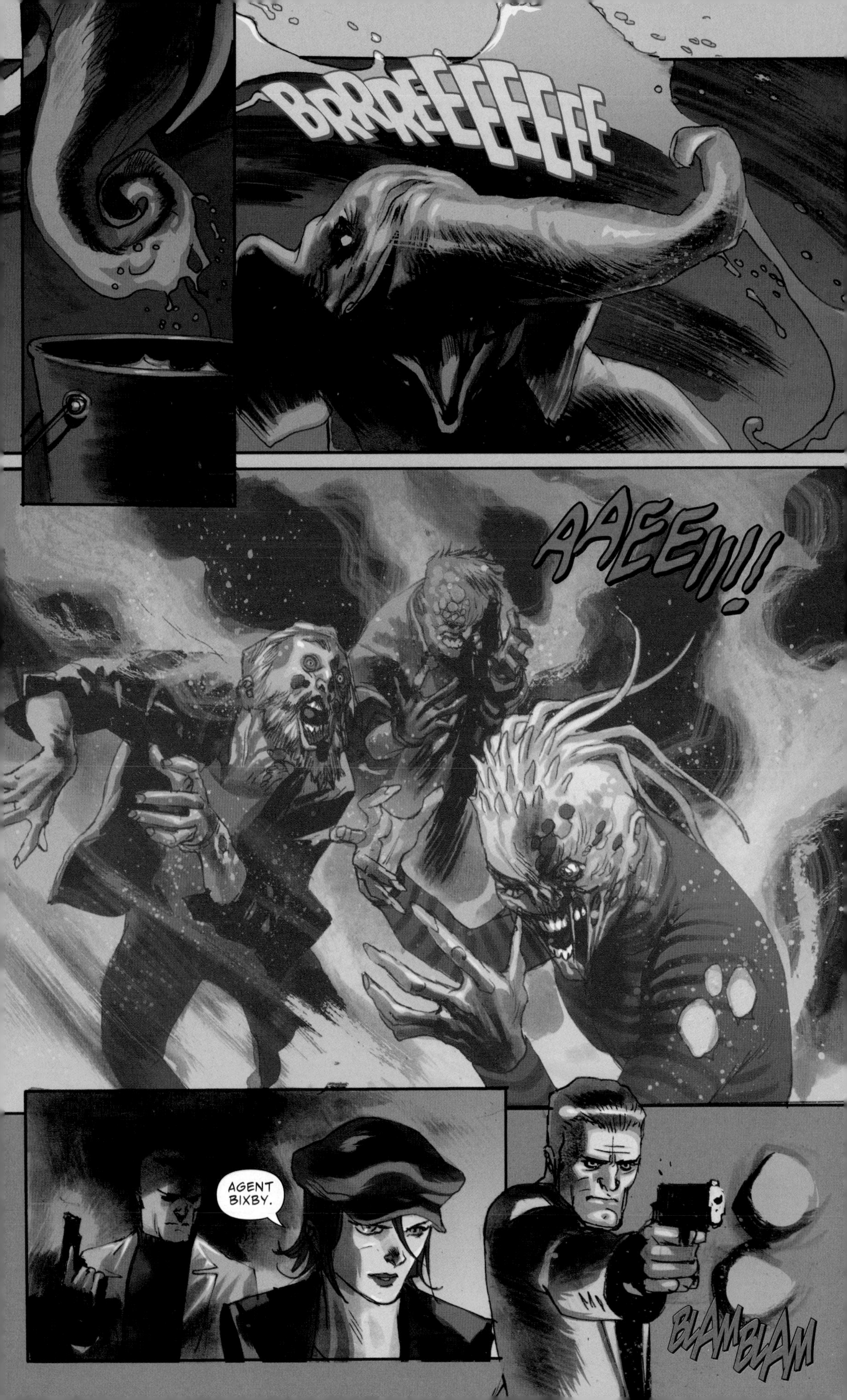
BRROEEEEEEEE
AAEEII!!
AGENT BIXBY.
BLAMBLAM

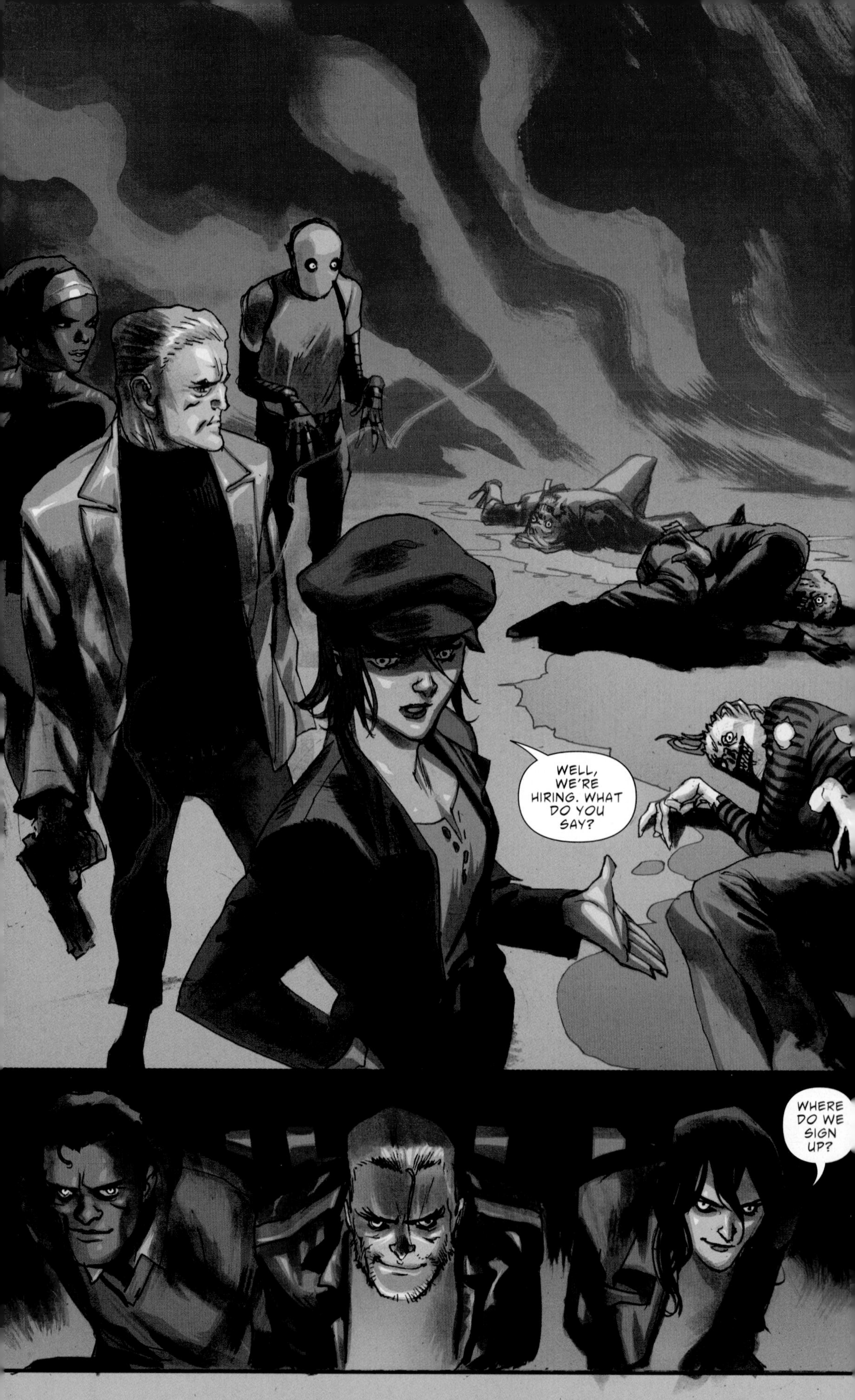
WELL, WE'RE HIRING. WHAT DO YOU SAY?
WHERE DO WE SIGN UP?

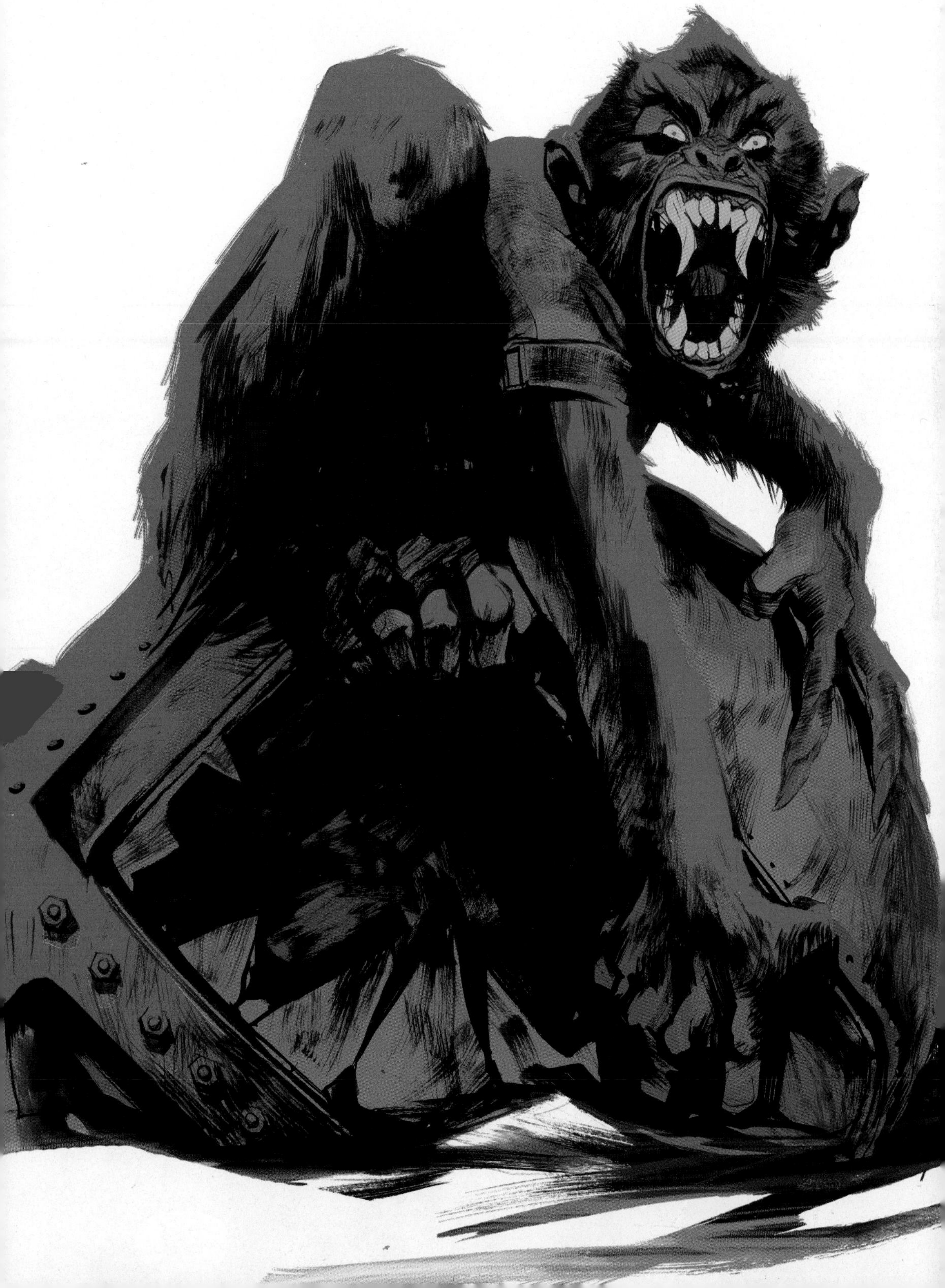

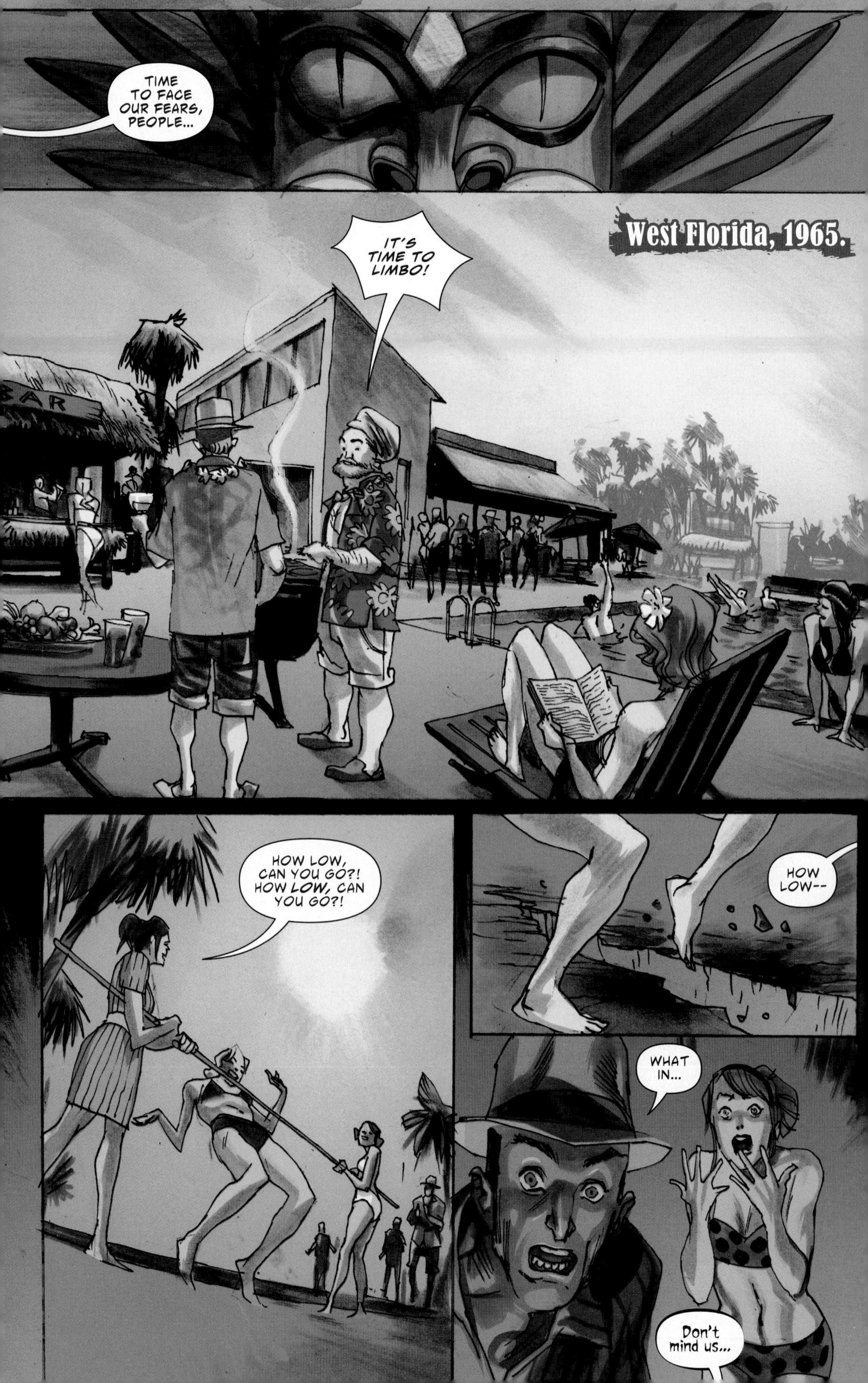
TIME TO FACE OUR FEARS, PEOPLE...
West Florida, 1965.
IT'S TIME TO LIMBO!
BAR
HOW LOW, CAN YOU GO?! HOW LOW, CAN YOU GO?!
HOW LOW--
WHAT IN...
Don't mind us...

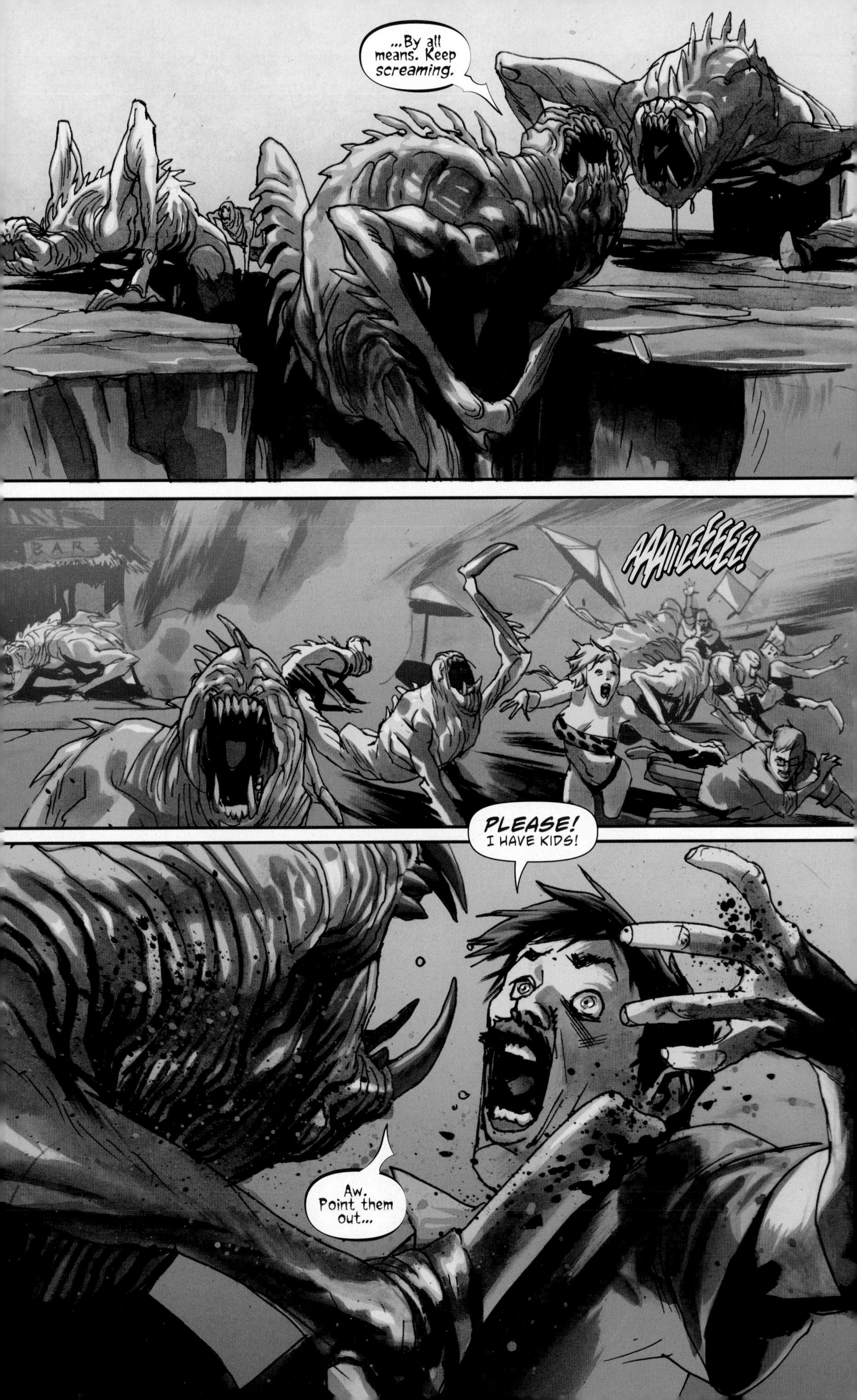
...By all means. Keep screaming.
AAAIIIEEEEE!
PLEASE! I HAVE KIDS!
Aw. Point them out...

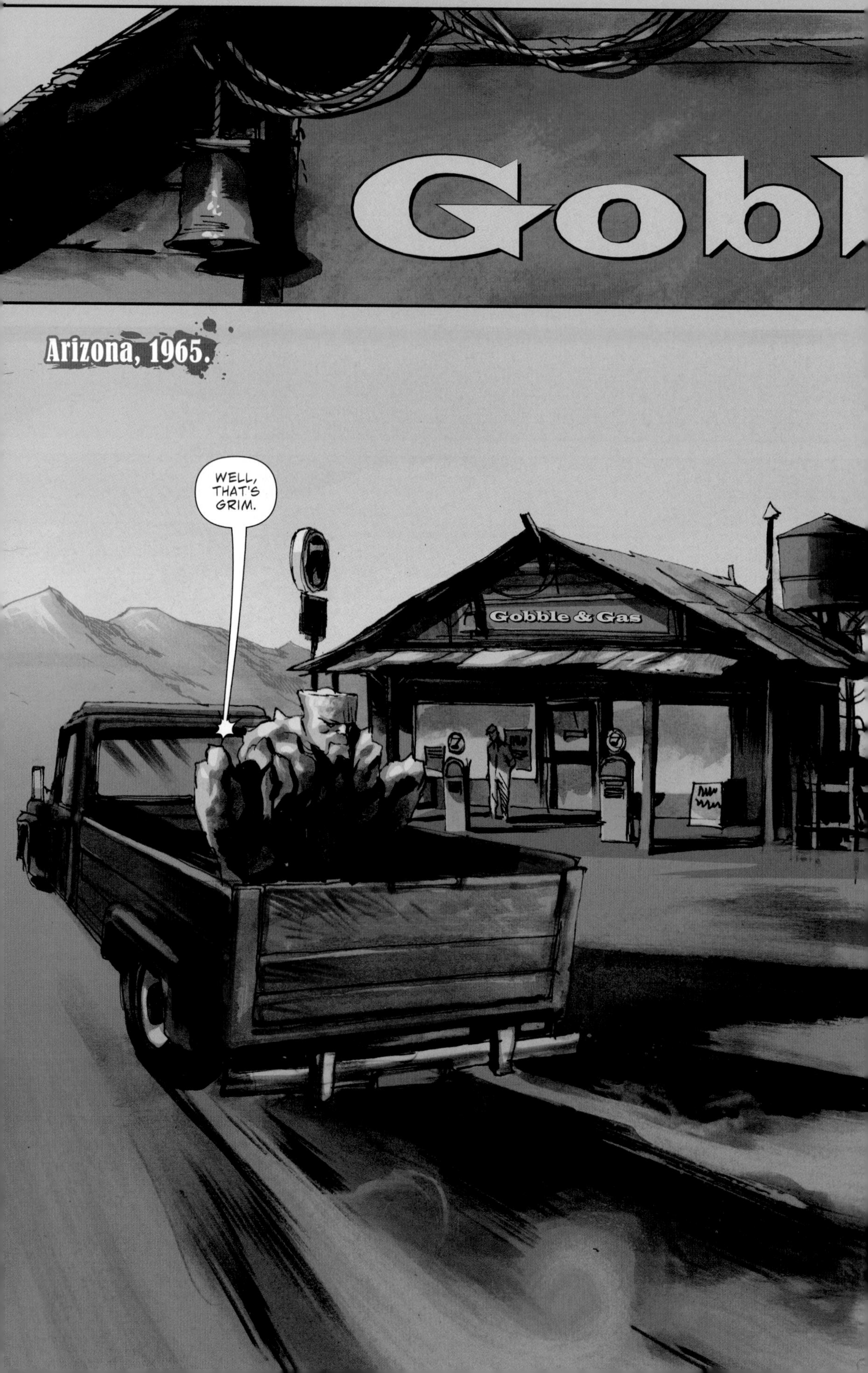
Arizona, 1965.
Gobble & Gas
WELL, THAT'S GRIM.

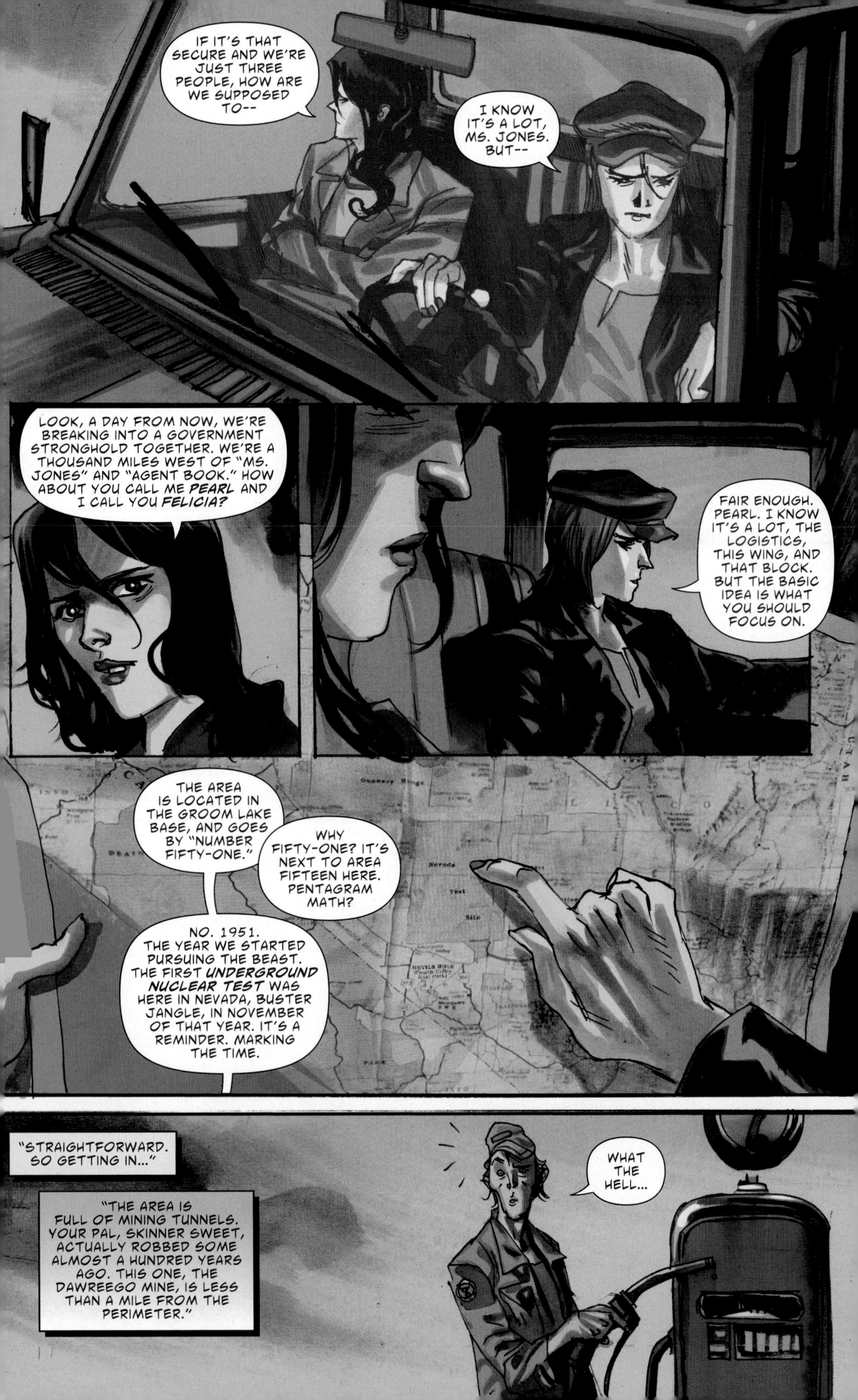
IF IT'S THAT SECURE AND WE'RE JUST THREE PEOPLE, HOW ARE WE SUPPOSED TO--
I KNOW IT'S A LOT, MS. JONES. BUT--
LOOK, A DAY FROM NOW, WE'RE BREAKING INTO A GOVERNMENT STRONGHOLD TOGETHER. WE'RE A THOUSAND MILES WEST OF "MS. JONES" AND "AGENT BOOK." HOW ABOUT YOU CALL ME *PEARL* AND I CALL YOU *FELICIA?*
FAIR ENOUGH. PEARL. I KNOW IT'S A LOT, THE LOGISTICS, THIS WING, AND THAT BLOCK. BUT THE BASIC IDEA IS WHAT YOU SHOULD FOCUS ON.
THE AREA IS LOCATED IN THE GROOM LAKE BASE, AND GOES BY "NUMBER FIFTY-ONE."
WHY FIFTY-ONE? IT'S NEXT TO AREA FIFTEEN HERE. PENTAGRAM MATH?
NO. 1951. THE YEAR WE STARTED PURSUING THE BEAST. THE FIRST ***UNDERGROUND NUCLEAR TEST*** WAS HERE IN NEVADA, BUSTER JANGLE, IN NOVEMBER OF THAT YEAR. IT'S A REMINDER. MARKING THE TIME.
"STRAIGHTFORWARD. SO GETTING IN..."
"THE AREA IS FULL OF MINING TUNNELS. YOUR PAL, SKINNER SWEET, ACTUALLY ROBBED SOME ALMOST A HUNDRED YEARS AGO. THIS ONE, THE DAWREEGO MINE, IS LESS THAN A MILE FROM THE PERIMETER."
WHAT THE HELL...

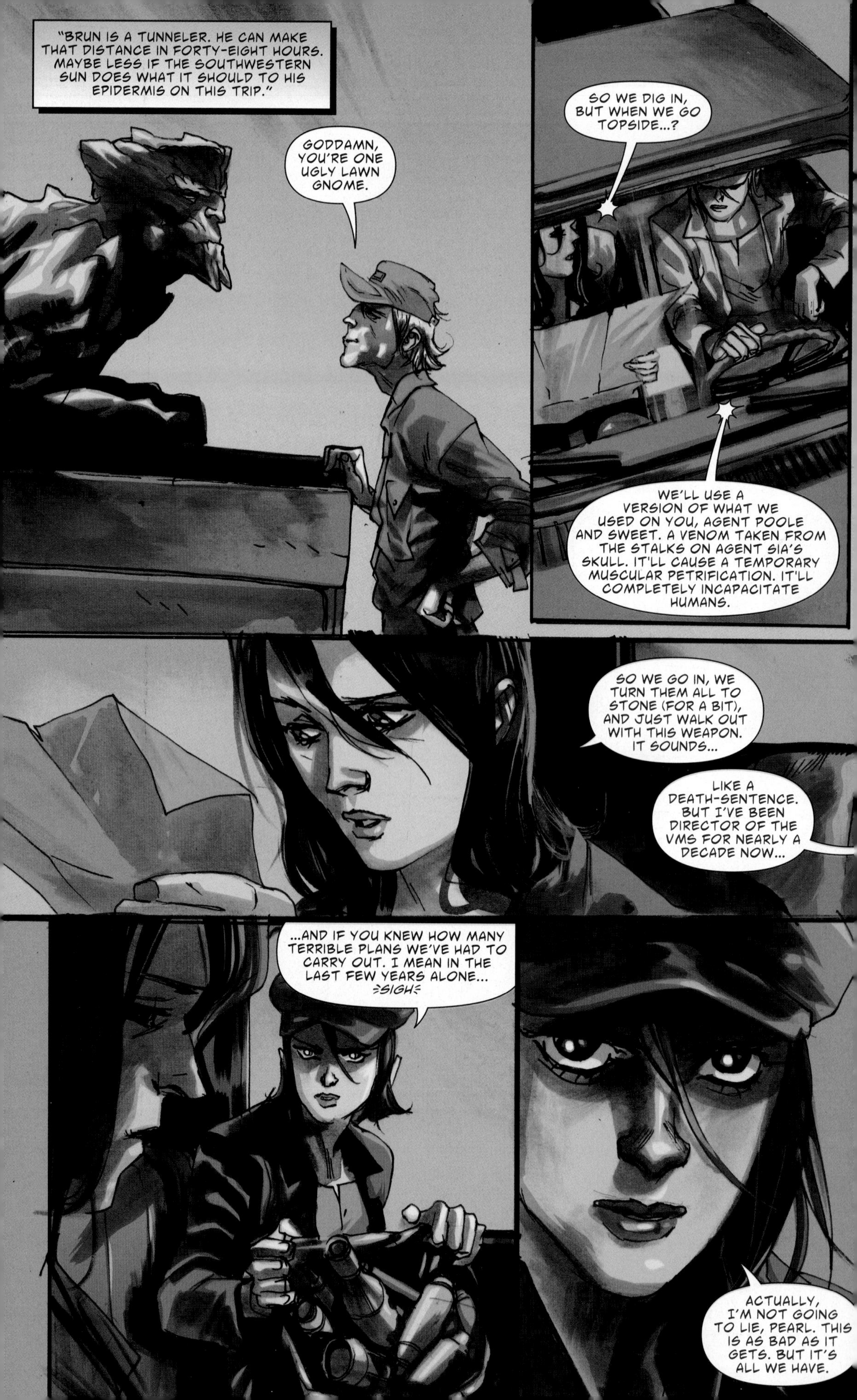
"BRUN IS A TUNNELER. HE CAN MAKE THAT DISTANCE IN FORTY-EIGHT HOURS. MAYBE LESS IF THE SOUTHWESTERN SUN DOES WHAT IT SHOULD TO HIS EPIDERMIS ON THIS TRIP."
GODDAMN, YOU'RE ONE UGLY LAWN GNOME.
SO WE DIG IN, BUT WHEN WE GO TOPSIDE...?
WE'LL USE A VERSION OF WHAT WE USED ON YOU, AGENT POOLE AND SWEET. A VENOM TAKEN FROM THE STALKS ON AGENT SIA'S SKULL. IT'LL CAUSE A TEMPORARY MUSCULAR PETRIFICATION. IT'LL COMPLETELY INCAPACITATE HUMANS.
SO WE GO IN, WE TURN THEM ALL TO STONE (FOR A BIT), AND JUST WALK OUT WITH THIS WEAPON. IT SOUNDS...
LIKE A DEATH-SENTENCE. BUT I'VE BEEN DIRECTOR OF THE VMS FOR NEARLY A DECADE NOW...
...AND IF YOU KNEW HOW MANY TERRIBLE PLANS WE'VE HAD TO CARRY OUT. I MEAN IN THE LAST FEW YEARS ALONE... SIGH
ACTUALLY, I'M NOT GOING TO LIE, PEARL. THIS IS AS BAD AS IT GETS. BUT IT'S ALL WE HAVE.

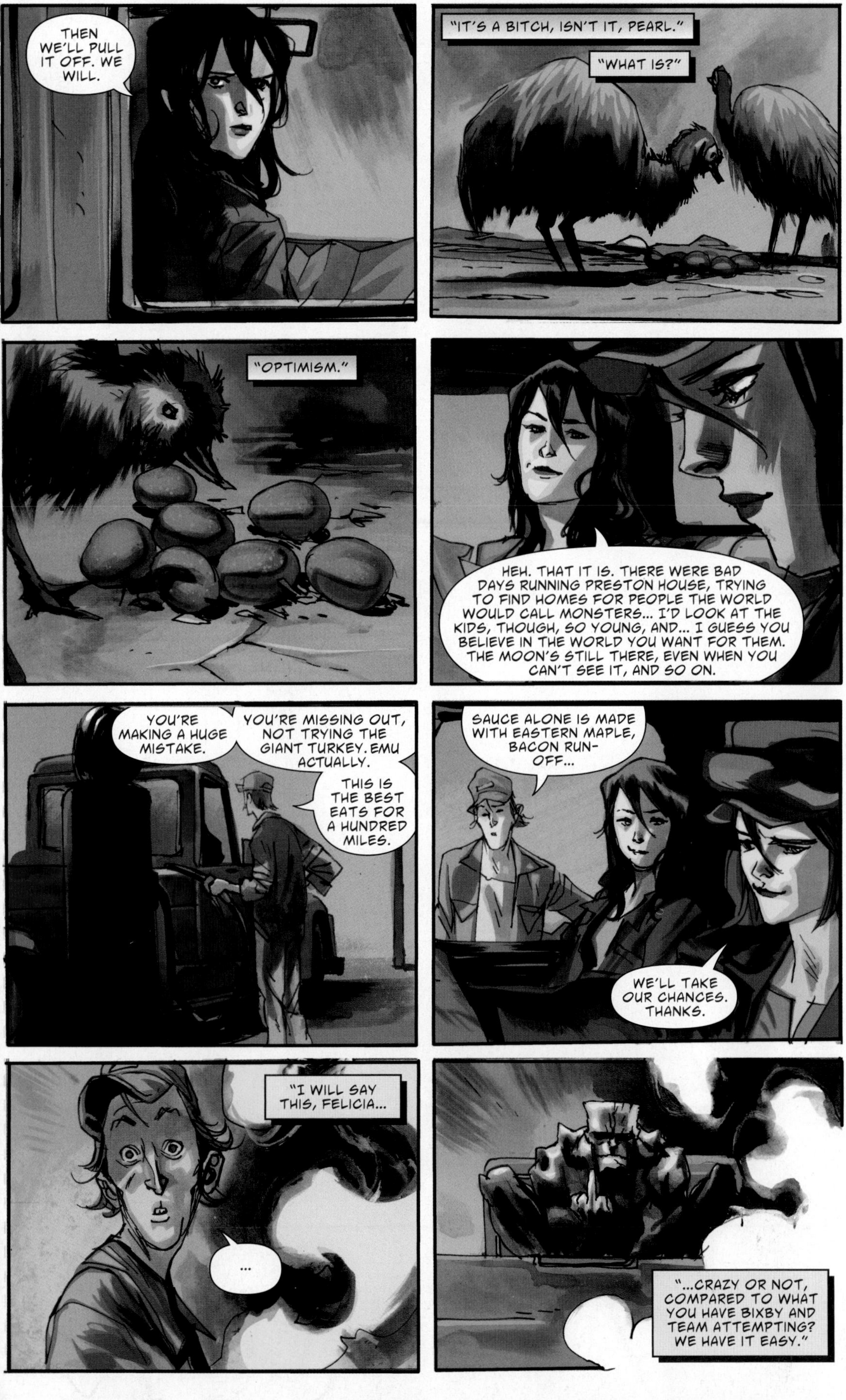
THEN WE'LL PULL IT OFF. WE WILL.
"IT'S A BITCH, ISN'T IT, PEARL."
"WHAT IS?"
"OPTIMISM."
HEH. THAT IT IS. THERE WERE BAD DAYS RUNNING PRESTON HOUSE, TRYING TO FIND HOMES FOR PEOPLE THE WORLD WOULD CALL MONSTERS... I'D LOOK AT THE KIDS, THOUGH, SO YOUNG, AND... I GUESS YOU BELIEVE IN THE WORLD YOU WANT FOR THEM. THE MOON'S STILL THERE, EVEN WHEN YOU CAN'T SEE IT, AND SO ON.
YOU'RE MAKING A HUGE MISTAKE.
YOU'RE MISSING OUT, NOT TRYING THE GIANT TURKEY. EMU ACTUALLY.
THIS IS THE BEST EATS FOR A HUNDRED MILES.
SAUCE ALONE IS MADE WITH EASTERN MAPLE, BACON RUN-OFF...
WE'LL TAKE OUR CHANCES. THANKS.
"I WILL SAY THIS, FELICIA...
...
"...CRAZY OR NOT, COMPARED TO WHAT YOU HAVE BIXBY AND TEAM ATTEMPTING? WE HAVE IT EASY."

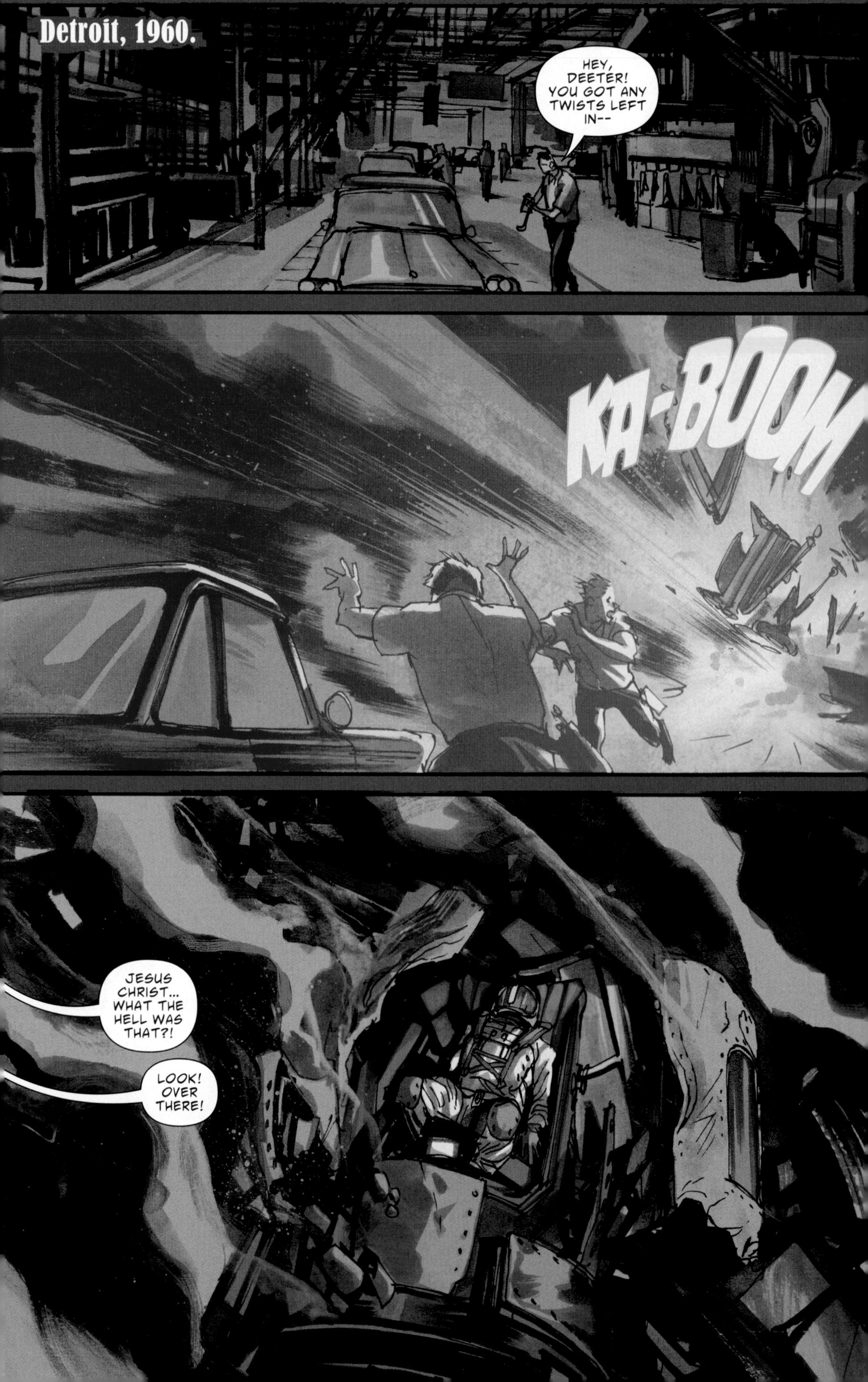
Detroit, 1960.
HEY, DEETER! YOU GOT ANY TWISTS LEFT IN--
KA-BOOM
JESUS CHRIST... WHAT THE HELL WAS THAT?!
LOOK! OVER THERE!

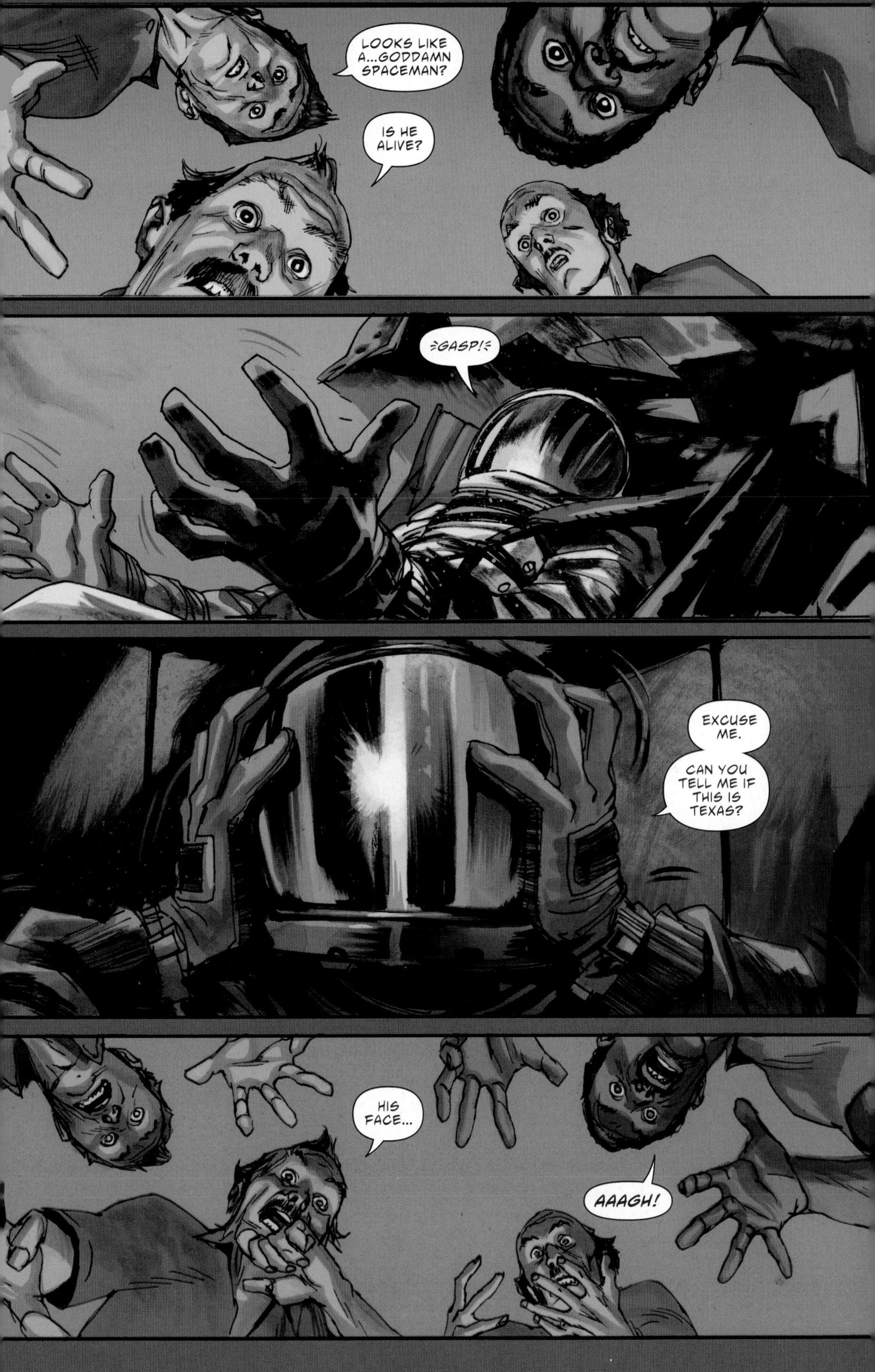
LOOKS LIKE A...GODDAMN SPACEMAN?
IS HE ALIVE?
≠GASP!≠
EXCUSE ME.
CAN YOU TELL ME IF THIS IS TEXAS?
HIS FACE...
AAAGH!

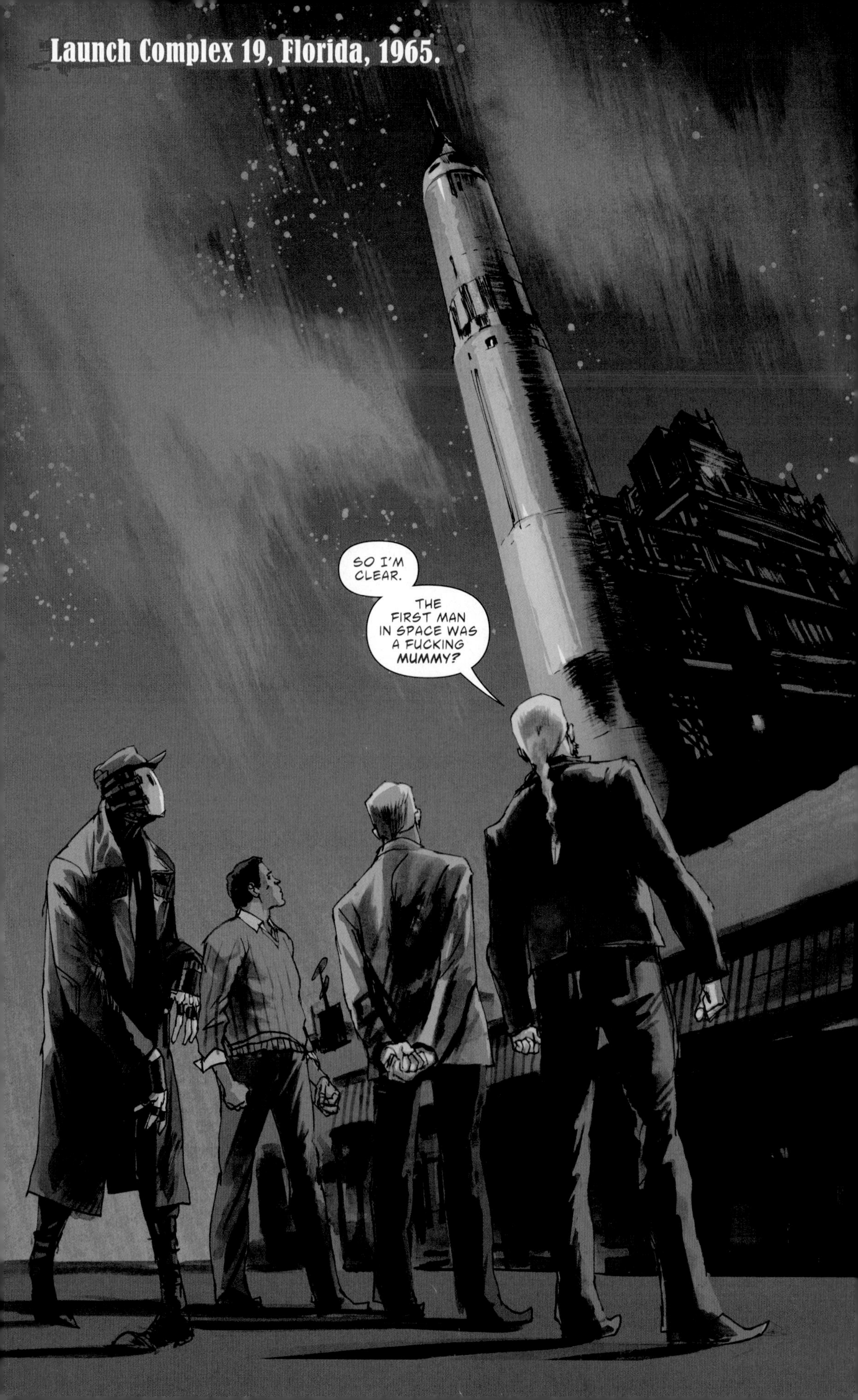
Launch Complex 19, Florida, 1965.
SO I'M CLEAR.
THE FIRST MAN IN SPACE WAS A FUCKING MUMMY?

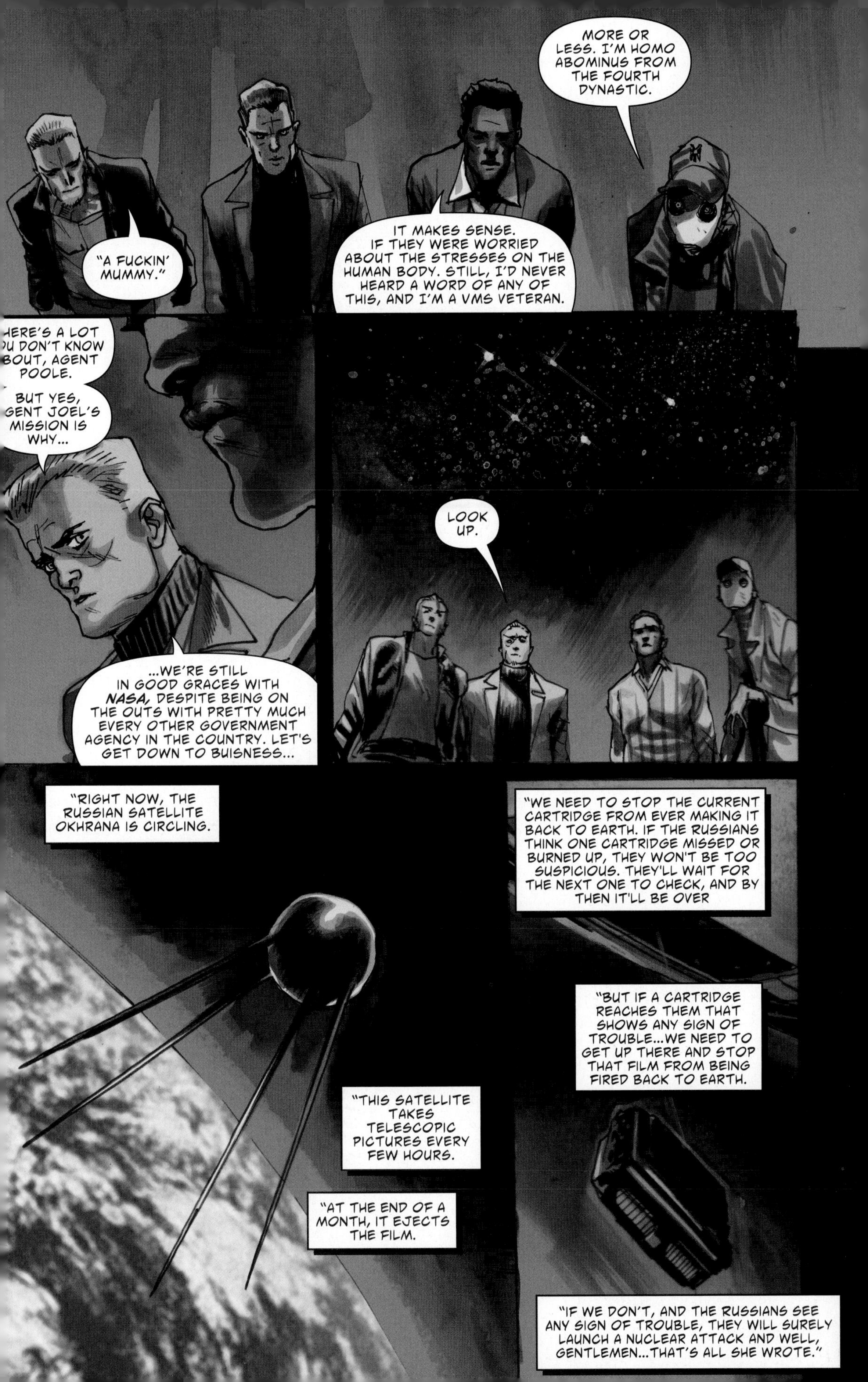
"A FUCKIN' MUMMY."
IT MAKES SENSE. IF THEY WERE WORRIED ABOUT THE STRESSES ON THE HUMAN BODY. STILL, I'D NEVER HEARD A WORD OF ANY OF THIS, AND I'M A VMS VETERAN.
MORE OR LESS. I'M HOMO ABOMINUS FROM THE FOURTH DYNASTIC.
HERE'S A LOT OU DON'T KNOW BOUT, AGENT POOLE.
BUT YES, GENT JOEL'S MISSION IS WHY...
...WE'RE STILL IN GOOD GRACES WITH NASA, DESPITE BEING ON THE OUTS WITH PRETTY MUCH EVERY OTHER GOVERNMENT AGENCY IN THE COUNTRY. LET'S GET DOWN TO BUISNESS...
LOOK UP.
"RIGHT NOW, THE RUSSIAN SATELLITE OKHRANA IS CIRCLING.
"THIS SATELLITE TAKES TELESCOPIC PICTURES EVERY FEW HOURS.
"AT THE END OF A MONTH, IT EJECTS THE FILM.
"WE NEED TO STOP THE CURRENT CARTRIDGE FROM EVER MAKING IT BACK TO EARTH. IF THE RUSSIANS THINK ONE CARTRIDGE MISSED OR BURNED UP, THEY WON'T BE TOO SUSPICIOUS. THEY'LL WAIT FOR THE NEXT ONE TO CHECK, AND BY THEN IT'LL BE OVER
"BUT IF A CARTRIDGE REACHES THEM THAT SHOWS ANY SIGN OF TROUBLE...WE NEED TO GET UP THERE AND STOP THAT FILM FROM BEING FIRED BACK TO EARTH.
"IF WE DON'T, AND THE RUSSIANS SEE ANY SIGN OF TROUBLE, THEY WILL SURELY LAUNCH A NUCLEAR ATTACK AND WELL, GENTLEMEN...THAT'S ALL SHE WROTE."

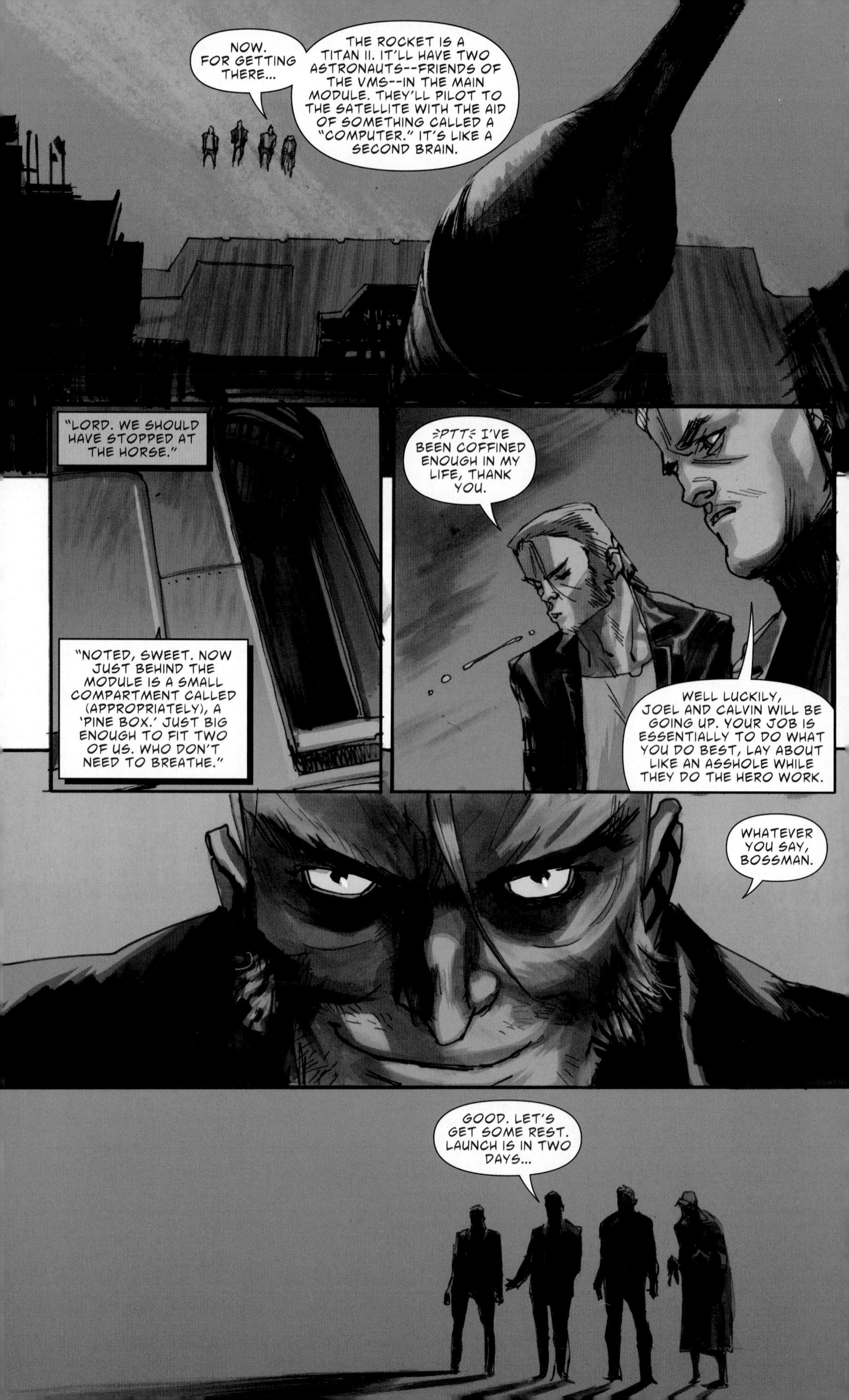
NOW. FOR GETTING THERE...
THE ROCKET IS A TITAN II. IT'LL HAVE TWO ASTRONAUTS--FRIENDS OF THE VMS--IN THE MAIN MODULE. THEY'LL PILOT TO THE SATELLITE WITH THE AID OF SOMETHING CALLED A "COMPUTER." IT'S LIKE A SECOND BRAIN.
"LORD. WE SHOULD HAVE STOPPED AT THE HORSE."
"NOTED, SWEET. NOW JUST BEHIND THE MODULE IS A SMALL COMPARTMENT CALLED (APPROPRIATELY), A 'PINE BOX.' JUST BIG ENOUGH TO FIT TWO OF US. WHO DON'T NEED TO BREATHE."
PTT I'VE BEEN COFFINED ENOUGH IN MY LIFE, THANK YOU.
WELL LUCKILY, JOEL AND CALVIN WILL BE GOING UP. YOUR JOB IS ESSENTIALLY TO DO WHAT YOU DO BEST, LAY ABOUT LIKE AN ASSHOLE WHILE THEY DO THE HERO WORK.
WHATEVER YOU SAY, BOSSMAN.
GOOD. LET'S GET SOME REST. LAUNCH IS IN TWO DAYS...

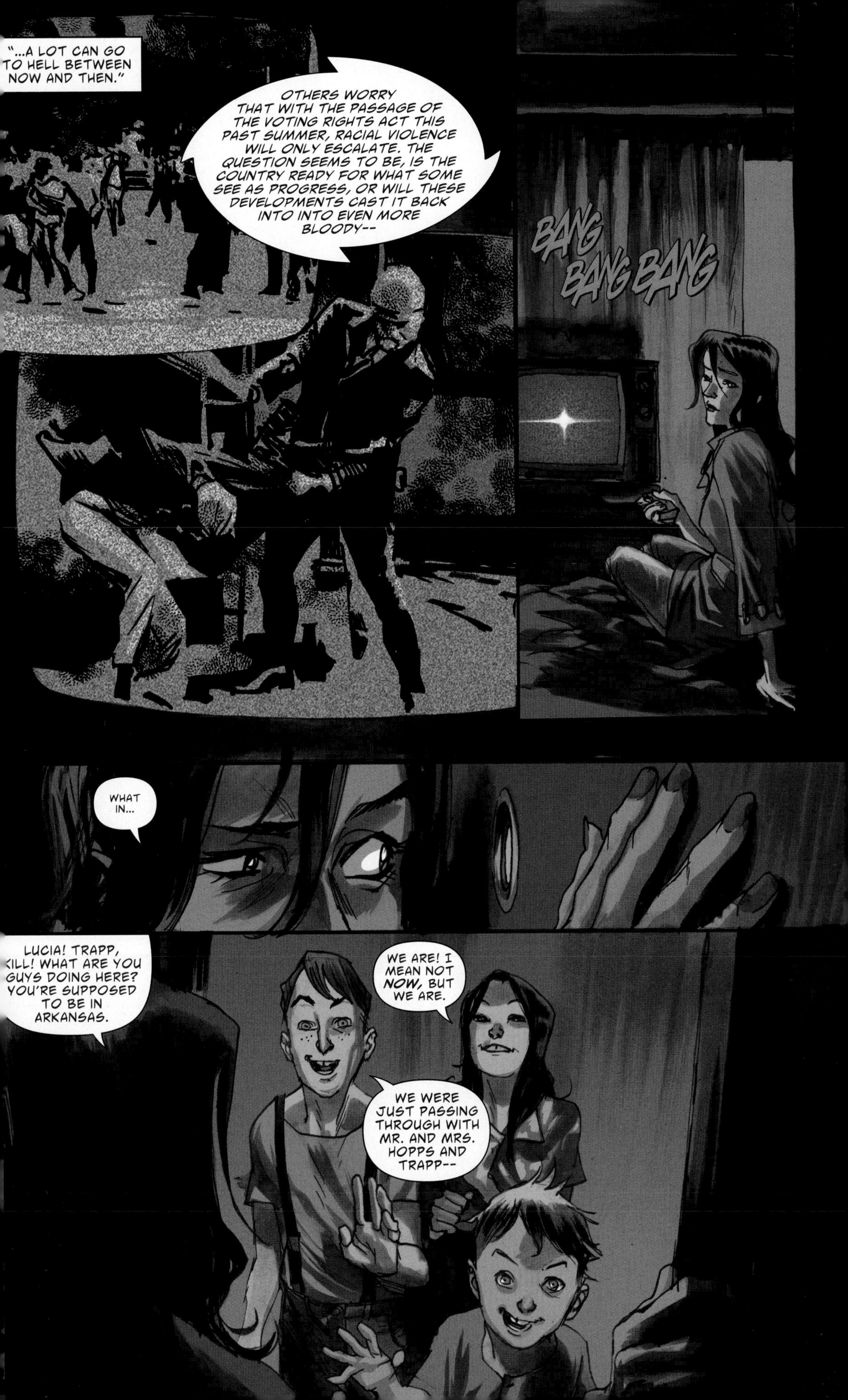
"...A LOT CAN GO TO HELL BETWEEN NOW AND THEN."
OTHERS WORRY THAT WITH THE PASSAGE OF THE VOTING RIGHTS ACT THIS PAST SUMMER, RACIAL VIOLENCE WILL ONLY ESCALATE. THE QUESTION SEEMS TO BE, IS THE COUNTRY READY FOR WHAT SOME SEE AS PROGRESS, OR WILL THESE DEVELOPMENTS CAST IT BACK INTO INTO EVEN MORE BLOODY--
BANG
BANG BANG
WHAT IN...
LUCIA! TRAPP, KILL! WHAT ARE YOU GUYS DOING HERE? YOU'RE SUPPOSED TO BE IN ARKANSAS.
WE ARE! I MEAN NOT NOW, BUT WE ARE.
WE WERE JUST PASSING THROUGH WITH MR. AND MRS. HOPPS AND TRAPP--

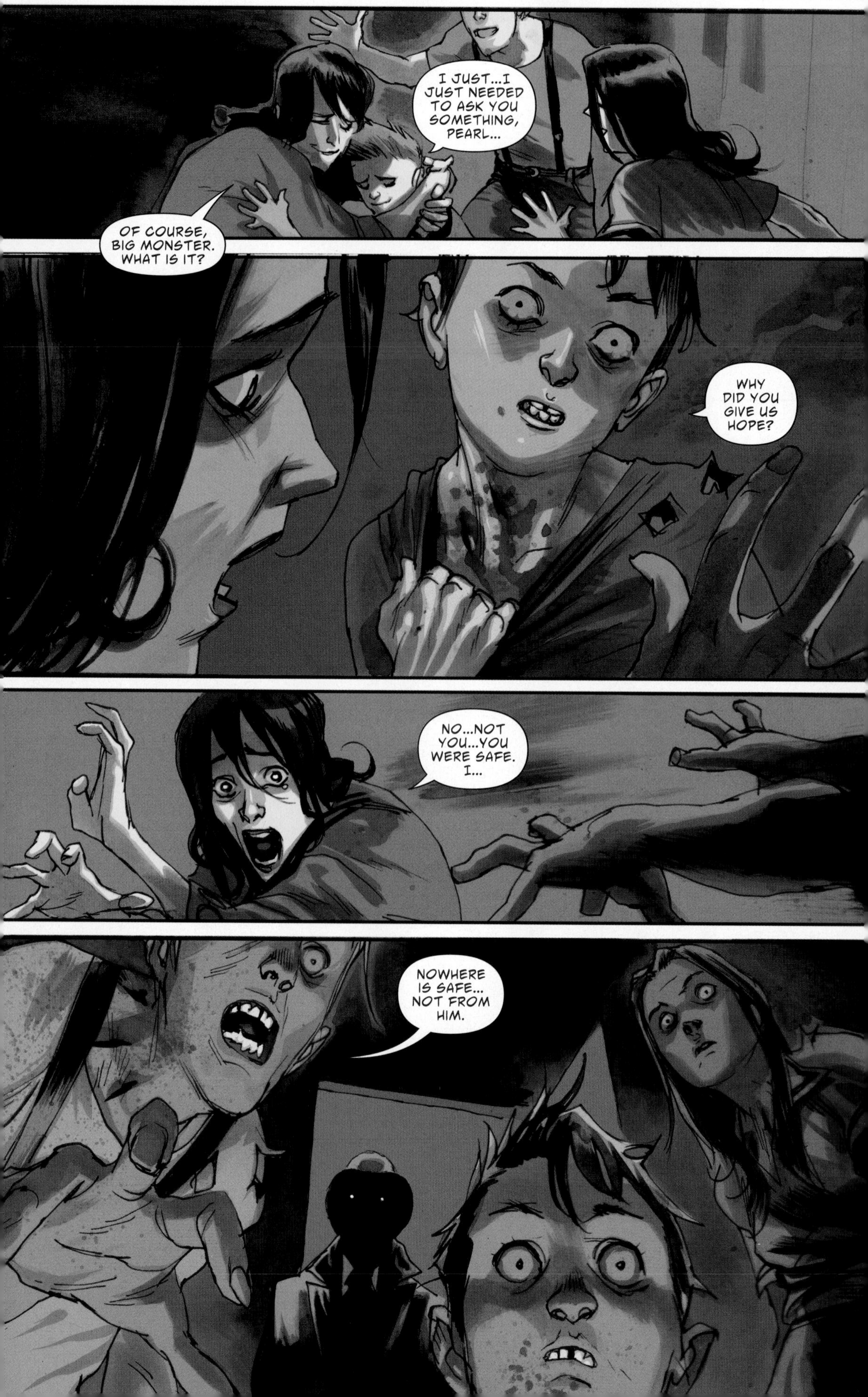
I JUST...I JUST NEEDED TO ASK YOU SOMETHING, PEARL...
OF COURSE, BIG MONSTER. WHAT IS IT?
WHY DID YOU GIVE US HOPE?
NO...NOT YOU...YOU WERE SAFE. I...
NOWHERE IS SAFE... NOT FROM HIM.

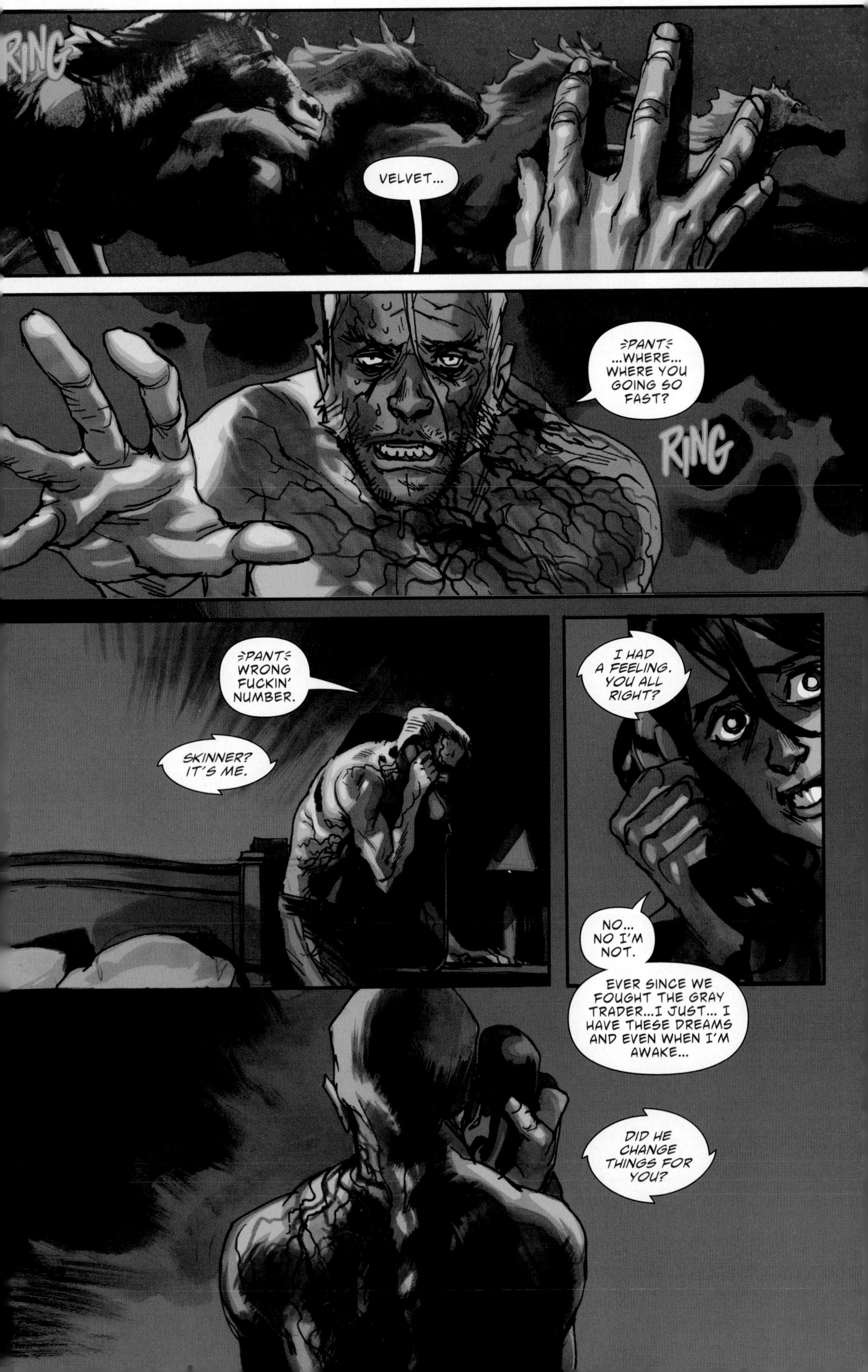
RING
VELVET...
≈PANT≈ ...WHERE... WHERE YOU GOING SO FAST?
RING
≈PANT≈ WRONG FUCKIN' NUMBER.
SKINNER? IT'S ME.
I HAD A FEELING. YOU ALL RIGHT?
NO... NO I'M NOT.
EVER SINCE WE FOUGHT THE GRAY TRADER...I JUST... I HAVE THESE DREAMS AND EVEN WHEN I'M AWAKE...
DID HE CHANGE THINGS FOR YOU?

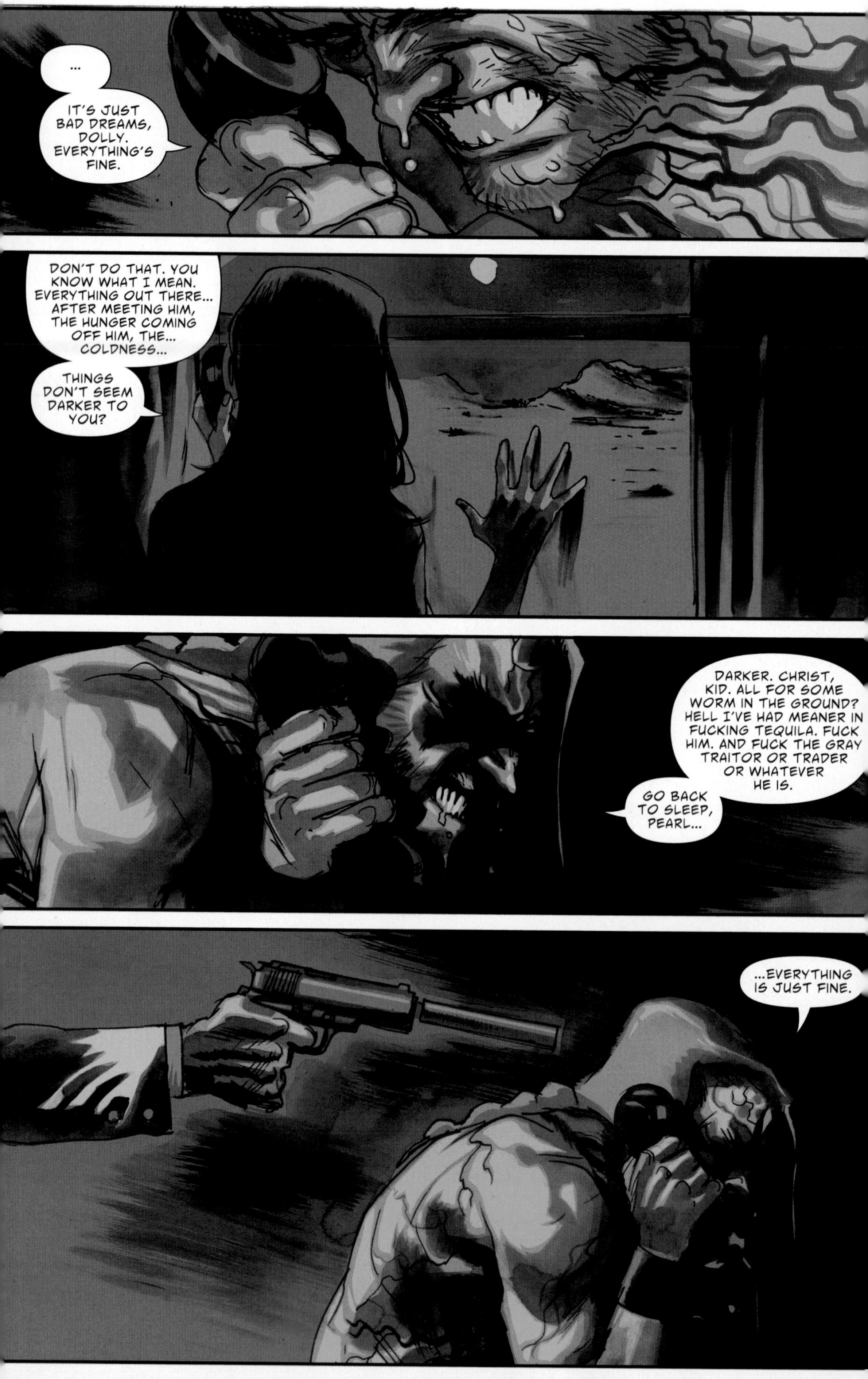
...
IT'S JUST BAD DREAMS, DOLLY. EVERYTHING'S FINE.
DON'T DO THAT. YOU KNOW WHAT I MEAN. EVERYTHING OUT THERE... AFTER MEETING HIM, THE HUNGER COMING OFF HIM, THE... COLDNESS...
THINGS DON'T SEEM DARKER TO YOU?
DARKER. CHRIST, KID. ALL FOR SOME WORM IN THE GROUND? HELL I'VE HAD MEANER IN FUCKING TEQUILA. FUCK HIM. AND FUCK THE GRAY TRAITOR OR TRADER OR WHATEVER HE IS.
GO BACK TO SLEEP, PEARL...
...EVERYTHING IS JUST FINE.

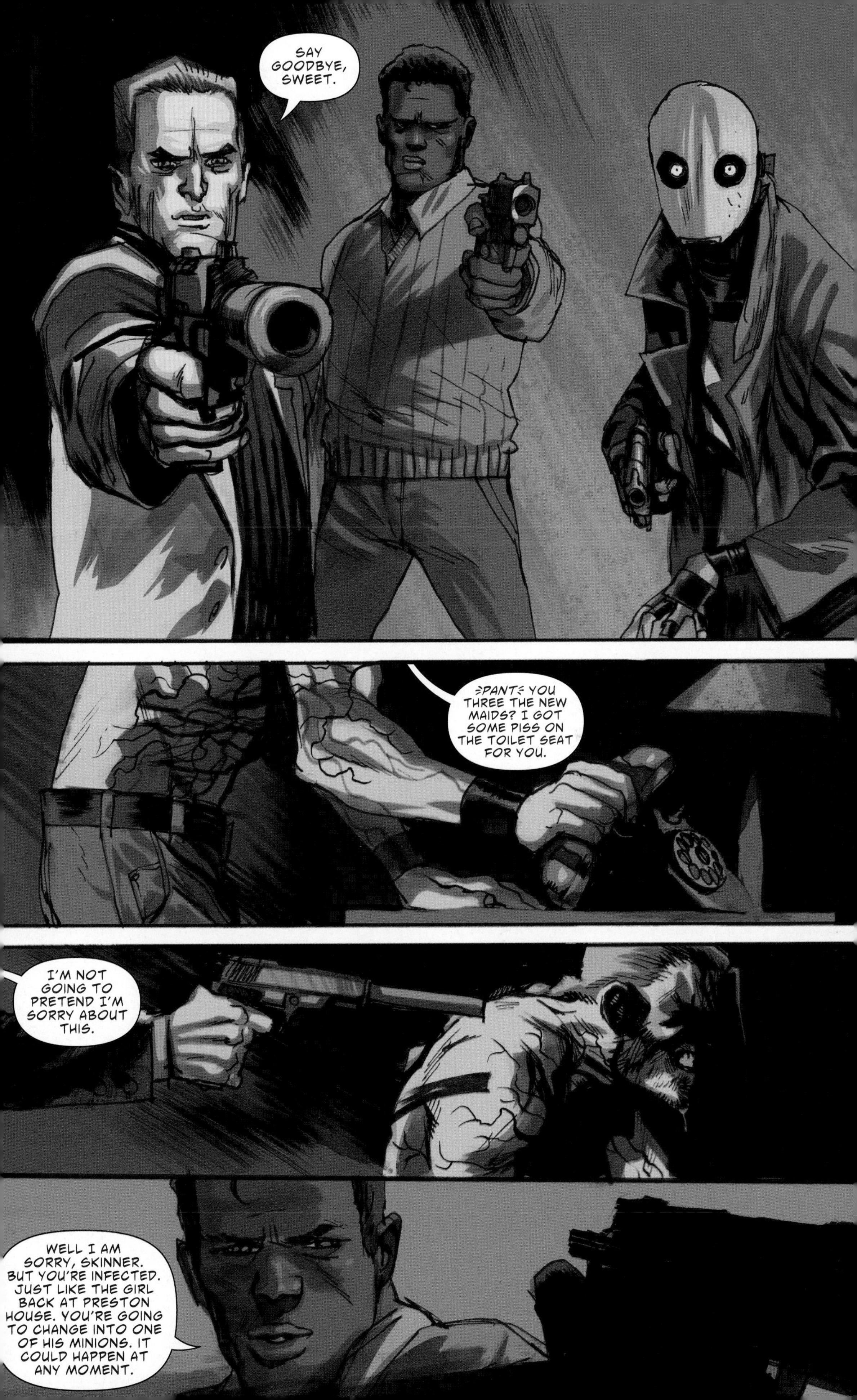
SAY GOODBYE, SWEET.
=PANT= YOU THREE THE NEW MAIDS? I GOT SOME PISS ON THE TOILET SEAT FOR YOU.
I'M NOT GOING TO PRETEND I'M SORRY ABOUT THIS.
WELL I AM SORRY, SKINNER. BUT YOU'RE INFECTED. JUST LIKE THE GIRL BACK AT PRESTON HOUSE. YOU'RE GOING TO CHANGE INTO ONE OF HIS MINIONS. IT COULD HAPPEN AT ANY MOMENT.

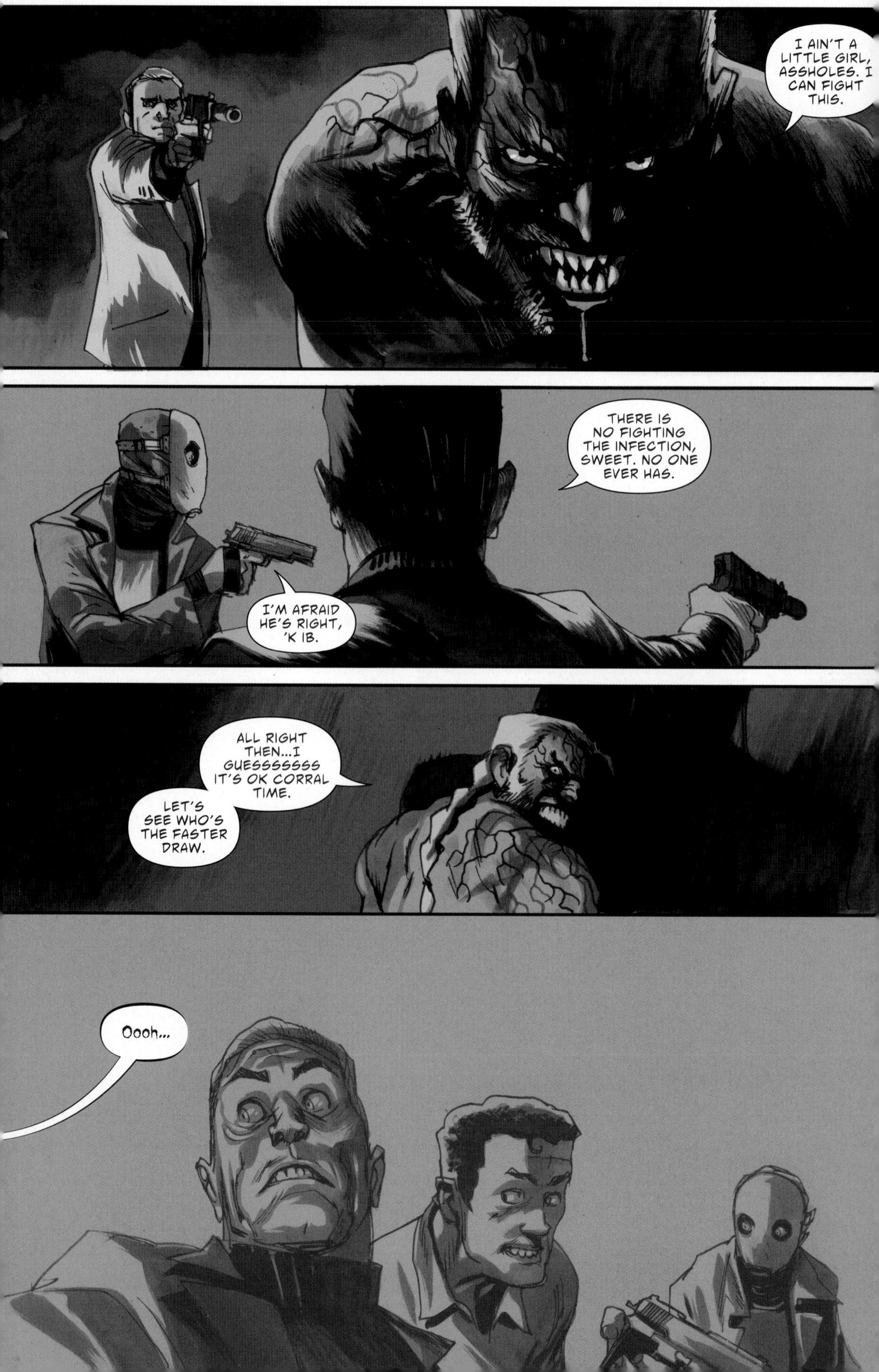
I AIN'T A LITTLE GIRL, ASSHOLES. I CAN FIGHT THIS.
THERE IS NO FIGHTING THE INFECTION, SWEET. NO ONE EVER HAS.
I'M AFRAID HE'S RIGHT, 'K IB.
ALL RIGHT THEN...I GUESSSSSSS IT'S OK CORRAL TIME.
LET'S SEE WHO'S THE FASTER DRAW.
Oooh...

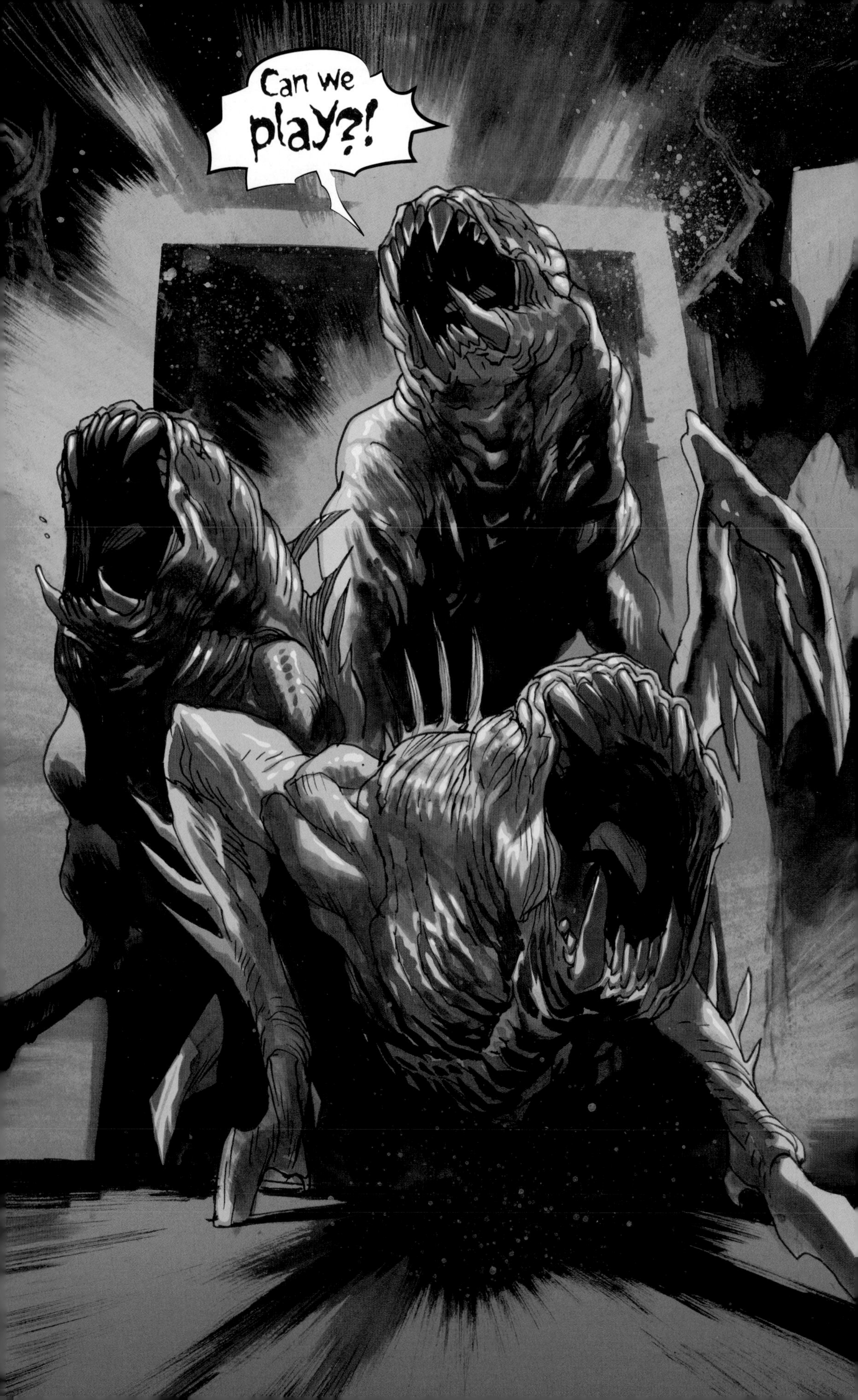
Can we play?!

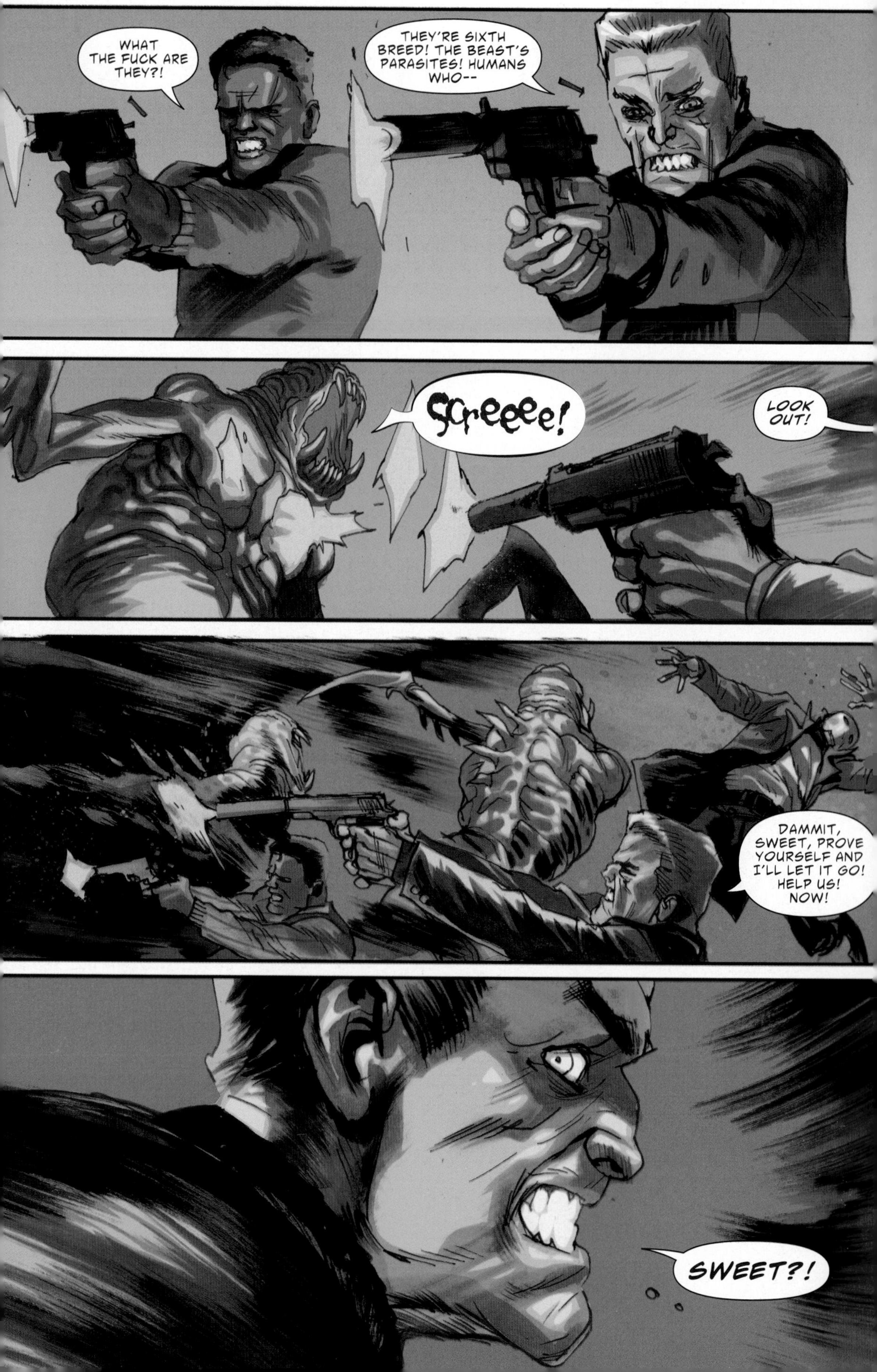
WHAT THE FUCK ARE THEY?!
THEY'RE SIXTH BREED! THE BEAST'S PARASITES! HUMANS WHO--
SCREEEE!
LOOK OUT!
DAMMIT, SWEET, PROVE YOURSELF AND I'LL LET IT GO! HELP US! NOW!
SWEET?!

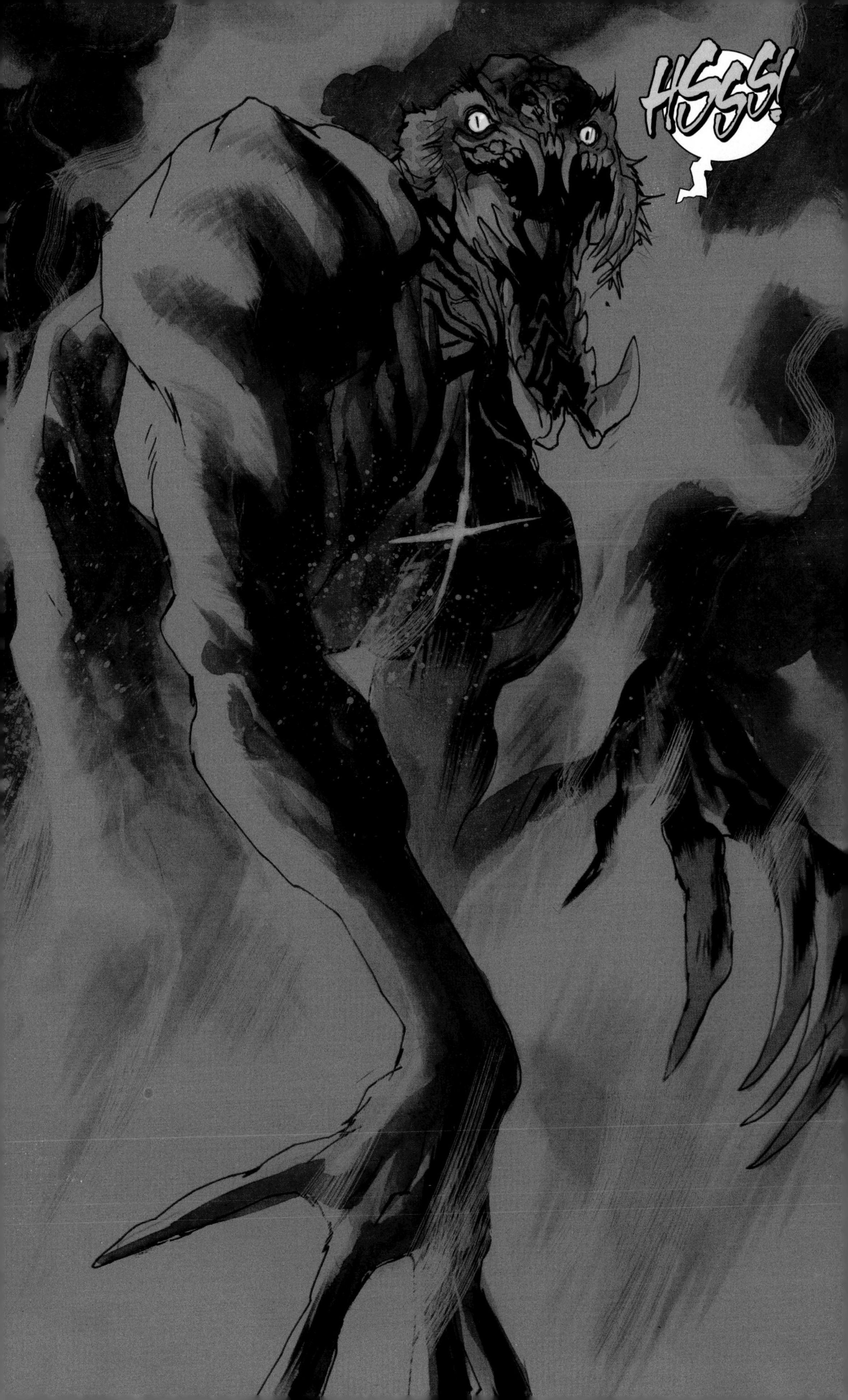
HSSS!

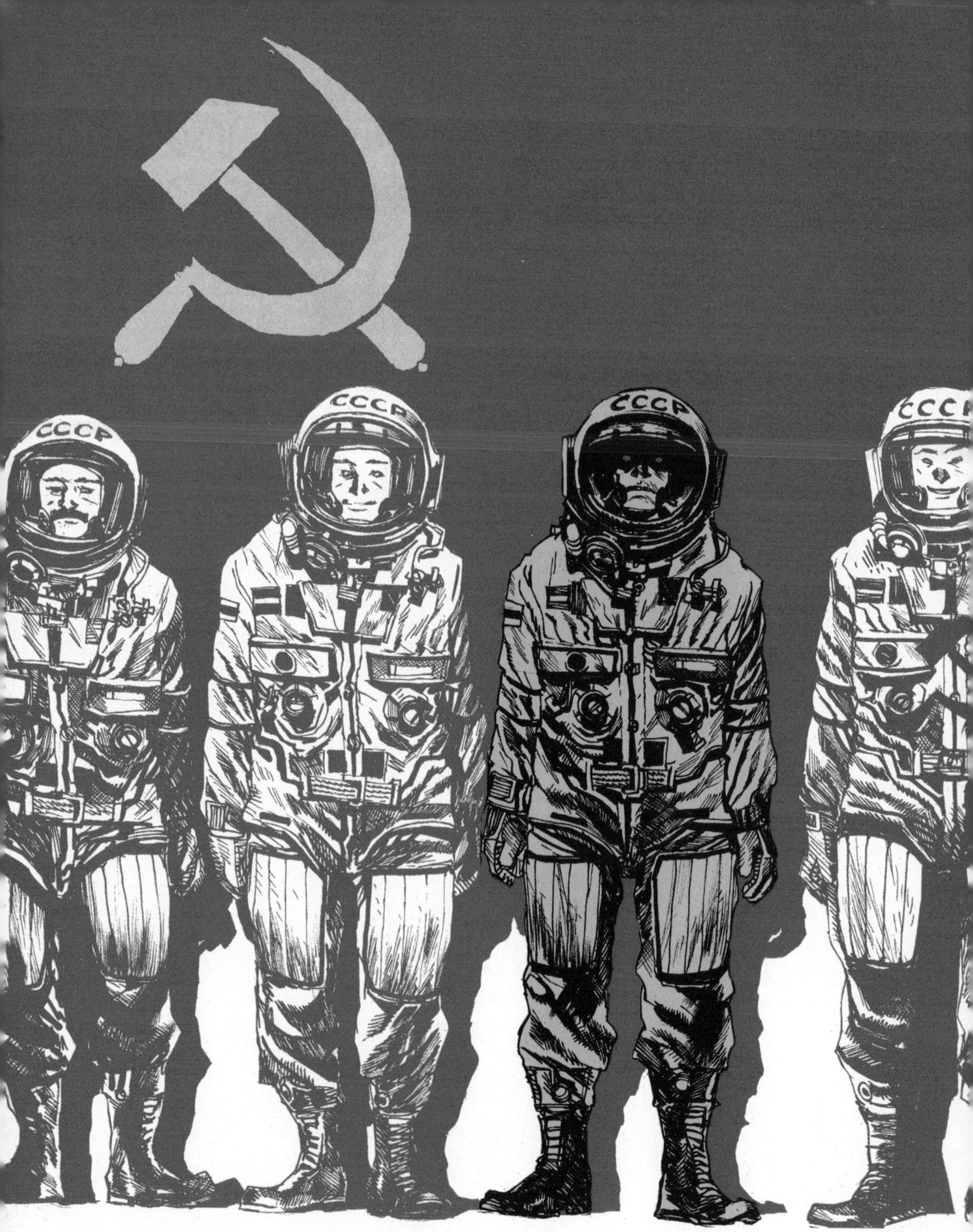
CCCP
CCCP
CCCP

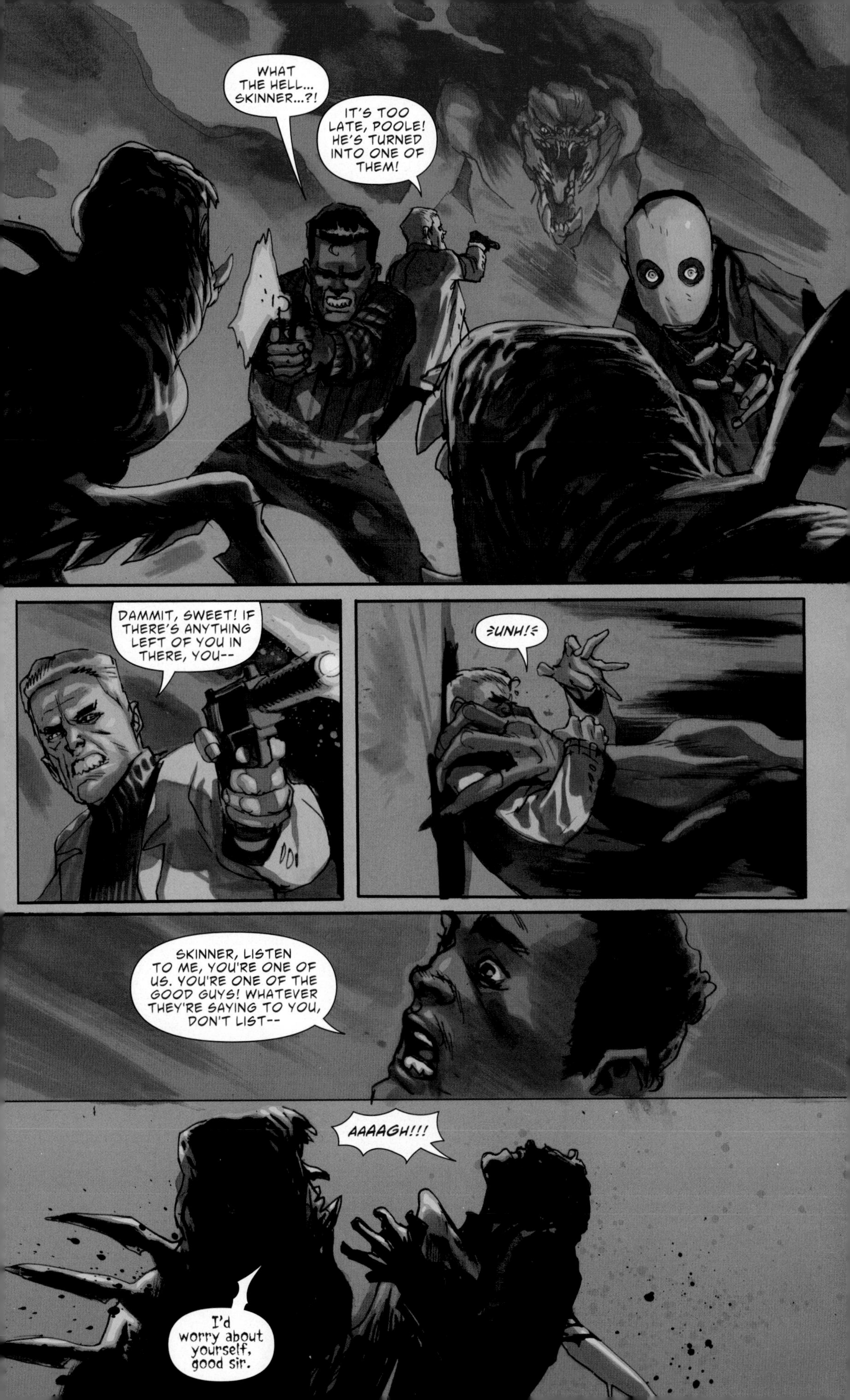
WHAT THE HELL... SKINNER...?!
IT'S TOO LATE, POOLE! HE'S TURNED INTO ONE OF THEM!
DAMMIT, SWEET! IF THERE'S ANYTHING LEFT OF YOU IN THERE, YOU--
UNH!
SKINNER, LISTEN TO ME, YOU'RE ONE OF US. YOU'RE ONE OF THE GOOD GUYS! WHATEVER THEY'RE SAYING TO YOU, DON'T LIST--
AAAAGH!!!
I'd worry about yourself, good sir.

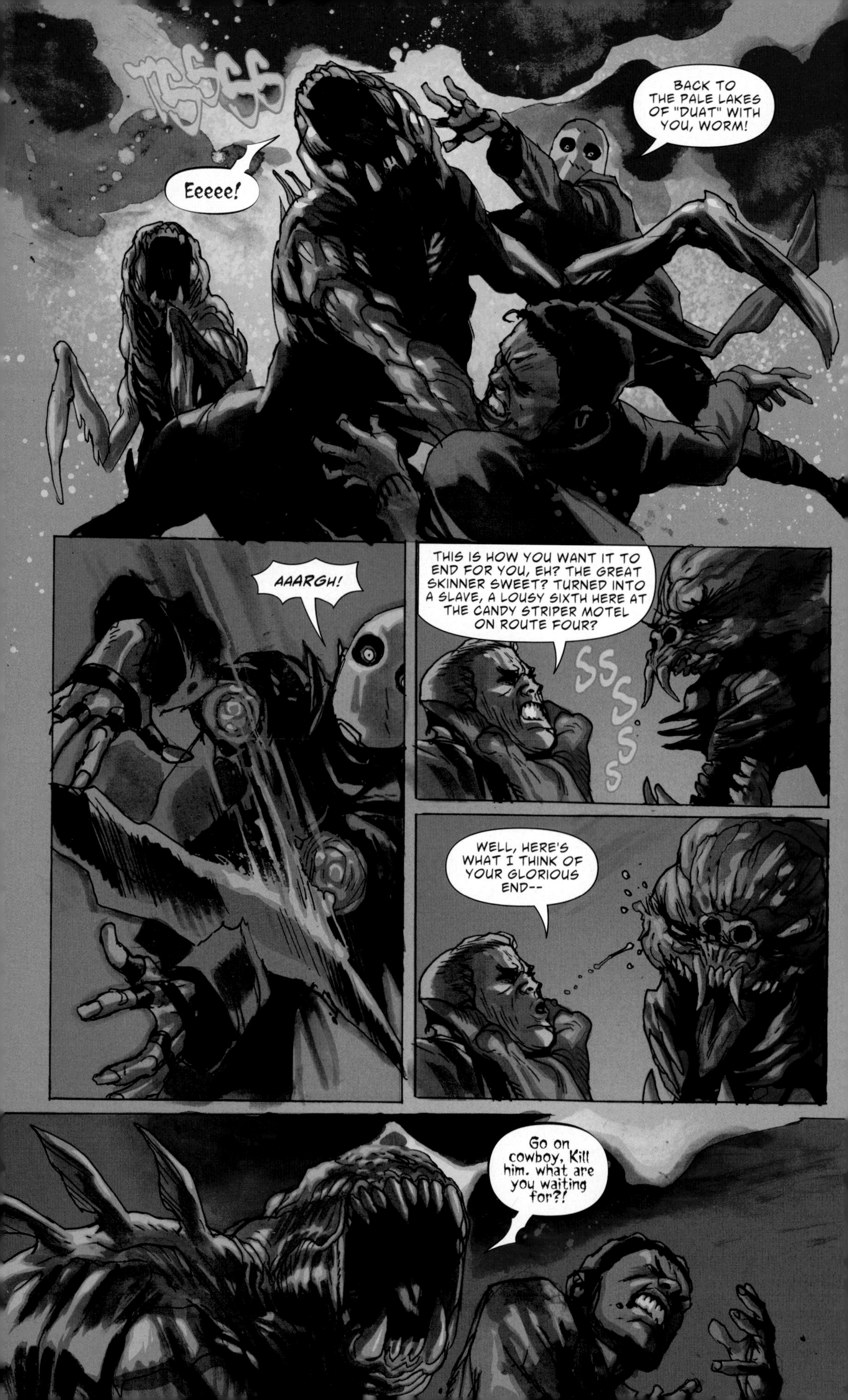
TSSSS
Eeeee!
BACK TO THE PALE LAKES OF "DUAT" WITH YOU, WORM!
AAARGH!
THIS IS HOW YOU WANT IT TO END FOR YOU, EH? THE GREAT SKINNER SWEET? TURNED INTO A SLAVE, A LOUSY SIXTH HERE AT THE CANDY STRIPER MOTEL ON ROUTE FOUR?
SSSSSS
WELL, HERE'S WHAT I THINK OF YOUR GLORIOUS END--
Go on cowboy, Kill him. what are you waiting for?!

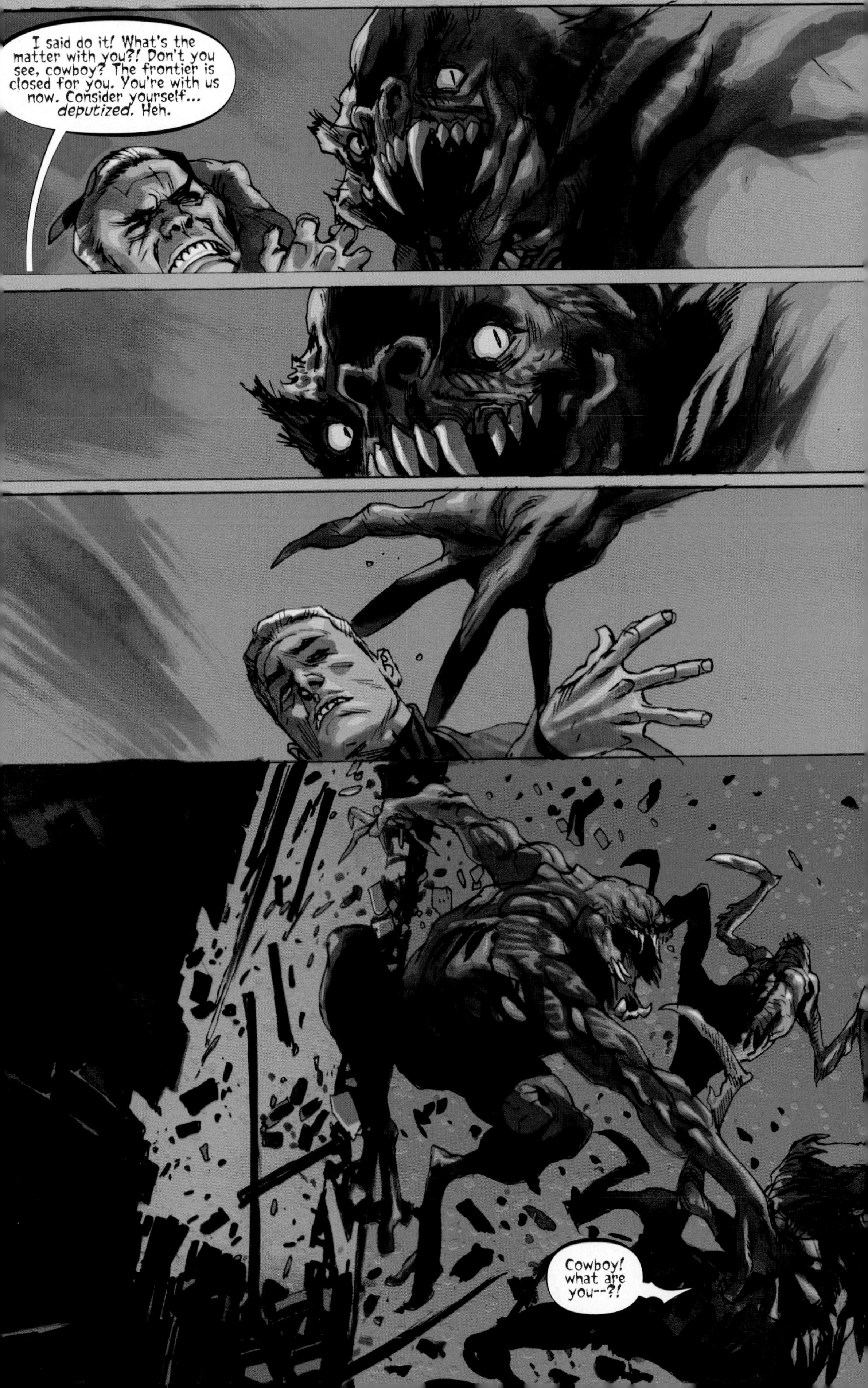
I said do it! What's the matter with you?! Don't you see, cowboy? The frontier is closed for you. You're with us now. Consider yourself... *deputized.* Heh.
Cowboy! what are you--?!

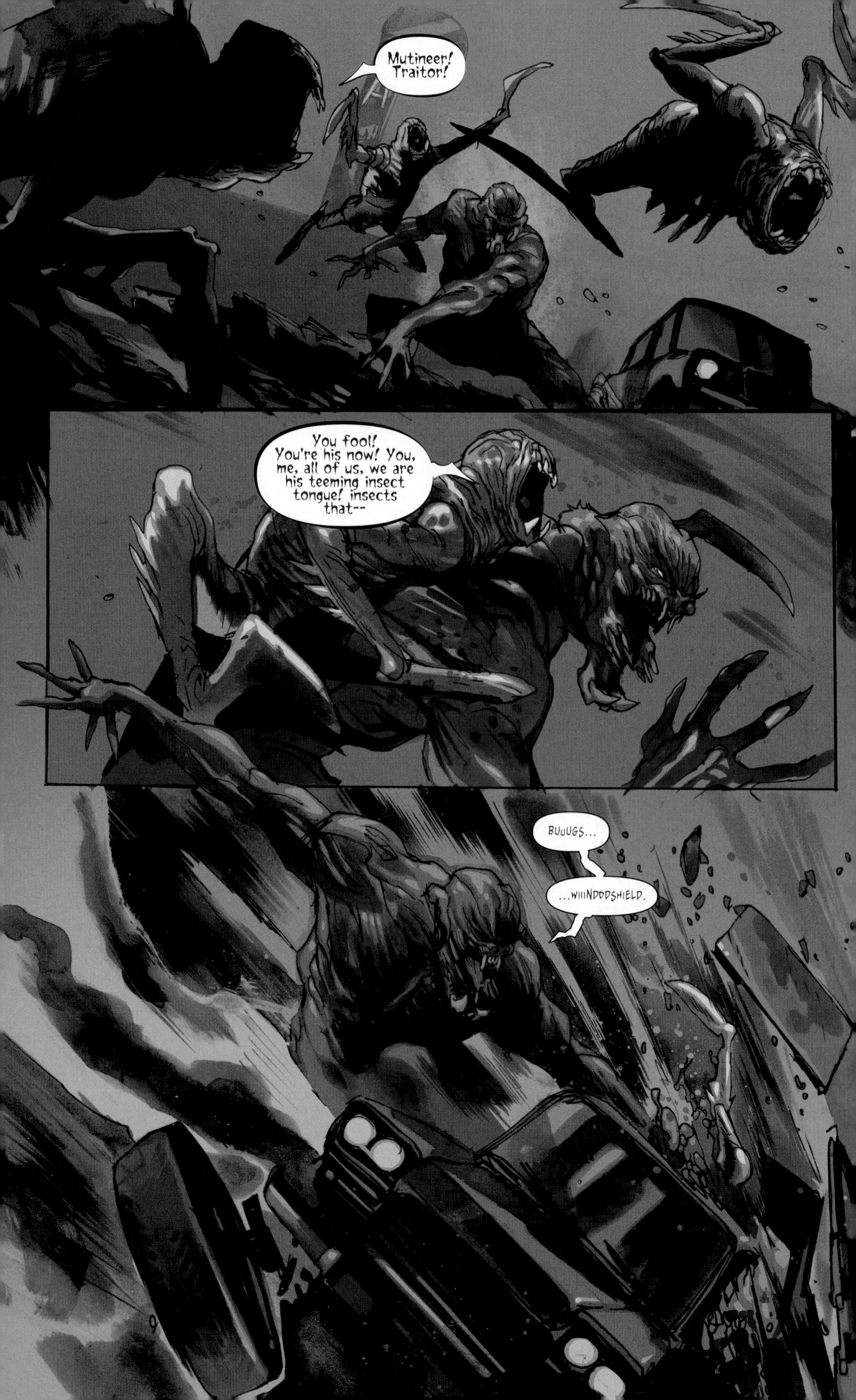
Mutineer! Traitor!
You fool! You're his now! You, me, all of us, we are his teeming insect tongue! insects that--
BUUUGS...
...WIIINDDDSHIELD.

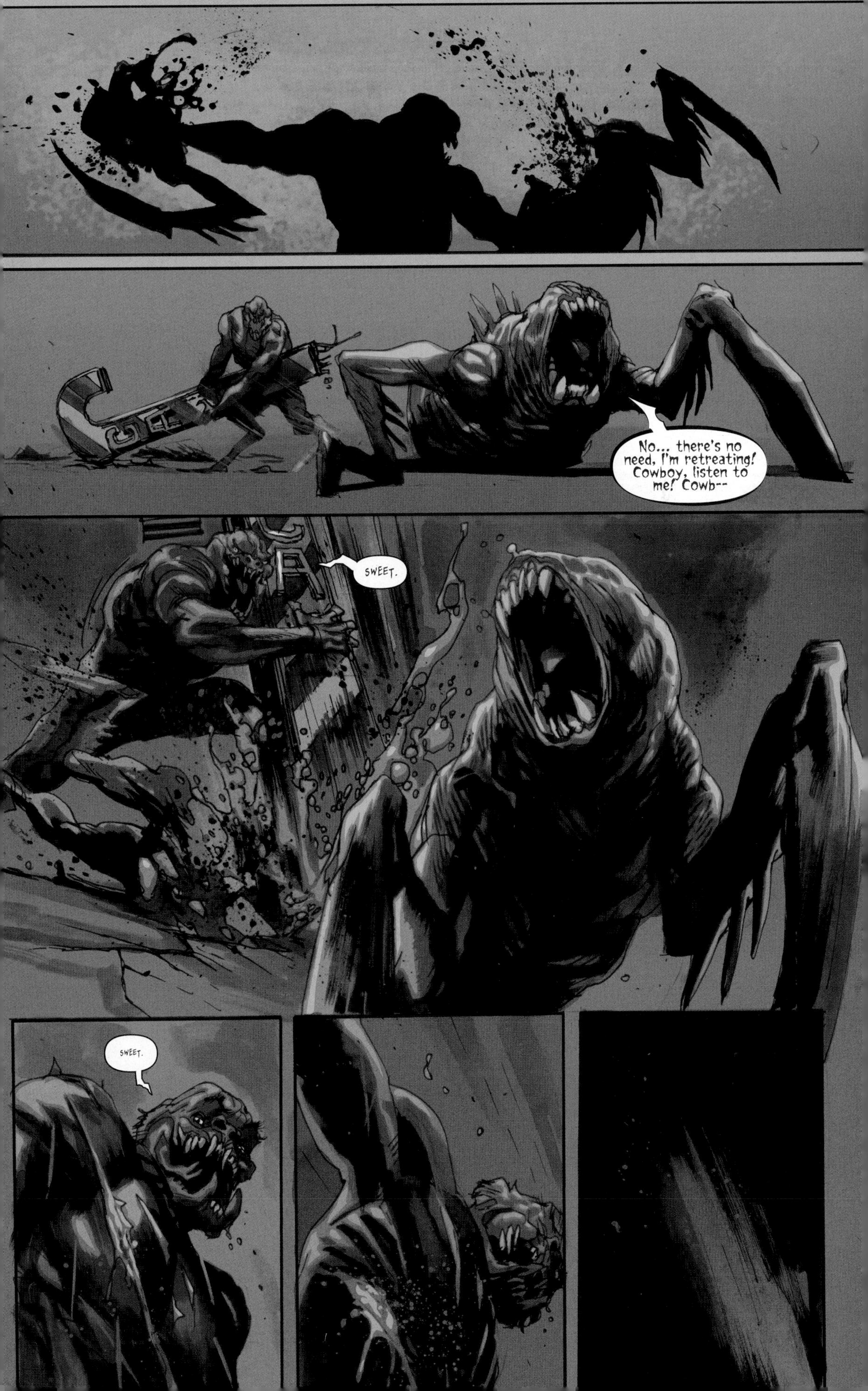
No... there's no need, I'm retreating! Cowboy, listen to me! Cowb--
SWEET.
SWEET.

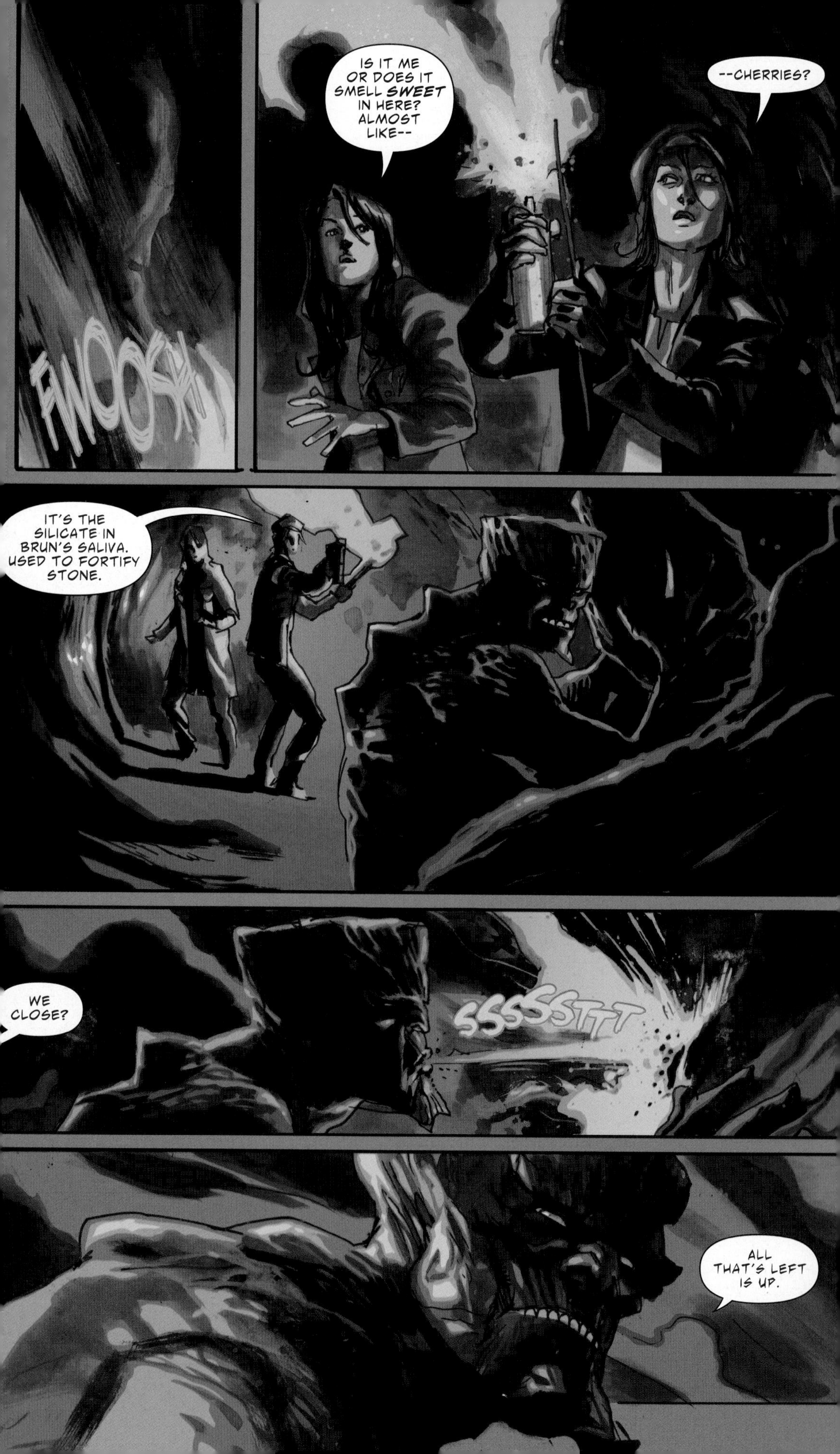
FWOOSH!
IS IT ME OR DOES IT SMELL **SWEET** IN HERE? ALMOST LIKE--
--CHERRIES?
IT'S THE SILICATE IN BRUN'S SALIVA. USED TO FORTIFY STONE.
WE CLOSE?
SSSSSTTT
ALL THAT'S LEFT IS UP.

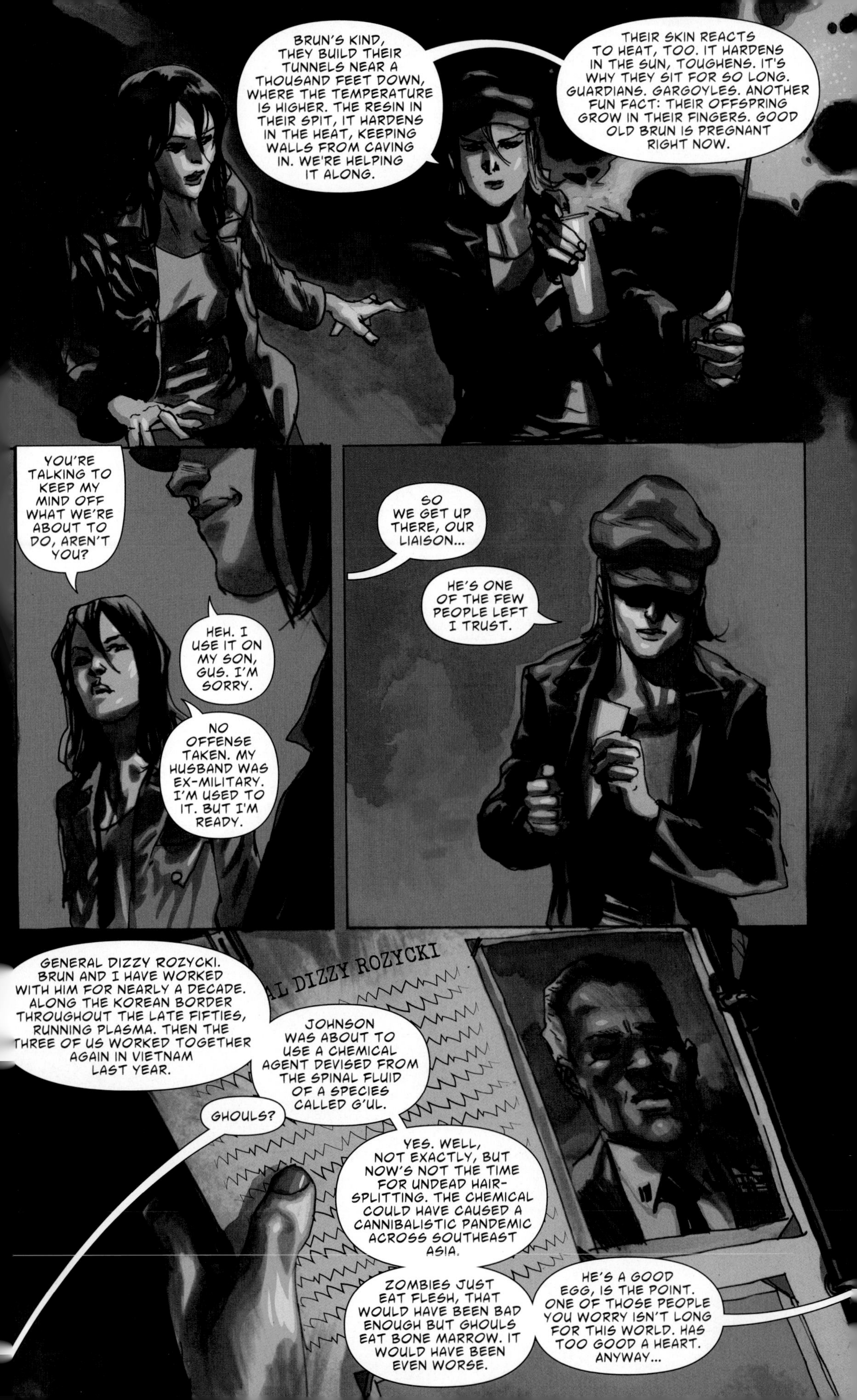
BRUN'S KIND, THEY BUILD THEIR TUNNELS NEAR A THOUSAND FEET DOWN, WHERE THE TEMPERATURE IS HIGHER. THE RESIN IN THEIR SPIT, IT HARDENS IN THE HEAT, KEEPING WALLS FROM CAVING IN. WE'RE HELPING IT ALONG.
THEIR SKIN REACTS TO HEAT, TOO. IT HARDENS IN THE SUN, TOUGHENS. IT'S WHY THEY SIT FOR SO LONG. GUARDIANS. GARGOYLES. ANOTHER FUN FACT: THEIR OFFSPRING GROW IN THEIR FINGERS. GOOD OLD BRUN IS PREGNANT RIGHT NOW.
YOU'RE TALKING TO KEEP MY MIND OFF WHAT WE'RE ABOUT TO DO, AREN'T YOU?
HEH. I USE IT ON MY SON, GUS. I'M SORRY.
NO OFFENSE TAKEN. MY HUSBAND WAS EX-MILITARY. I'M USED TO IT. BUT I'M READY.
SO WE GET UP THERE, OUR LIAISON...
HE'S ONE OF THE FEW PEOPLE LEFT I TRUST.
GENERAL DIZZY ROZYCKI. BRUN AND I HAVE WORKED WITH HIM FOR NEARLY A DECADE. ALONG THE KOREAN BORDER THROUGHOUT THE LATE FIFTIES, RUNNING PLASMA. THEN THE THREE OF US WORKED TOGETHER AGAIN IN VIETNAM LAST YEAR.
AL DIZZY ROZYCKI
JOHNSON WAS ABOUT TO USE A CHEMICAL AGENT DEVISED FROM THE SPINAL FLUID OF A SPECIES CALLED G'UL.
GHOULS?
YES. WELL, NOT EXACTLY, BUT NOW'S NOT THE TIME FOR UNDEAD HAIR-SPLITTING. THE CHEMICAL COULD HAVE CAUSED A CANNIBALISTIC PANDEMIC ACROSS SOUTHEAST ASIA.
ZOMBIES JUST EAT FLESH, THAT WOULD HAVE BEEN BAD ENOUGH BUT GHOULS EAT BONE MARROW. IT WOULD HAVE BEEN EVEN WORSE.
HE'S A GOOD EGG, IS THE POINT. ONE OF THOSE PEOPLE YOU WORRY ISN'T LONG FOR THIS WORLD. HAS TOO GOOD A HEART. ANYWAY...

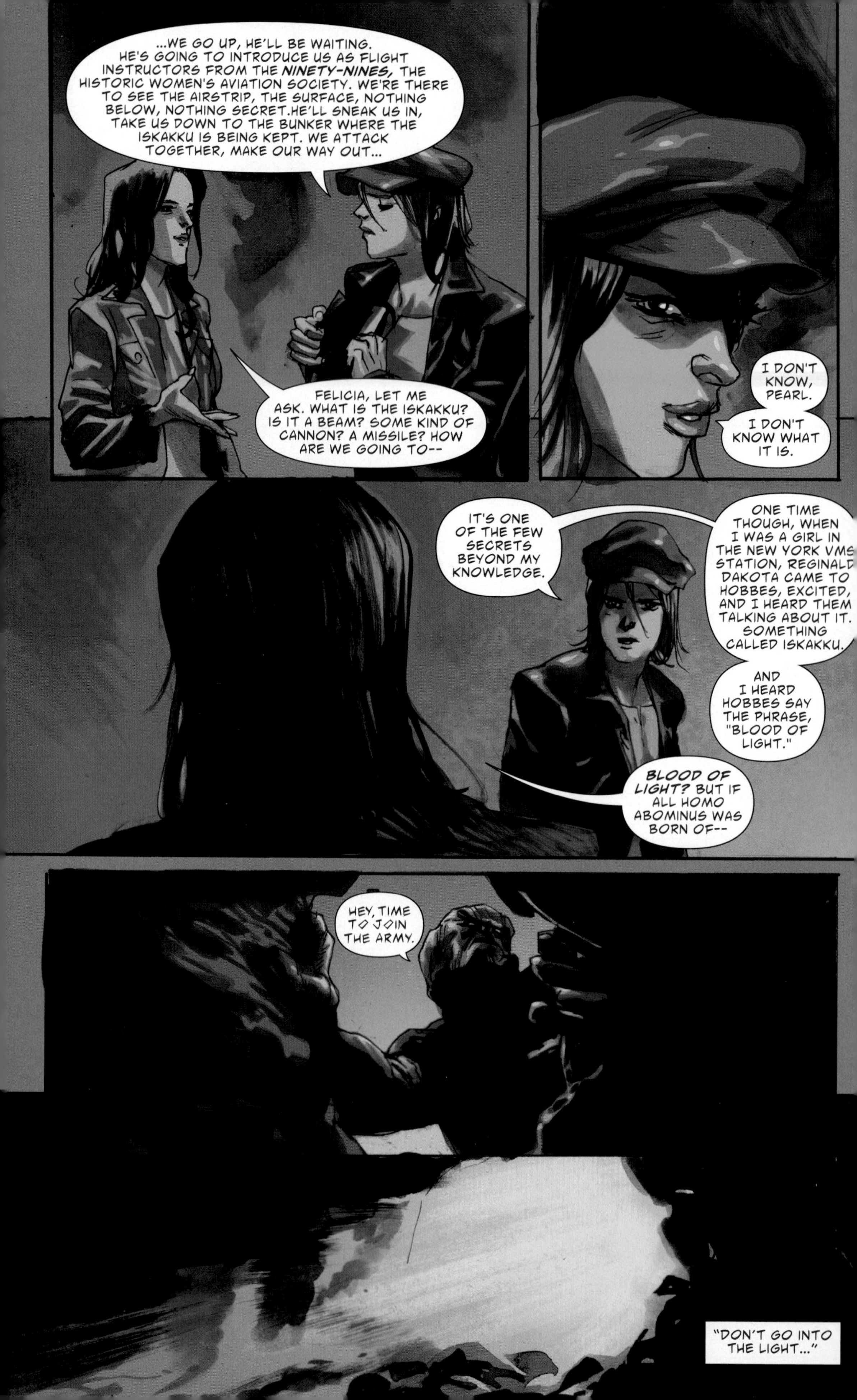
...WE GO UP, HE'LL BE WAITING. HE'S GOING TO INTRODUCE US AS FLIGHT INSTRUCTORS FROM THE *NINETY-NINES,* THE HISTORIC WOMEN'S AVIATION SOCIETY. WE'RE THERE TO SEE THE AIRSTRIP, THE SURFACE, NOTHING BELOW, NOTHING SECRET.HE'LL SNEAK US IN, TAKE US DOWN TO THE BUNKER WHERE THE ISKAKKU IS BEING KEPT. WE ATTACK TOGETHER, MAKE OUR WAY OUT...
FELICIA, LET ME ASK. WHAT IS THE ISKAKKU? IS IT A BEAM? SOME KIND OF CANNON? A MISSILE? HOW ARE WE GOING TO--
I DON'T KNOW, PEARL.
I DON'T KNOW WHAT IT IS.
IT'S ONE OF THE FEW SECRETS BEYOND MY KNOWLEDGE.
ONE TIME THOUGH, WHEN I WAS A GIRL IN THE NEW YORK VMS STATION, REGINALD DAKOTA CAME TO HOBBES, EXCITED, AND I HEARD THEM TALKING ABOUT IT. SOMETHING CALLED ISKAKKU.
AND I HEARD HOBBES SAY THE PHRASE, "BLOOD OF LIGHT."
BLOOD OF LIGHT? BUT IF ALL HOMO ABOMINUS WAS BORN OF--
HEY, TIME TO JOIN THE ARMY.
"DON'T GO INTO THE LIGHT..."

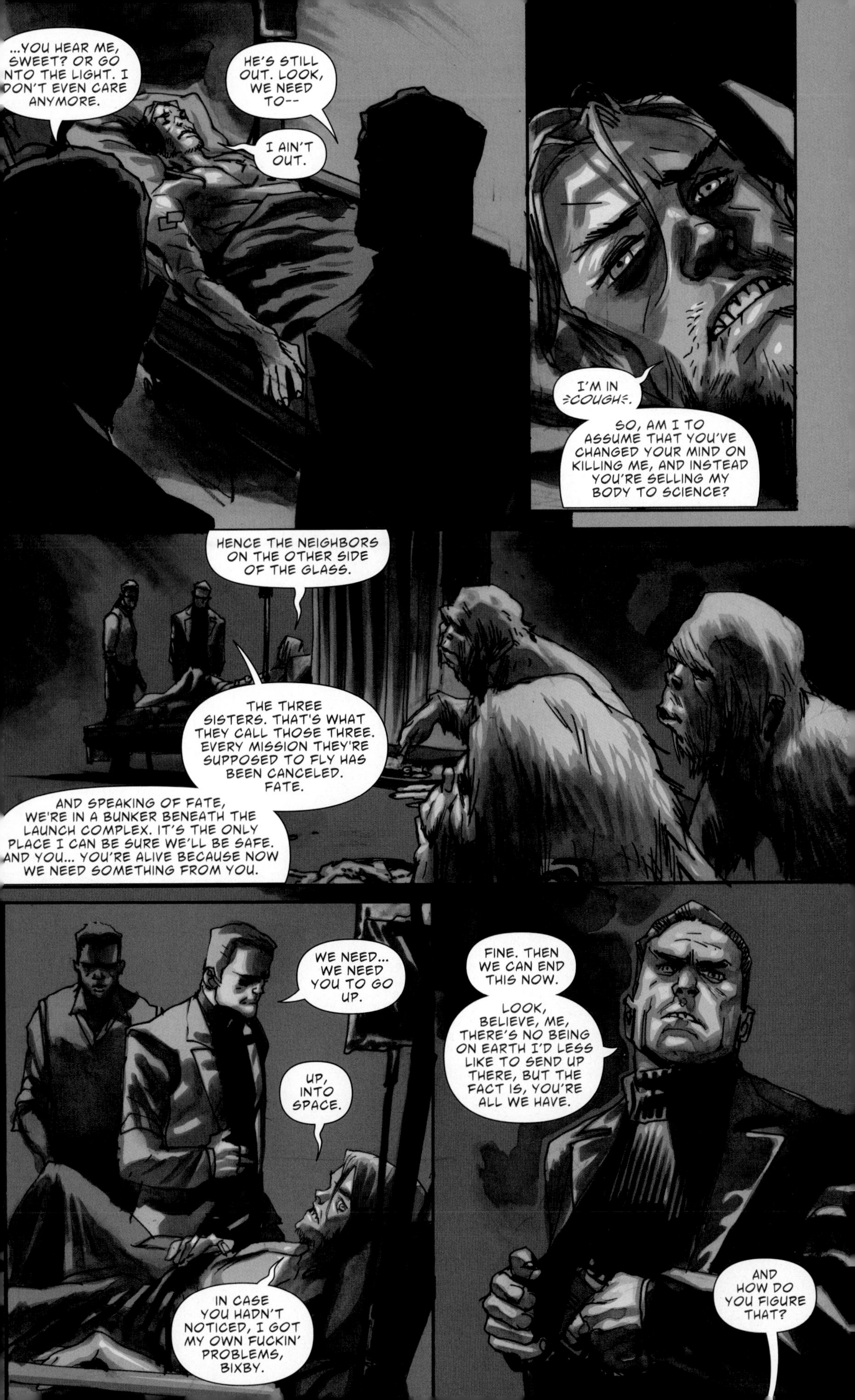
...YOU HEAR ME, SWEET? OR GO NTO THE LIGHT. I DON'T EVEN CARE ANYMORE.
HE'S STILL OUT. LOOK, WE NEED TO--
I AIN'T OUT.
I'M IN =COUGH=.
SO, AM I TO ASSUME THAT YOU'VE CHANGED YOUR MIND ON KILLING ME, AND INSTEAD YOU'RE SELLING MY BODY TO SCIENCE?
HENCE THE NEIGHBORS ON THE OTHER SIDE OF THE GLASS.
THE THREE SISTERS. THAT'S WHAT THEY CALL THOSE THREE. EVERY MISSION THEY'RE SUPPOSED TO FLY HAS BEEN CANCELED. FATE.
AND SPEAKING OF FATE, WE'RE IN A BUNKER BENEATH THE LAUNCH COMPLEX. IT'S THE ONLY PLACE I CAN BE SURE WE'LL BE SAFE. AND YOU... YOU'RE ALIVE BECAUSE NOW WE NEED SOMETHING FROM YOU.
WE NEED... WE NEED YOU TO GO UP.
UP, INTO SPACE.
IN CASE YOU HADN'T NOTICED, I GOT MY OWN FUCKIN' PROBLEMS, BIXBY.
FINE. THEN WE CAN END THIS NOW.
LOOK, BELIEVE, ME, THERE'S NO BEING ON EARTH I'D LESS LIKE TO SEND UP THERE, BUT THE FACT IS, YOU'RE ALL WE HAVE.
AND HOW DO YOU FIGURE THAT?

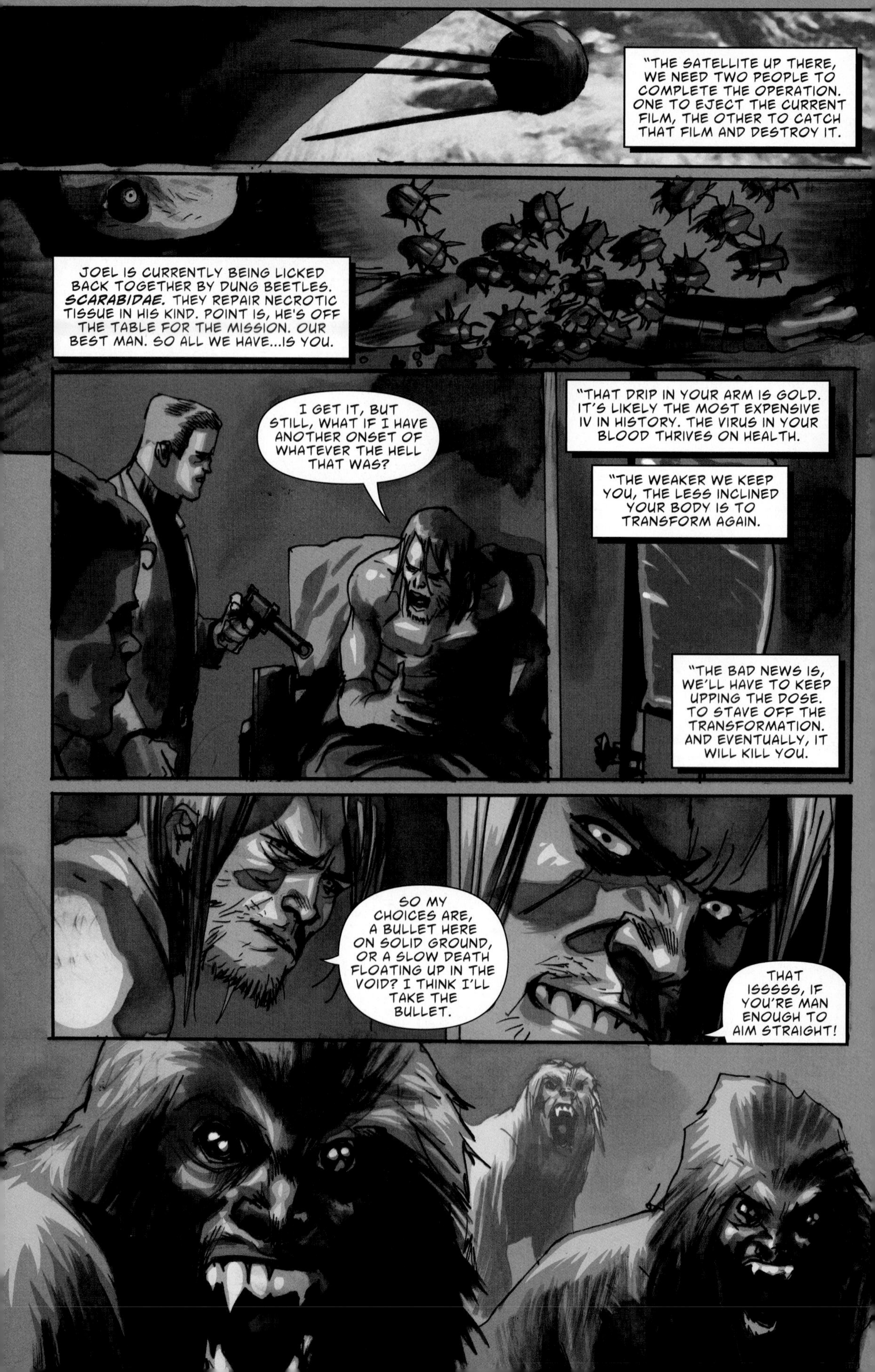
"THE SATELLITE UP THERE, WE NEED TWO PEOPLE TO COMPLETE THE OPERATION. ONE TO EJECT THE CURRENT FILM, THE OTHER TO CATCH THAT FILM AND DESTROY IT.
JOEL IS CURRENTLY BEING LICKED BACK TOGETHER BY DUNG BEETLES. SCARABIDAE. THEY REPAIR NECROTIC TISSUE IN HIS KIND. POINT IS, HE'S OFF THE TABLE FOR THE MISSION. OUR BEST MAN. SO ALL WE HAVE...IS YOU.
I GET IT, BUT STILL, WHAT IF I HAVE ANOTHER ONSET OF WHATEVER THE HELL THAT WAS?
"THAT DRIP IN YOUR ARM IS GOLD. IT'S LIKELY THE MOST EXPENSIVE IV IN HISTORY. THE VIRUS IN YOUR BLOOD THRIVES ON HEALTH.
"THE WEAKER WE KEEP YOU, THE LESS INCLINED YOUR BODY IS TO TRANSFORM AGAIN.
"THE BAD NEWS IS, WE'LL HAVE TO KEEP UPPING THE DOSE. TO STAVE OFF THE TRANSFORMATION. AND EVENTUALLY, IT WILL KILL YOU.
SO MY CHOICES ARE, A BULLET HERE ON SOLID GROUND, OR A SLOW DEATH FLOATING UP IN THE VOID? I THINK I'LL TAKE THE BULLET.
THAT ISSSSS, IF YOU'RE MAN ENOUGH TO AIM STRAIGHT!

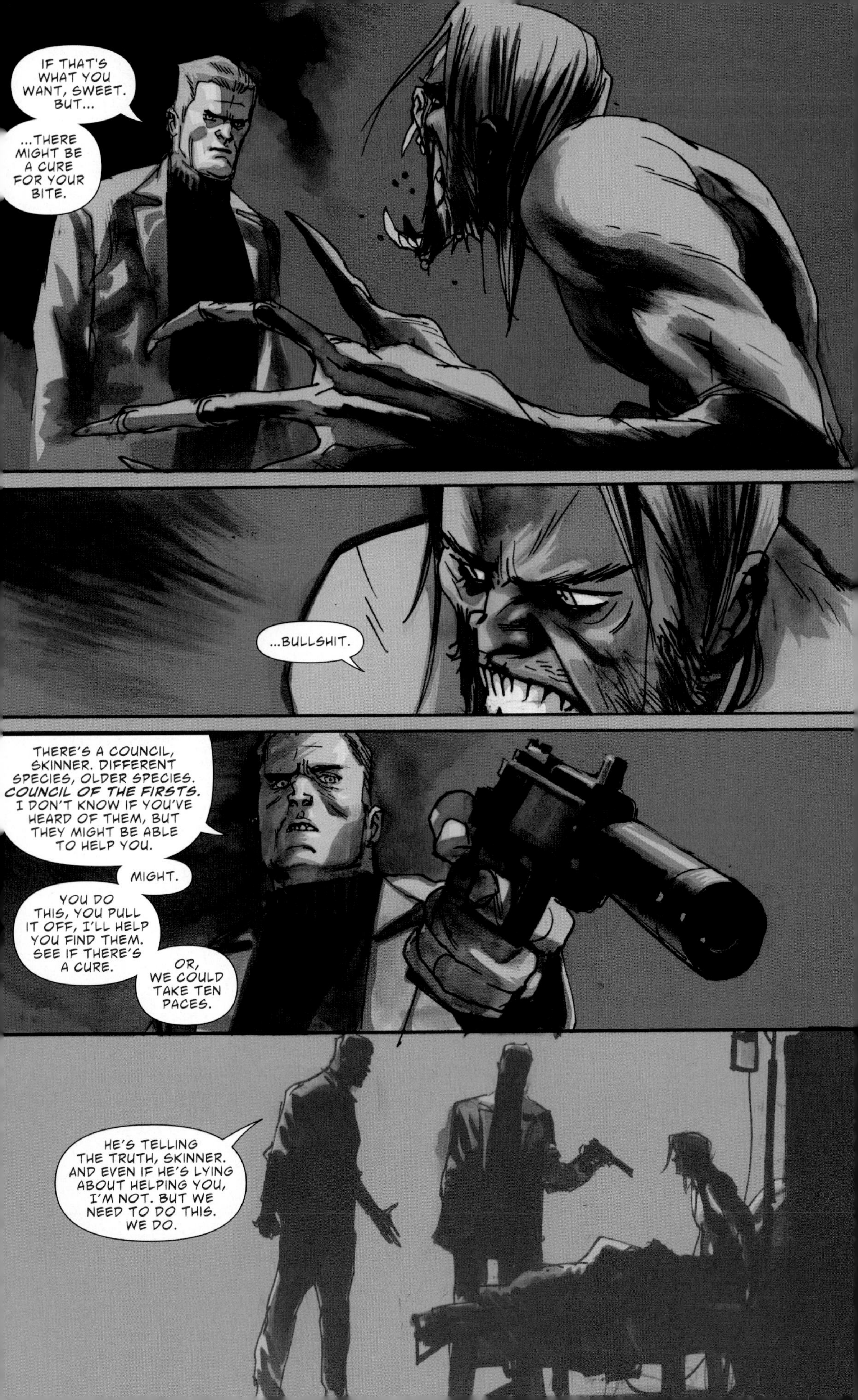
IF THAT'S WHAT YOU WANT, SWEET. BUT...
...THERE MIGHT BE A CURE FOR YOUR BITE.
...BULLSHIT.
THERE'S A COUNCIL, SKINNER. DIFFERENT SPECIES, OLDER SPECIES. *COUNCIL OF THE FIRSTS.* I DON'T KNOW IF YOU'VE HEARD OF THEM, BUT THEY MIGHT BE ABLE TO HELP YOU.
MIGHT.
YOU DO THIS, YOU PULL IT OFF, I'LL HELP YOU FIND THEM. SEE IF THERE'S A CURE.
OR, WE COULD TAKE TEN PACES.
HE'S TELLING THE TRUTH, SKINNER. AND EVEN IF HE'S LYING ABOUT HELPING YOU, I'M NOT. BUT WE NEED TO DO THIS. WE DO.

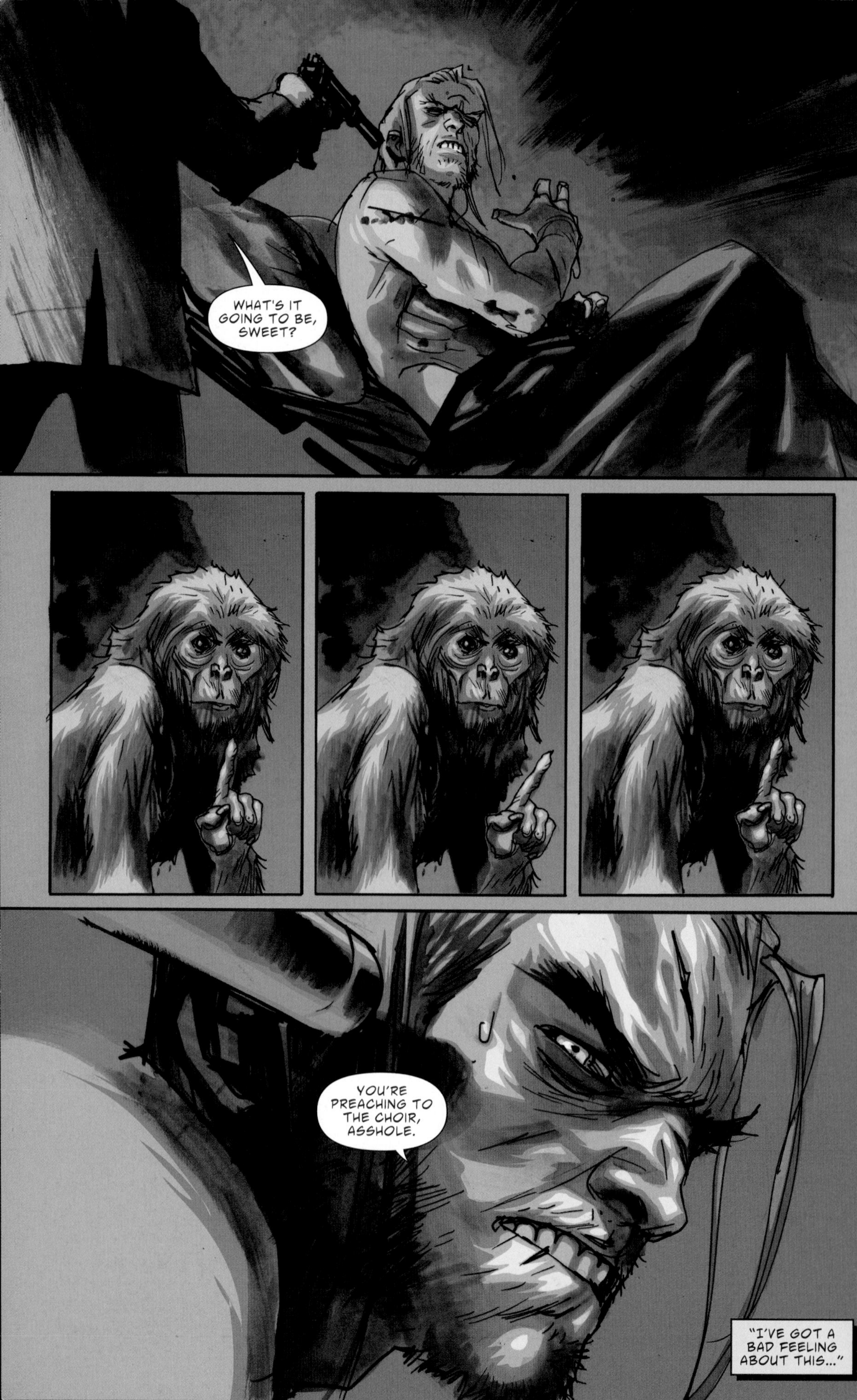
WHAT'S IT GOING TO BE, SWEET?
YOU'RE PREACHING TO THE CHOIR, ASSHOLE.
"I'VE GOT A BAD FEELING ABOUT THIS..."

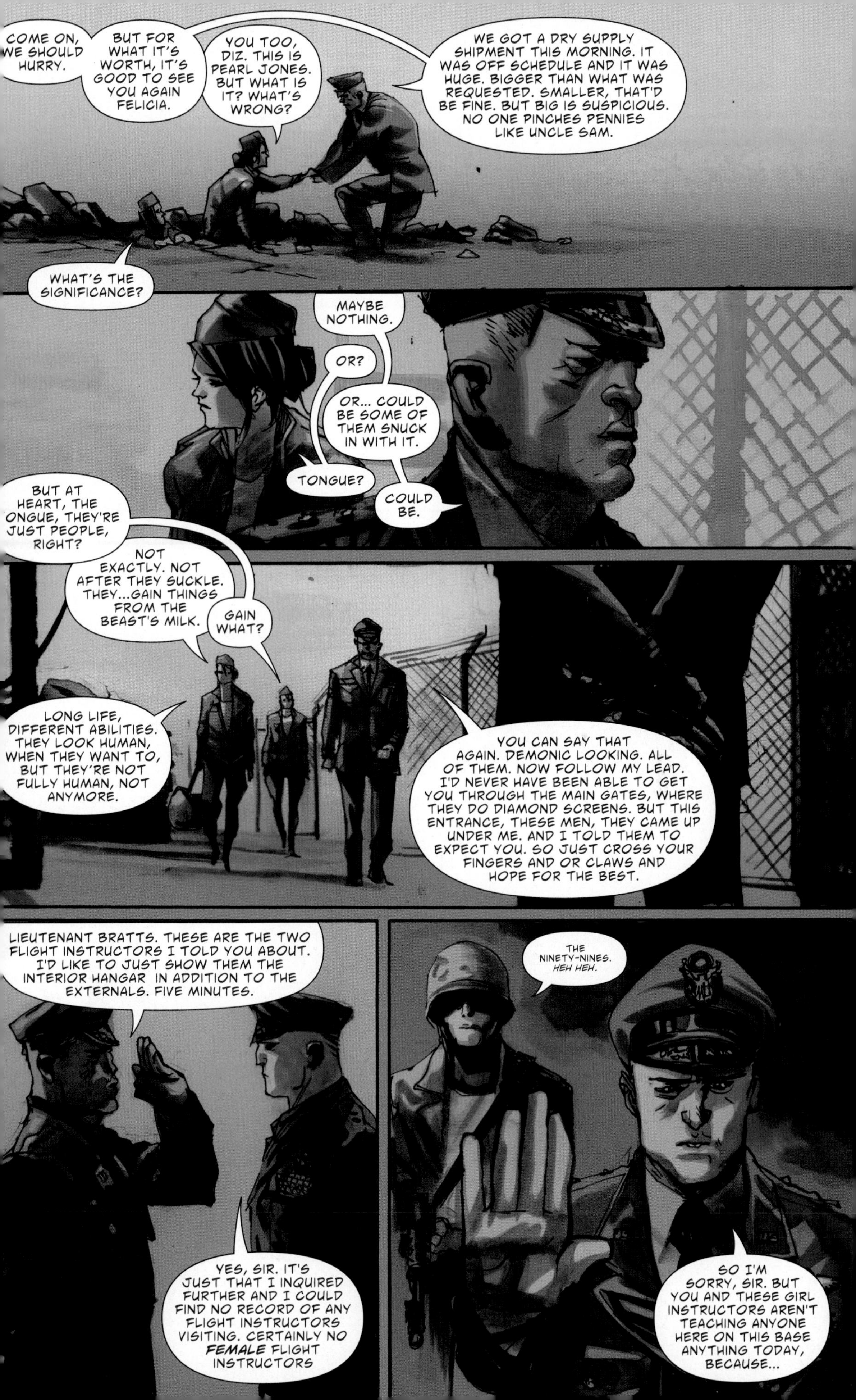

COME ON, WE SHOULD HURRY.
BUT FOR WHAT IT'S WORTH, IT'S GOOD TO SEE YOU AGAIN FELICIA.
YOU TOO, DIZ. THIS IS PEARL JONES. BUT WHAT IS IT? WHAT'S WRONG?
WE GOT A DRY SUPPLY SHIPMENT THIS MORNING. IT WAS OFF SCHEDULE AND IT WAS HUGE. BIGGER THAN WHAT WAS REQUESTED. SMALLER, THAT'D BE FINE. BUT BIG IS SUSPICIOUS. NO ONE PINCHES PENNIES LIKE UNCLE SAM.
WHAT'S THE SIGNIFICANCE?
MAYBE NOTHING.
OR?
OR... COULD BE SOME OF THEM SNUCK IN WITH IT.
TONGUE?
COULD BE.
BUT AT HEART, THE ONGUE, THEY'RE JUST PEOPLE, RIGHT?
NOT EXACTLY. NOT AFTER THEY SUCKLE. THEY...GAIN THINGS FROM THE BEAST'S MILK.
GAIN WHAT?
LONG LIFE, DIFFERENT ABILITIES. THEY LOOK HUMAN, WHEN THEY WANT TO, BUT THEY'RE NOT FULLY HUMAN, NOT ANYMORE.
YOU CAN SAY THAT AGAIN. DEMONIC LOOKING. ALL OF THEM. NOW FOLLOW MY LEAD. I'D NEVER HAVE BEEN ABLE TO GET YOU THROUGH THE MAIN GATES, WHERE THEY DO DIAMOND SCREENS. BUT THIS ENTRANCE, THESE MEN, THEY CAME UP UNDER ME. AND I TOLD THEM TO EXPECT YOU. SO JUST CROSS YOUR FINGERS AND OR CLAWS AND HOPE FOR THE BEST.
LIEUTENANT BRATTS. THESE ARE THE TWO FLIGHT INSTRUCTORS I TOLD YOU ABOUT. I'D LIKE TO JUST SHOW THEM THE INTERIOR HANGAR IN ADDITION TO THE EXTERNALS. FIVE MINUTES.
YES, SIR. IT'S JUST THAT I INQUIRED FURTHER AND I COULD FIND NO RECORD OF ANY FLIGHT INSTRUCTORS VISITING. CERTAINLY NO *FEMALE* FLIGHT INSTRUCTORS
THE NINETY-NINES. *HEH HEH.*
SO I'M SORRY, SIR. BUT YOU AND THESE GIRL INSTRUCTORS AREN'T TEACHING ANYONE HERE ON THIS BASE ANYTHING TODAY, BECAUSE...

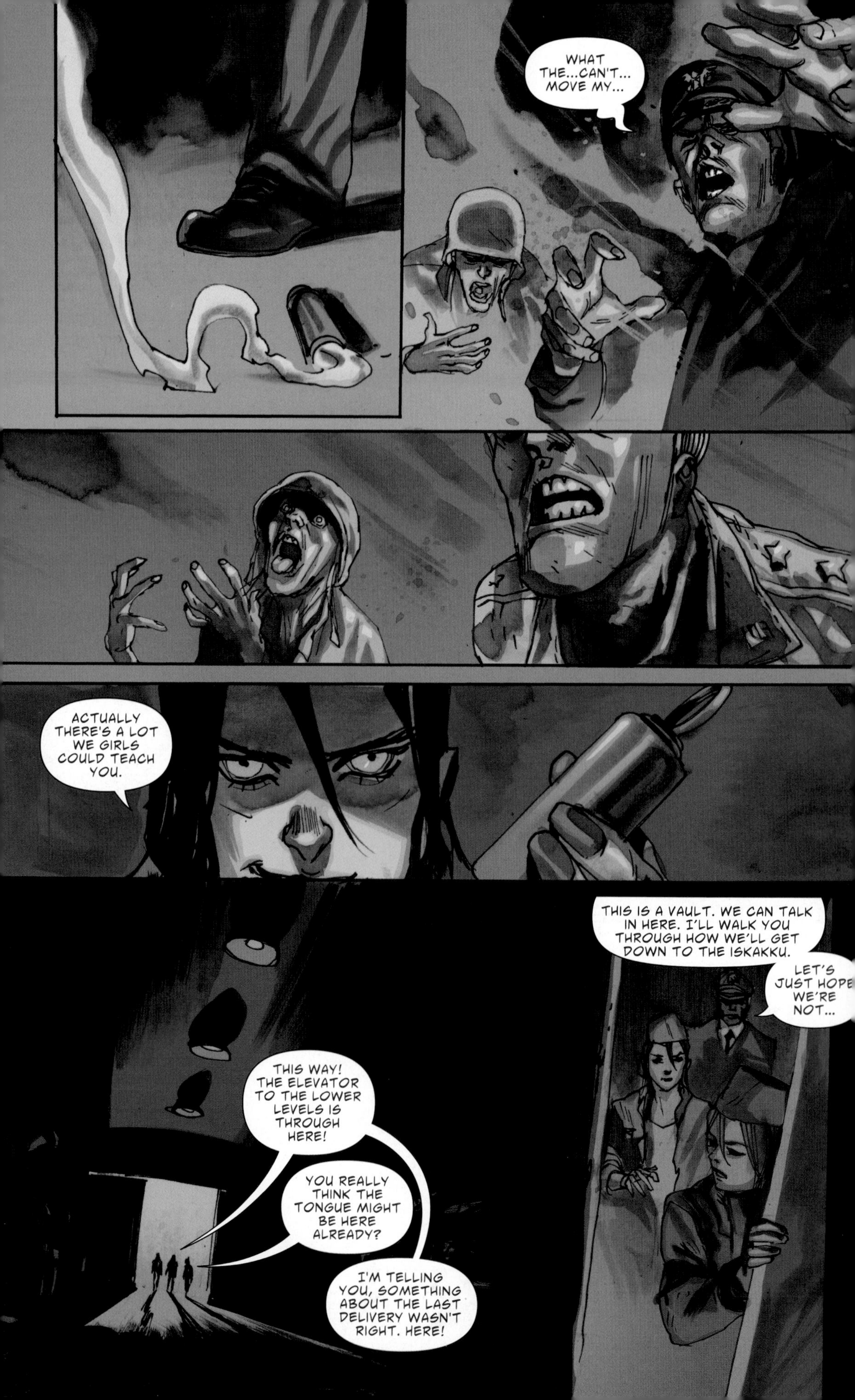
WHAT THE...CAN'T... MOVE MY...
ACTUALLY THERE'S A LOT WE GIRLS COULD TEACH YOU.
THIS WAY! THE ELEVATOR TO THE LOWER LEVELS IS THROUGH HERE!
YOU REALLY THINK THE TONGUE MIGHT BE HERE ALREADY?
I'M TELLING YOU, SOMETHING ABOUT THE LAST DELIVERY WASN'T RIGHT. HERE!
THIS IS A VAULT. WE CAN TALK IN HERE. I'LL WALK YOU THROUGH HOW WE'LL GET DOWN TO THE ISKAKKU.
LET'S JUST HOPE WE'RE NOT...

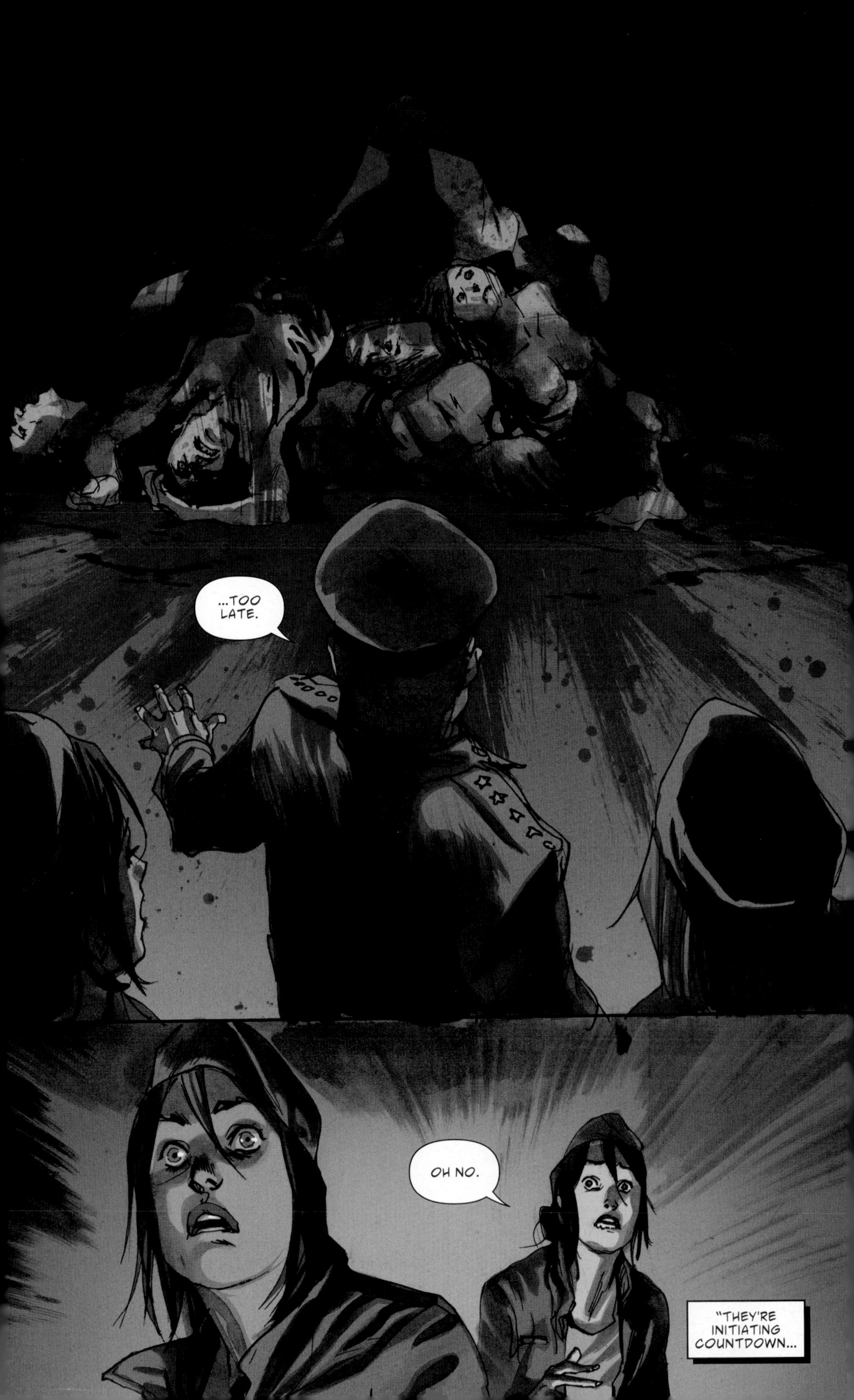
...TOO LATE.
OH NO.
"THEY'RE INITIATING COUNTDOWN...

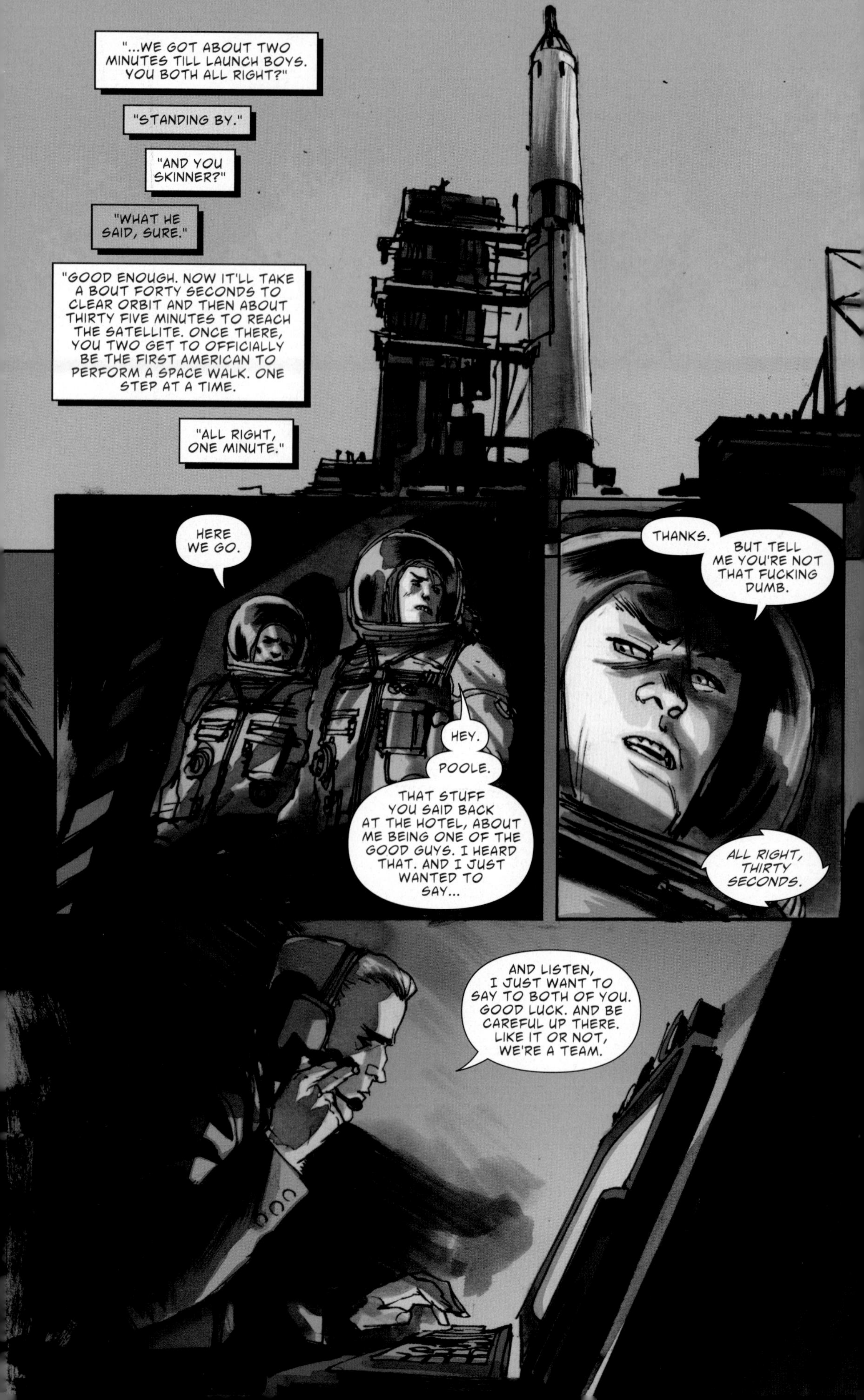
"...WE GOT ABOUT TWO MINUTES TILL LAUNCH BOYS. YOU BOTH ALL RIGHT?"
"STANDING BY."
"AND YOU SKINNER?"
"WHAT HE SAID, SURE."
"GOOD ENOUGH. NOW IT'LL TAKE A BOUT FORTY SECONDS TO CLEAR ORBIT AND THEN ABOUT THIRTY FIVE MINUTES TO REACH THE SATELLITE. ONCE THERE, YOU TWO GET TO OFFICIALLY BE THE FIRST AMERICAN TO PERFORM A SPACE WALK. ONE STEP AT A TIME.
"ALL RIGHT, ONE MINUTE."
HERE WE GO.
HEY.
POOLE.
THAT STUFF YOU SAID BACK AT THE HOTEL, ABOUT ME BEING ONE OF THE GOOD GUYS. I HEARD THAT. AND I JUST WANTED TO SAY...
THANKS.
BUT TELL ME YOU'RE NOT THAT FUCKING DUMB.
ALL RIGHT, THIRTY SECONDS.
AND LISTEN, I JUST WANT TO SAY TO BOTH OF YOU. GOOD LUCK. AND BE CAREFUL UP THERE. LIKE IT OR NOT, WE'RE A TEAM.

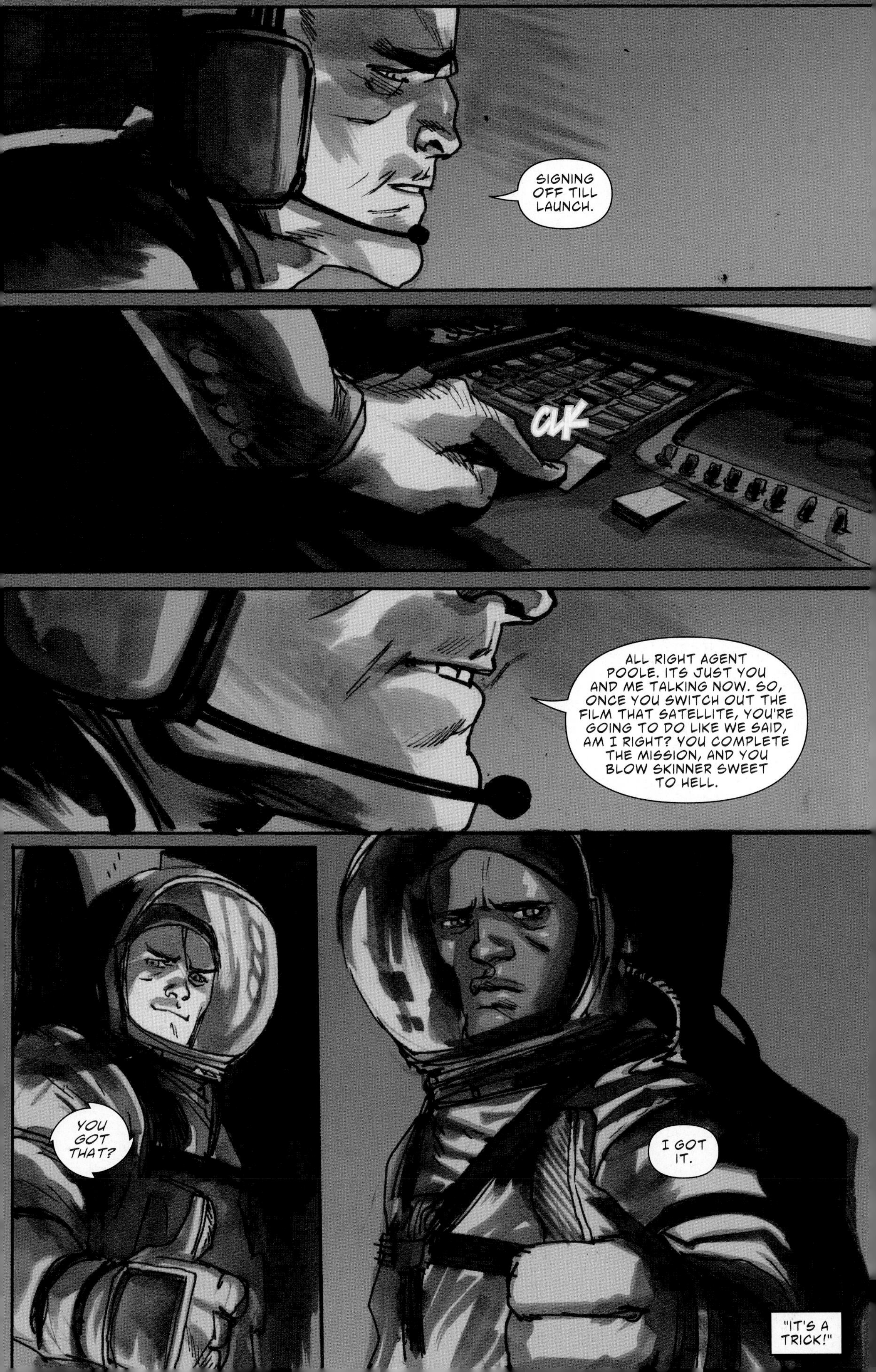
SIGNING OFF TILL LAUNCH.
CLK
ALL RIGHT AGENT POOLE. ITS JUST YOU AND ME TALKING NOW. SO, ONCE YOU SWITCH OUT THE FILM THAT SATELLITE, YOU'RE GOING TO DO LIKE WE SAID, AM I RIGHT? YOU COMPLETE THE MISSION, AND YOU BLOW SKINNER SWEET TO HELL.
YOU GOT THAT?
I GOT IT.
"IT'S A TRICK!"

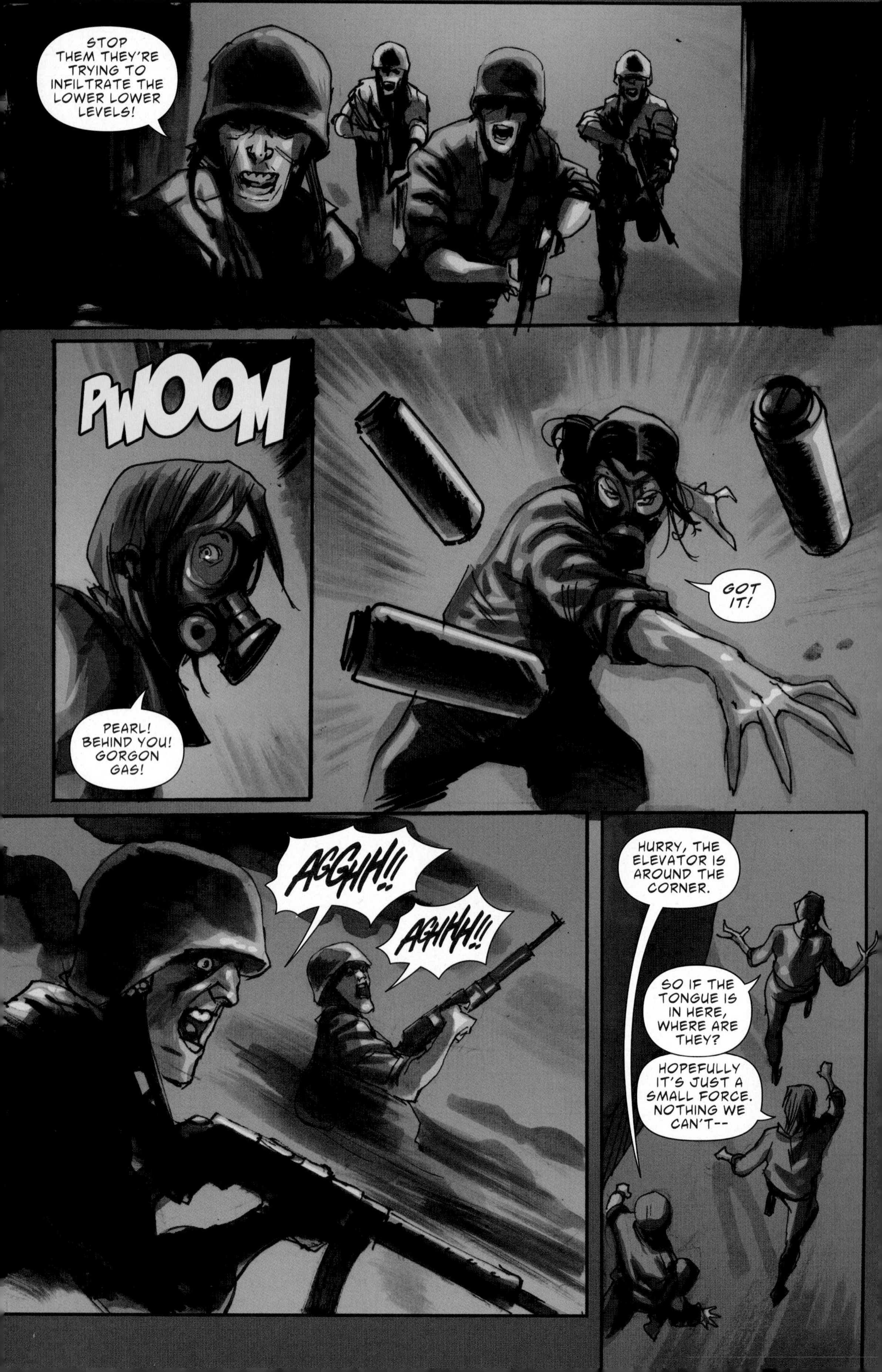
STOP THEM THEY'RE TRYING TO INFILTRATE THE LOWER LOWER LEVELS!
PWOOM
PEARL! BEHIND YOU! GORGON GAS!
GOT IT!
AGGHH!!
AGHHH!!
HURRY, THE ELEVATOR IS AROUND THE CORNER.
SO IF THE TONGUE IS IN HERE, WHERE ARE THEY?
HOPEFULLY IT'S JUST A SMALL FORCE. NOTHING WE CAN'T--

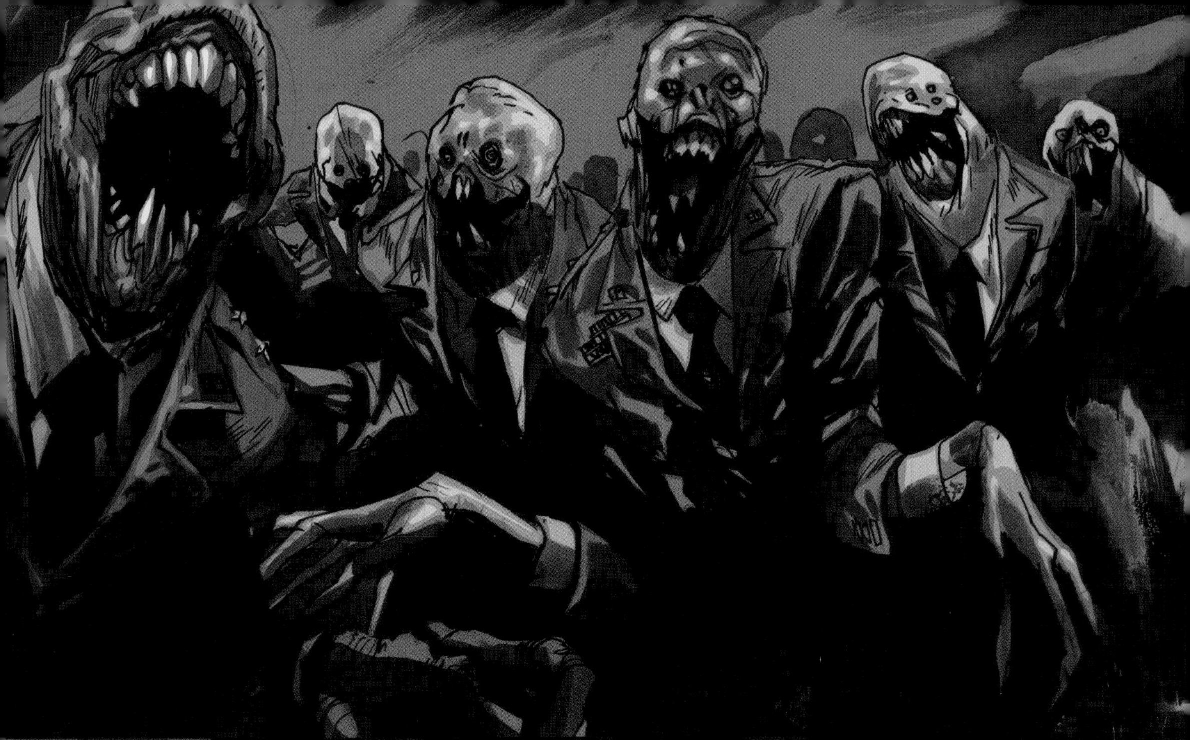

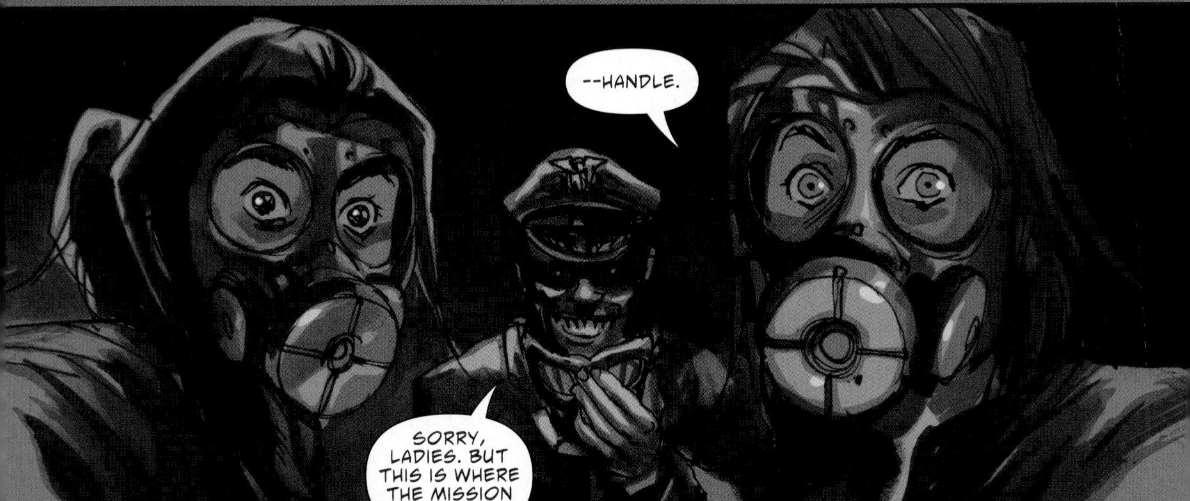
--HANDLE.
SORRY, LADIES. BUT THIS IS WHERE THE MISSION ENDS.

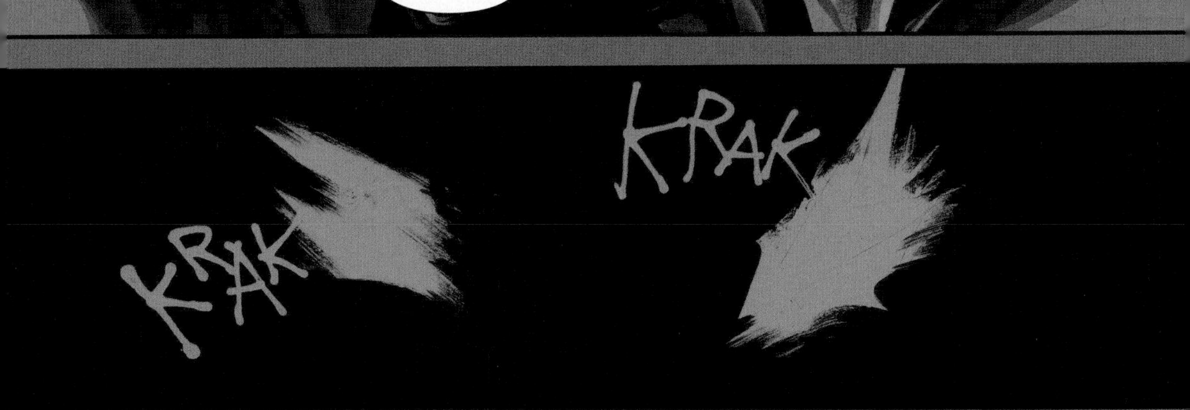
KRAK
KRAK

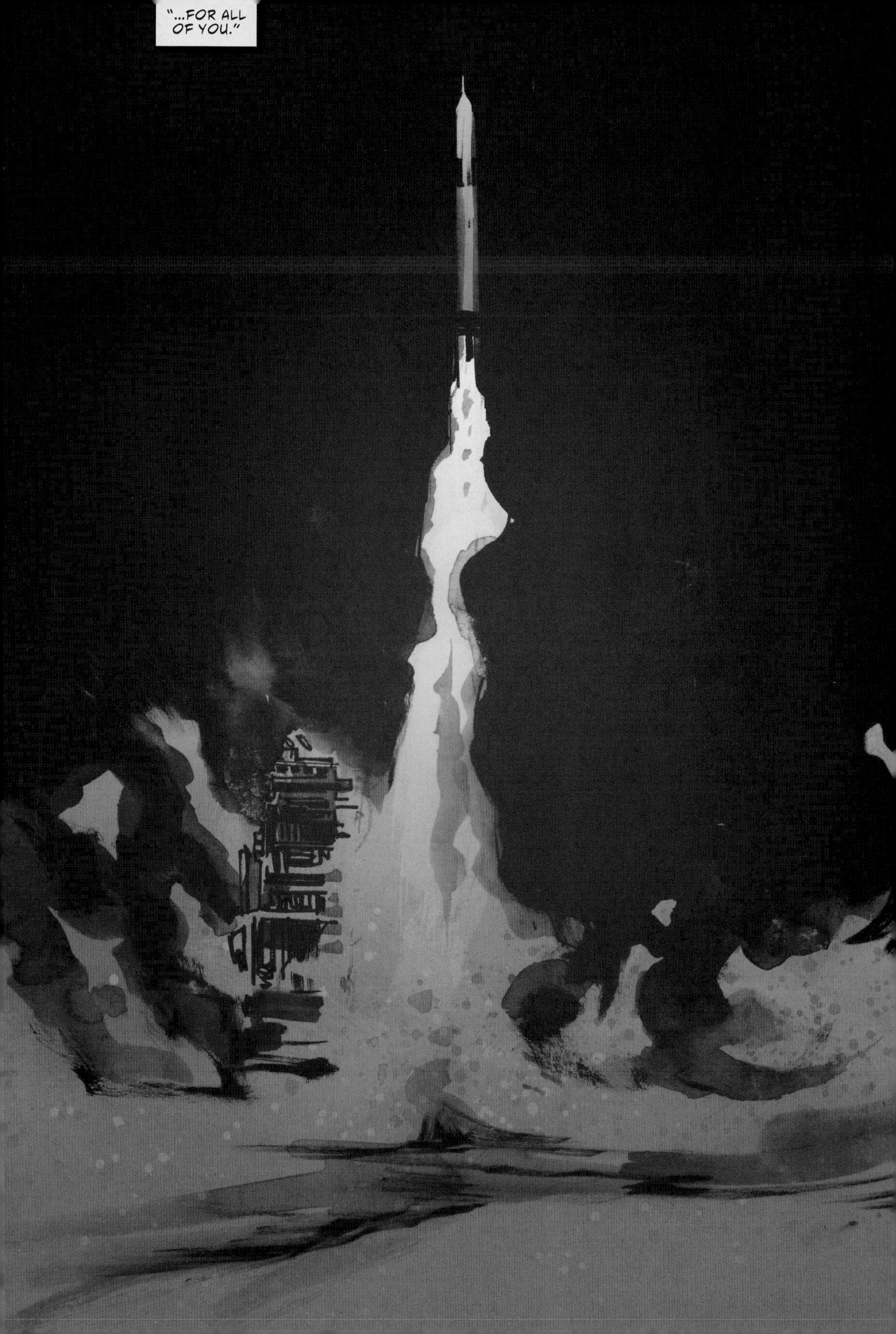
"...FOR ALL OF YOU."

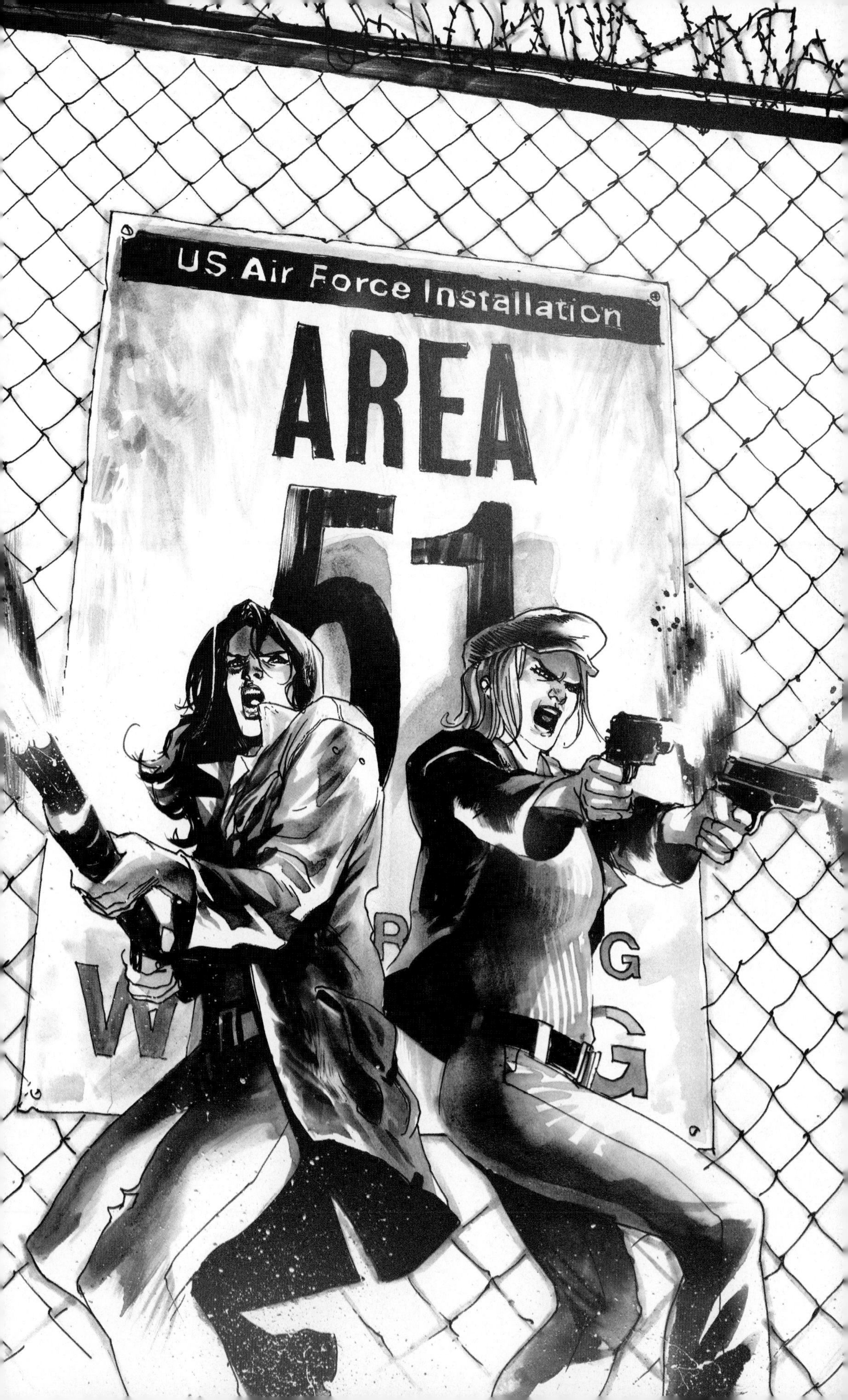
US Air Force Installation
AREA
51

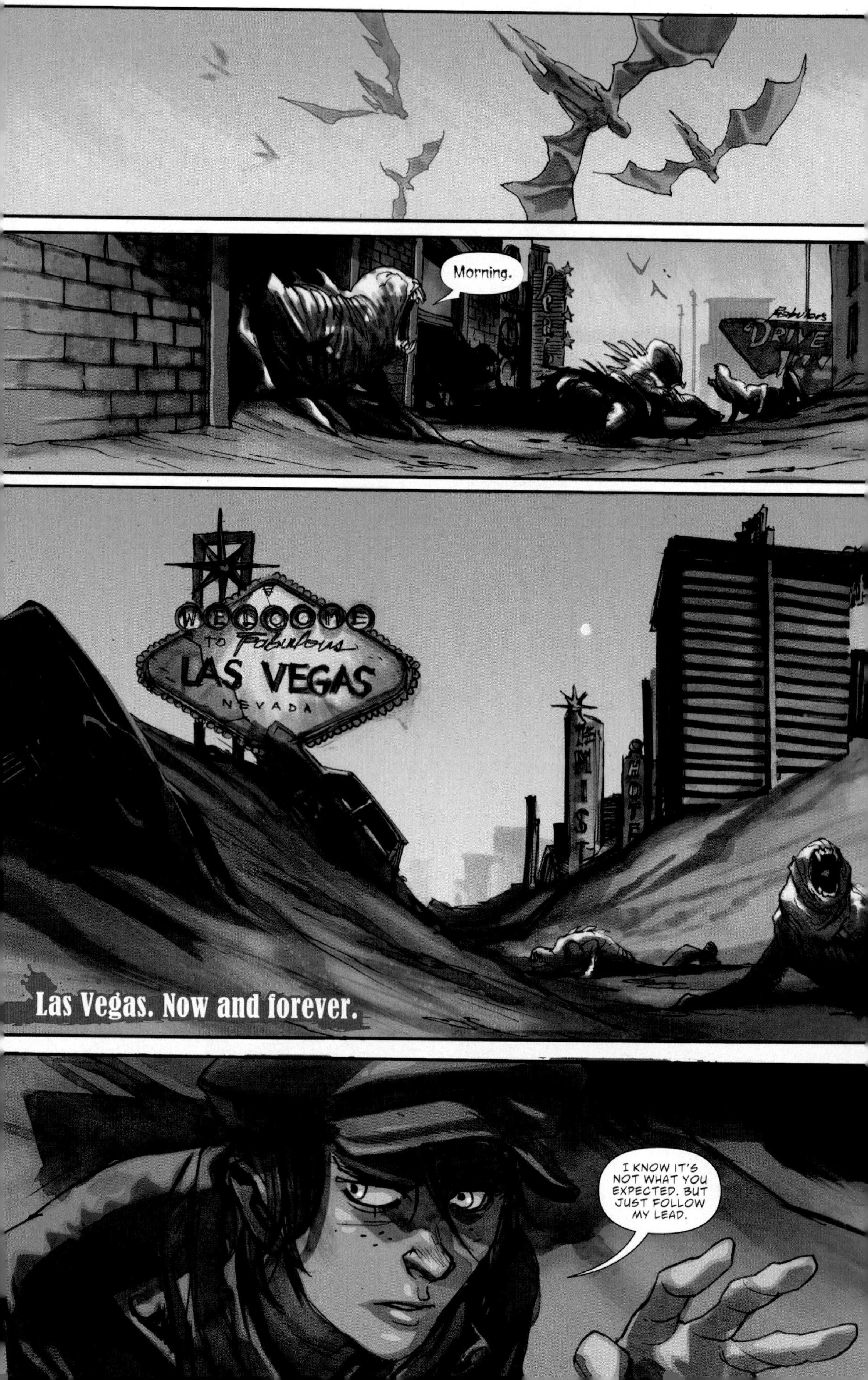
Morning.
WELCOME TO Fabulous LAS VEGAS NEVADA
Las Vegas. Now and forever.
I KNOW IT'S NOT WHAT YOU EXPECTED. BUT JUST FOLLOW MY LEAD.

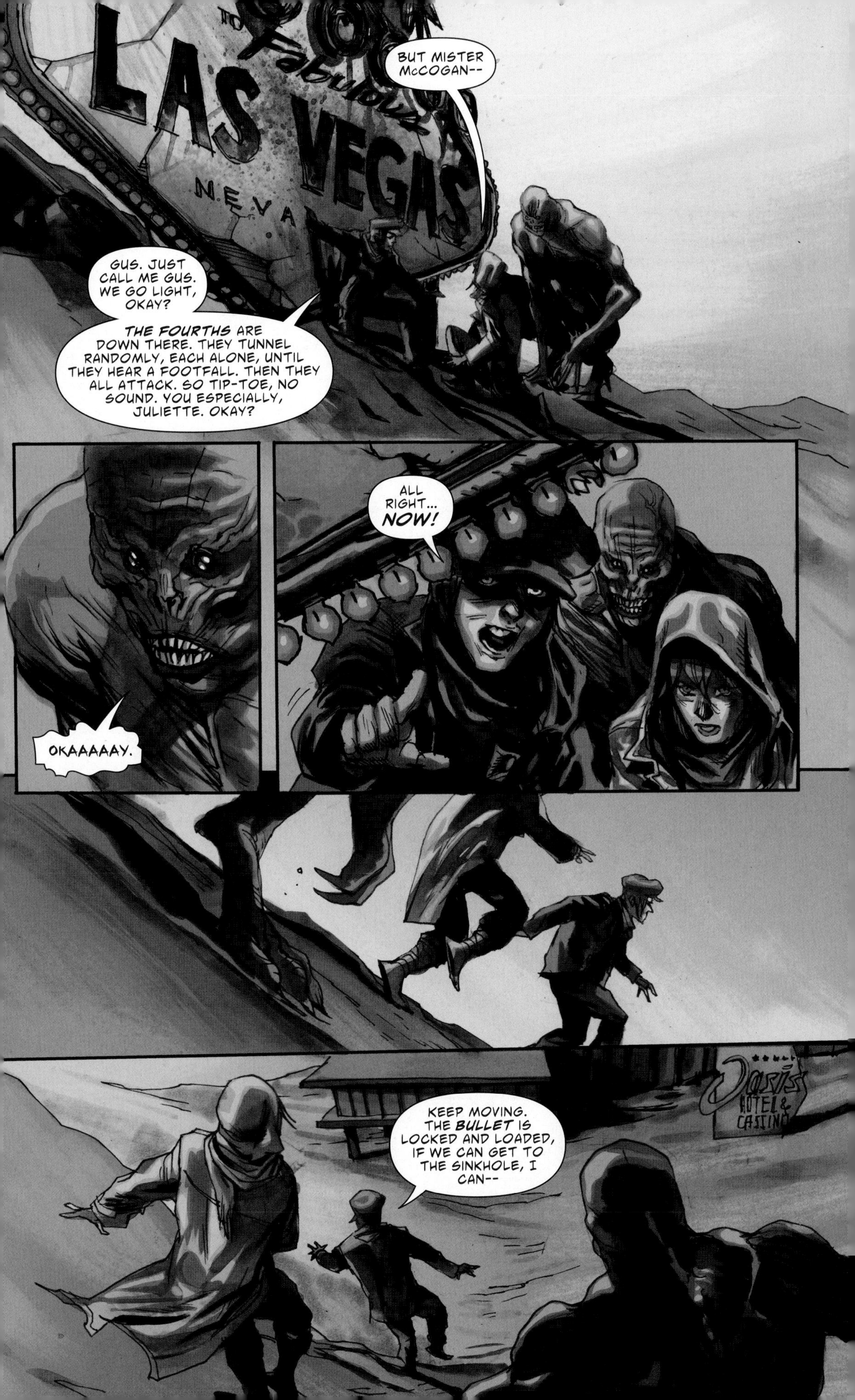

TO Fabulous LAS VEGAS NEVA
BUT MISTER McCOGAN--
GUS. JUST CALL ME GUS. WE GO LIGHT, OKAY?
THE FOURTHS ARE DOWN THERE. THEY TUNNEL RANDOMLY, EACH ALONE, UNTIL THEY HEAR A FOOTFALL. THEN THEY ALL ATTACK. SO TIP-TOE, NO SOUND. YOU ESPECIALLY, JULIETTE. OKAY?
OKAAAAAY.
ALL RIGHT... NOW!
Oasis HOTEL & CASINO
KEEP MOVING. THE BULLET IS LOCKED AND LOADED, IF WE CAN GET TO THE SINKHOLE, I CAN--

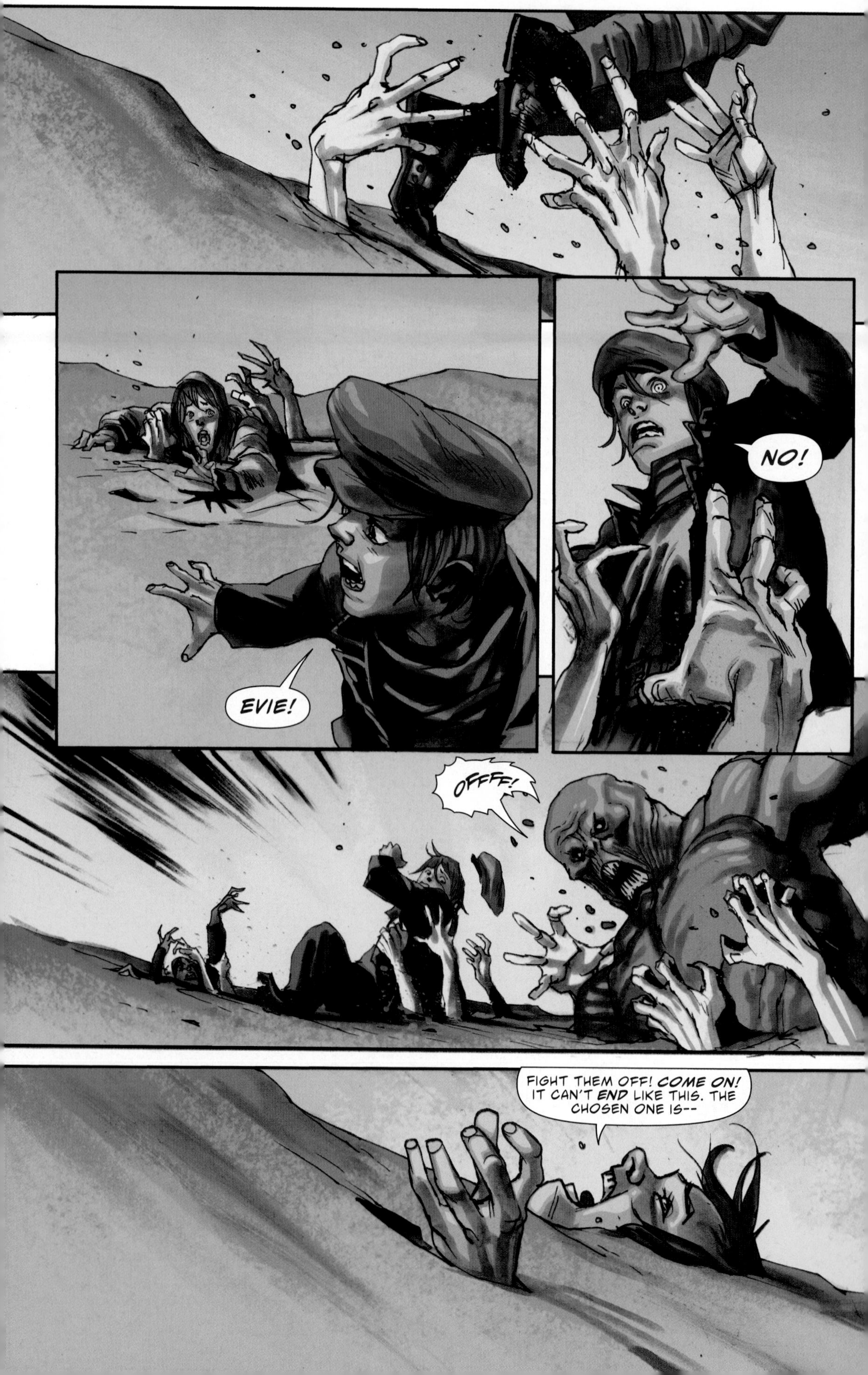
EVIE!
NO!
OFFFF!
FIGHT THEM OFF! COME ON! IT CAN'T END LIKE THIS. THE CHOSEN ONE IS--

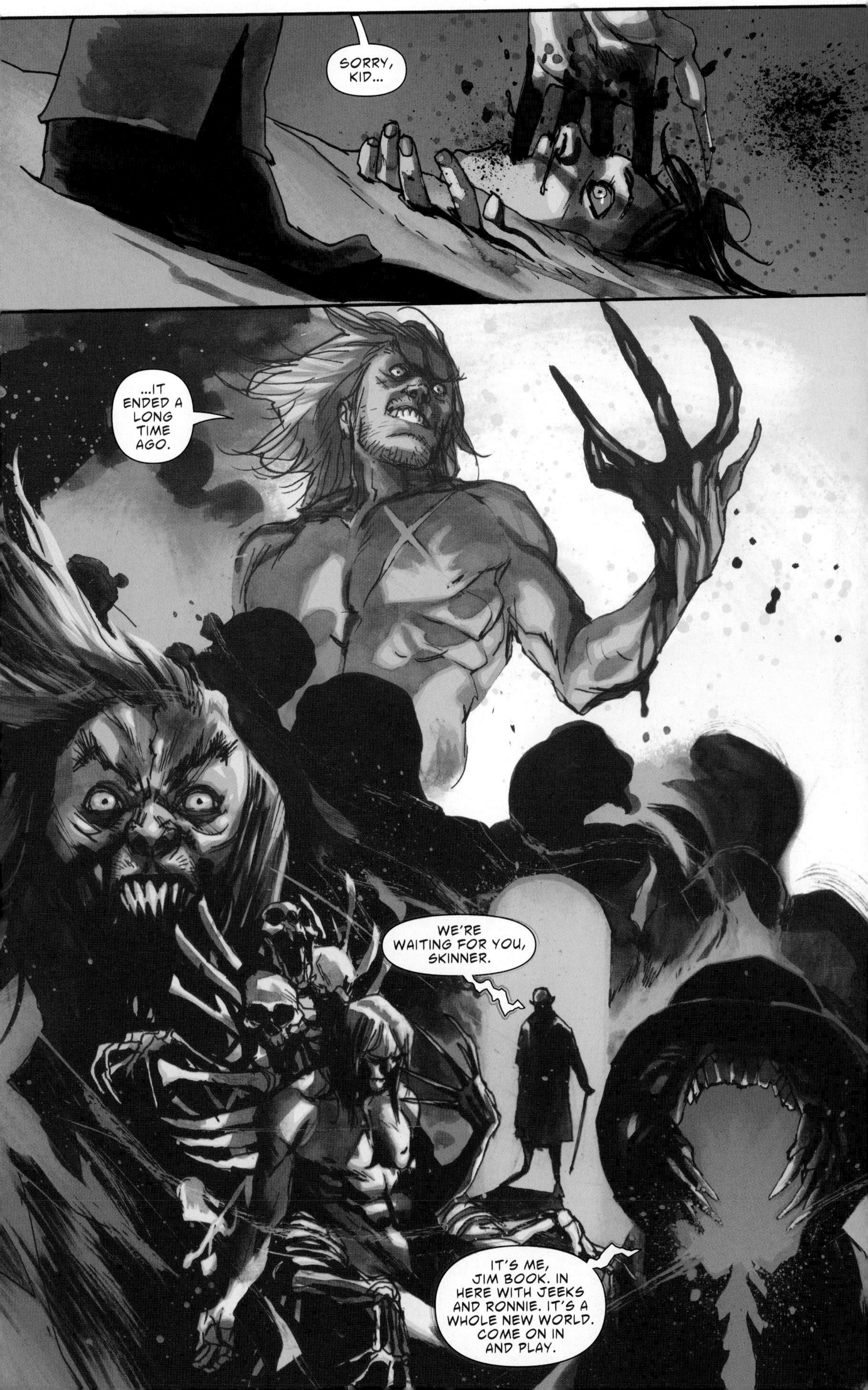
SORRY, KID...
...IT ENDED A LONG TIME AGO.
WE'RE WAITING FOR YOU, SKINNER.
IT'S ME, JIM BOOK. IN HERE WITH JEEKS AND RONNIE. IT'S A WHOLE NEW WORLD. COME ON IN AND PLAY.

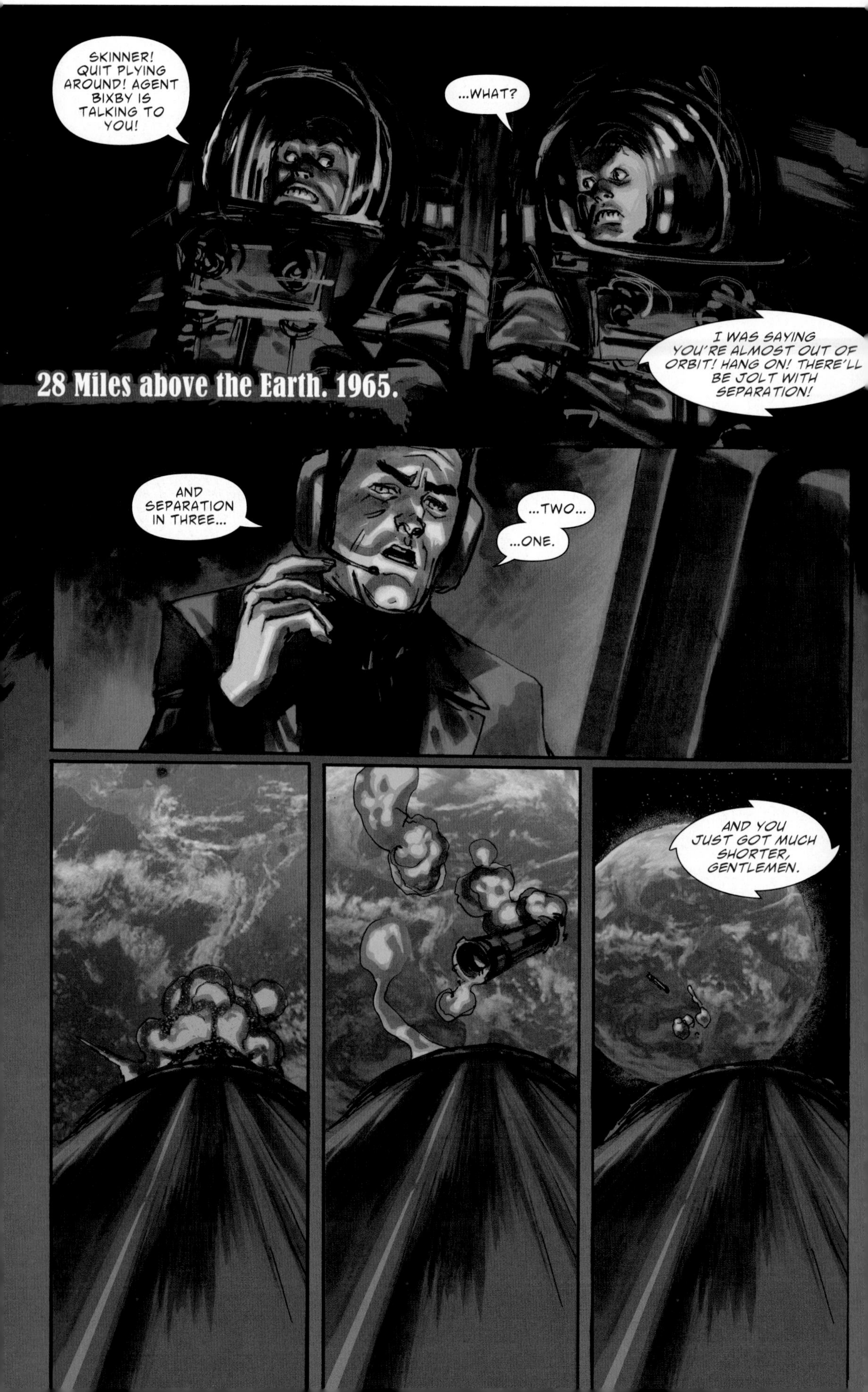
SKINNER! QUIT PLYING AROUND! AGENT BIXBY IS TALKING TO YOU!
...WHAT?
I WAS SAYING YOU'RE ALMOST OUT OF ORBIT! HANG ON! THERE'LL BE JOLT WITH SEPARATION!
28 Miles above the Earth. 1965.
AND SEPARATION IN THREE...
...TWO...
...ONE.
AND YOU JUST GOT MUCH SHORTER, GENTLEMEN.

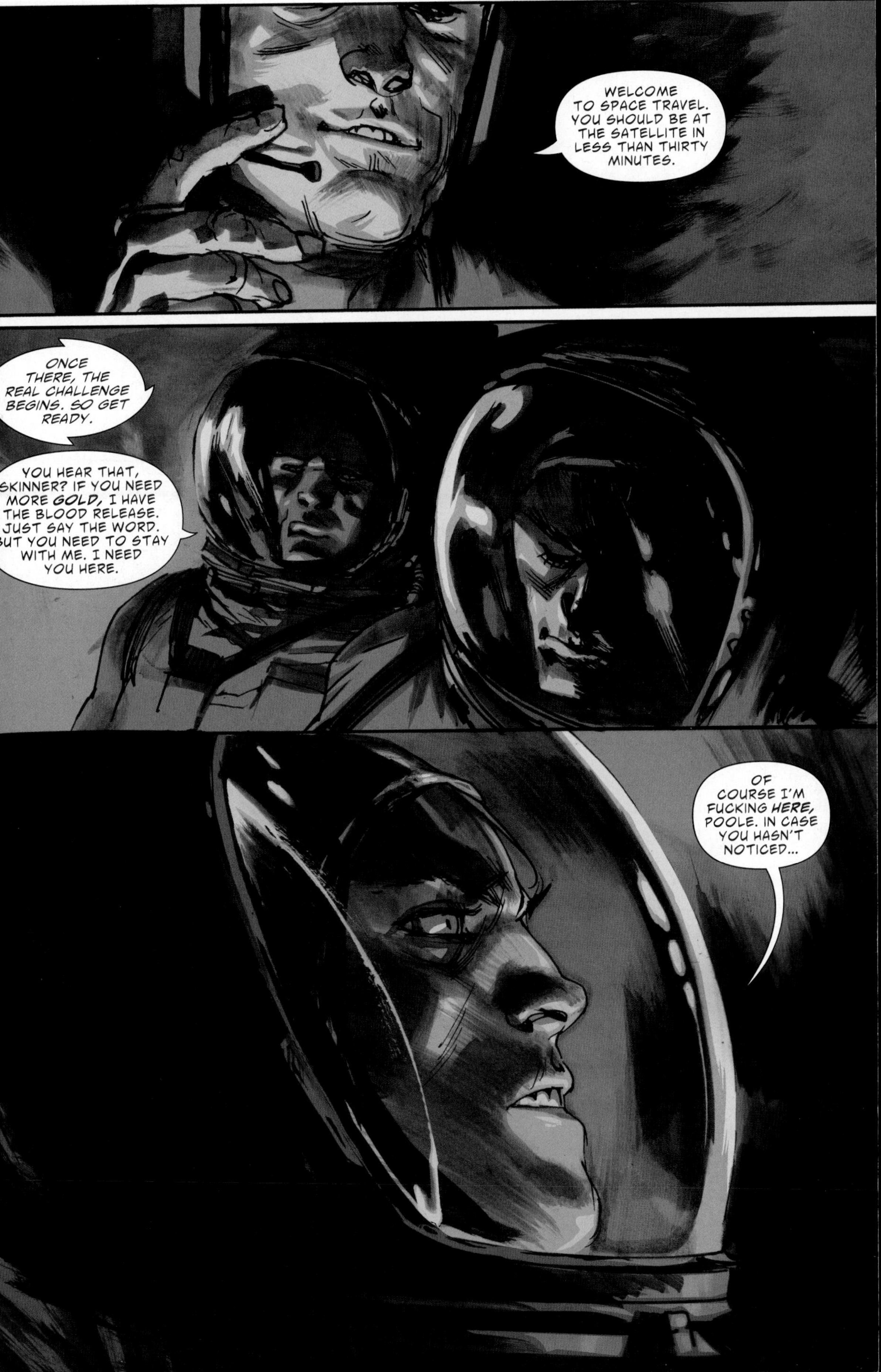
WELCOME TO SPACE TRAVEL. YOU SHOULD BE AT THE SATELLITE IN LESS THAN THIRTY MINUTES.
ONCE THERE, THE REAL CHALLENGE BEGINS. SO GET READY.
YOU HEAR THAT, SKINNER? IF YOU NEED MORE GOLD, I HAVE THE BLOOD RELEASE. JUST SAY THE WORD. BUT YOU NEED TO STAY WITH ME. I NEED YOU HERE.
OF COURSE I'M FUCKING HERE, POOLE. IN CASE YOU HASN'T NOTICED...

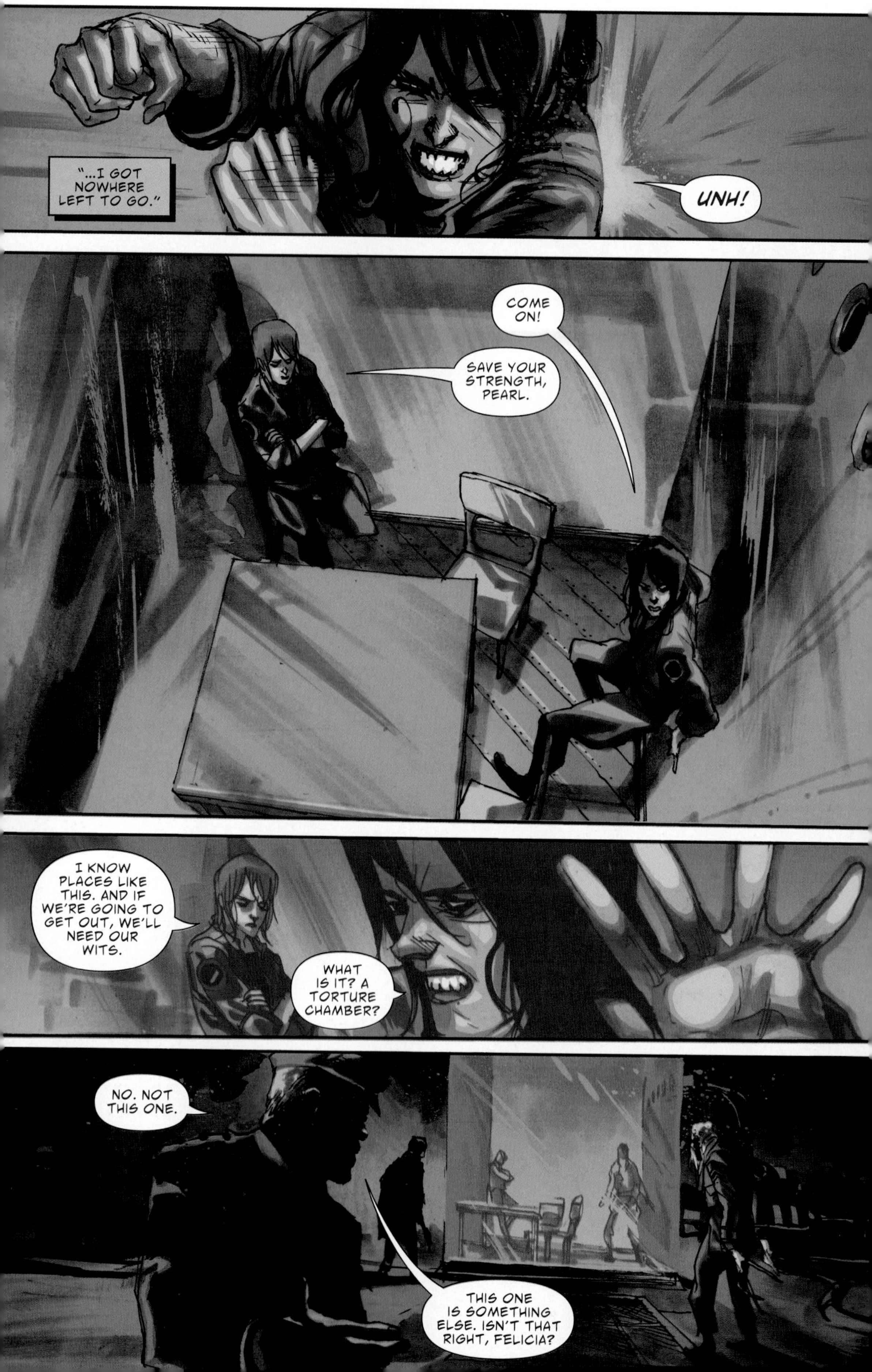
"...I GOT NOWHERE LEFT TO GO."
UNH!
COME ON!
SAVE YOUR STRENGTH, PEARL.
I KNOW PLACES LIKE THIS. AND IF WE'RE GOING TO GET OUT, WE'LL NEED OUR WITS.
WHAT IS IT? A TORTURE CHAMBER?
NO. NOT THIS ONE.
THIS ONE IS SOMETHING ELSE. ISN'T THAT RIGHT, FELICIA?

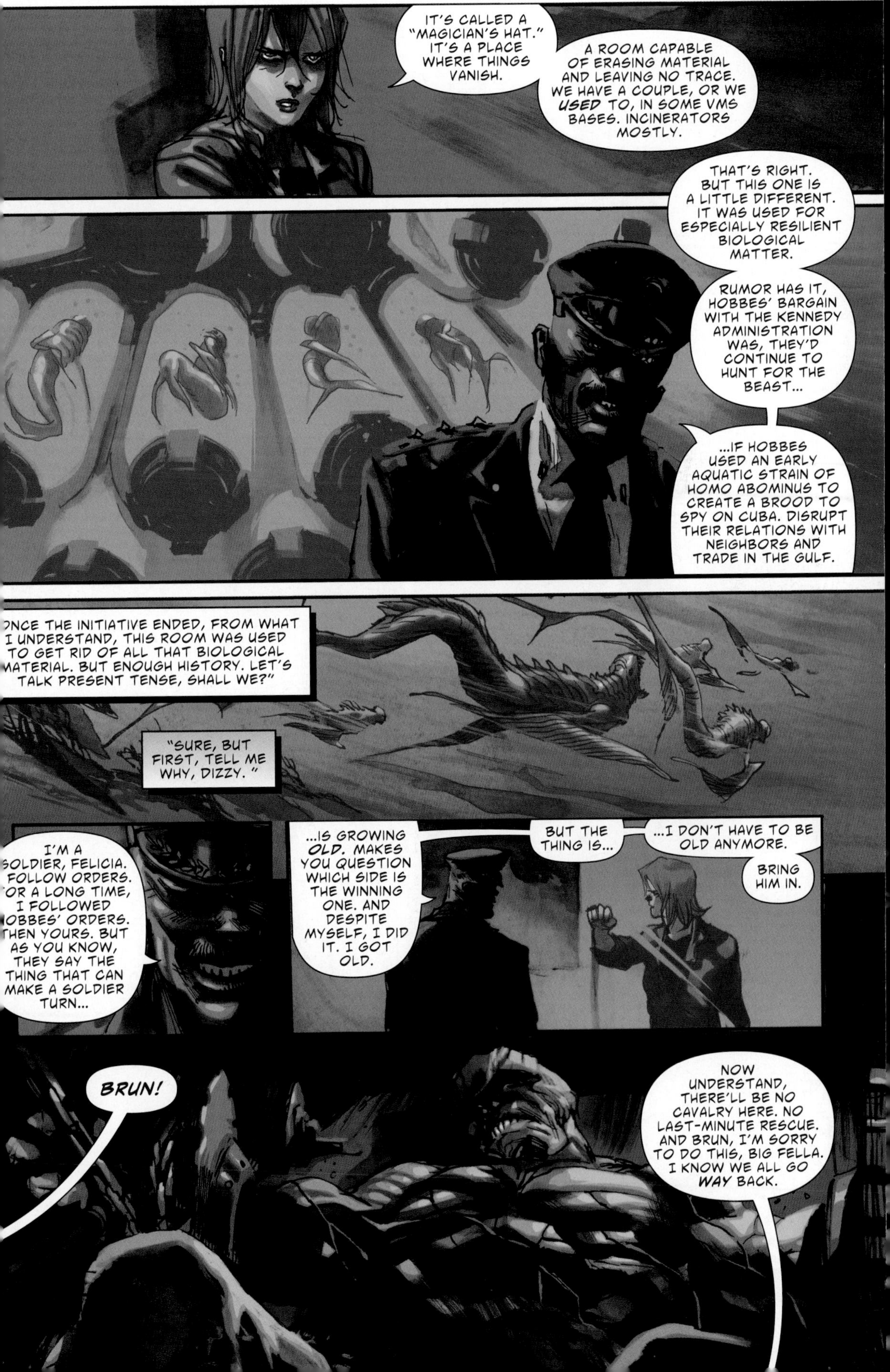
IT'S CALLED A "MAGICIAN'S HAT." IT'S A PLACE WHERE THINGS VANISH.
A ROOM CAPABLE OF ERASING MATERIAL AND LEAVING NO TRACE. WE HAVE A COUPLE, OR WE USED TO, IN SOME VMS BASES. INCINERATORS MOSTLY.
THAT'S RIGHT. BUT THIS ONE IS A LITTLE DIFFERENT. IT WAS USED FOR ESPECIALLY RESILIENT BIOLOGICAL MATTER.
RUMOR HAS IT, HOBBES' BARGAIN WITH THE KENNEDY ADMINISTRATION WAS, THEY'D CONTINUE TO HUNT FOR THE BEAST...
...IF HOBBES USED AN EARLY AQUATIC STRAIN OF HOMO ABOMINUS TO CREATE A BROOD TO SPY ON CUBA. DISRUPT THEIR RELATIONS WITH NEIGHBORS AND TRADE IN THE GULF.
ONCE THE INITIATIVE ENDED, FROM WHAT I UNDERSTAND, THIS ROOM WAS USED TO GET RID OF ALL THAT BIOLOGICAL MATERIAL. BUT ENOUGH HISTORY. LET'S TALK PRESENT TENSE, SHALL WE?"
"SURE, BUT FIRST, TELL ME WHY, DIZZY."
I'M A SOLDIER, FELICIA. I FOLLOW ORDERS. FOR A LONG TIME, I FOLLOWED HOBBES' ORDERS. THEN YOURS. BUT AS YOU KNOW, THEY SAY THE THING THAT CAN MAKE A SOLDIER TURN...
...IS GROWING OLD. MAKES YOU QUESTION WHICH SIDE IS THE WINNING ONE. AND DESPITE MYSELF, I DID IT. I GOT OLD.
BUT THE THING IS...
...I DON'T HAVE TO BE OLD ANYMORE.
BRING HIM IN.
BRUN!
NOW UNDERSTAND, THERE'LL BE NO CAVALRY HERE. NO LAST-MINUTE RESCUE. AND BRUN, I'M SORRY TO DO THIS, BIG FELLA. I KNOW WE ALL GO WAY BACK.

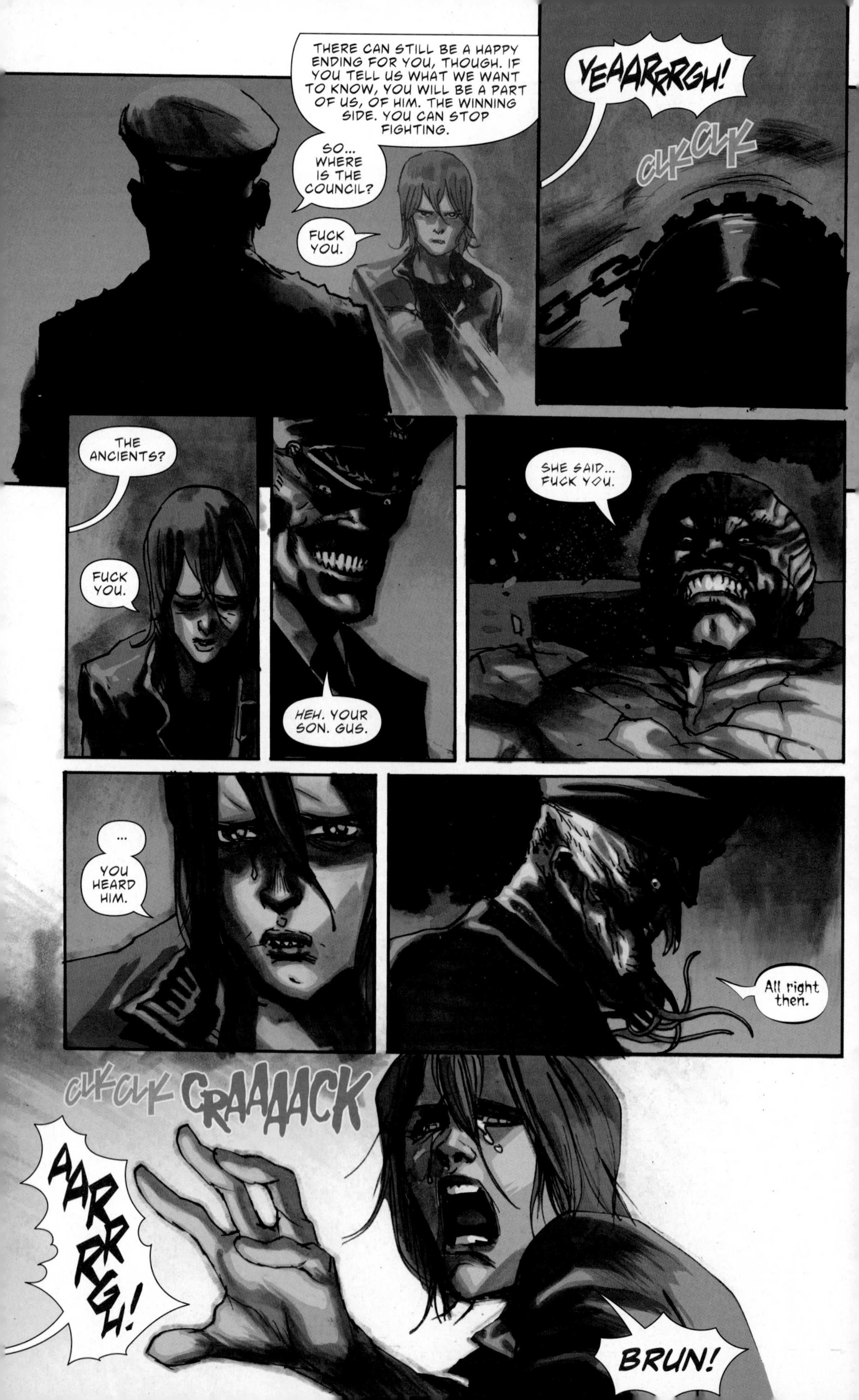

THERE CAN STILL BE A HAPPY ENDING FOR YOU, THOUGH. IF YOU TELL US WHAT WE WANT TO KNOW, YOU WILL BE A PART OF US, OF HIM. THE WINNING SIDE. YOU CAN STOP FIGHTING.
SO... WHERE IS THE COUNCIL?
FUCK YOU.
YEAARRRGH!
CLK CLK
THE ANCIENTS?
FUCK YOU.
HEH. YOUR SON. GUS.
SHE SAID... FUCK YOU.
... YOU HEARD HIM.
All right then.
CLK CLK CRAAAACK
AARRRGH!
BRUN!

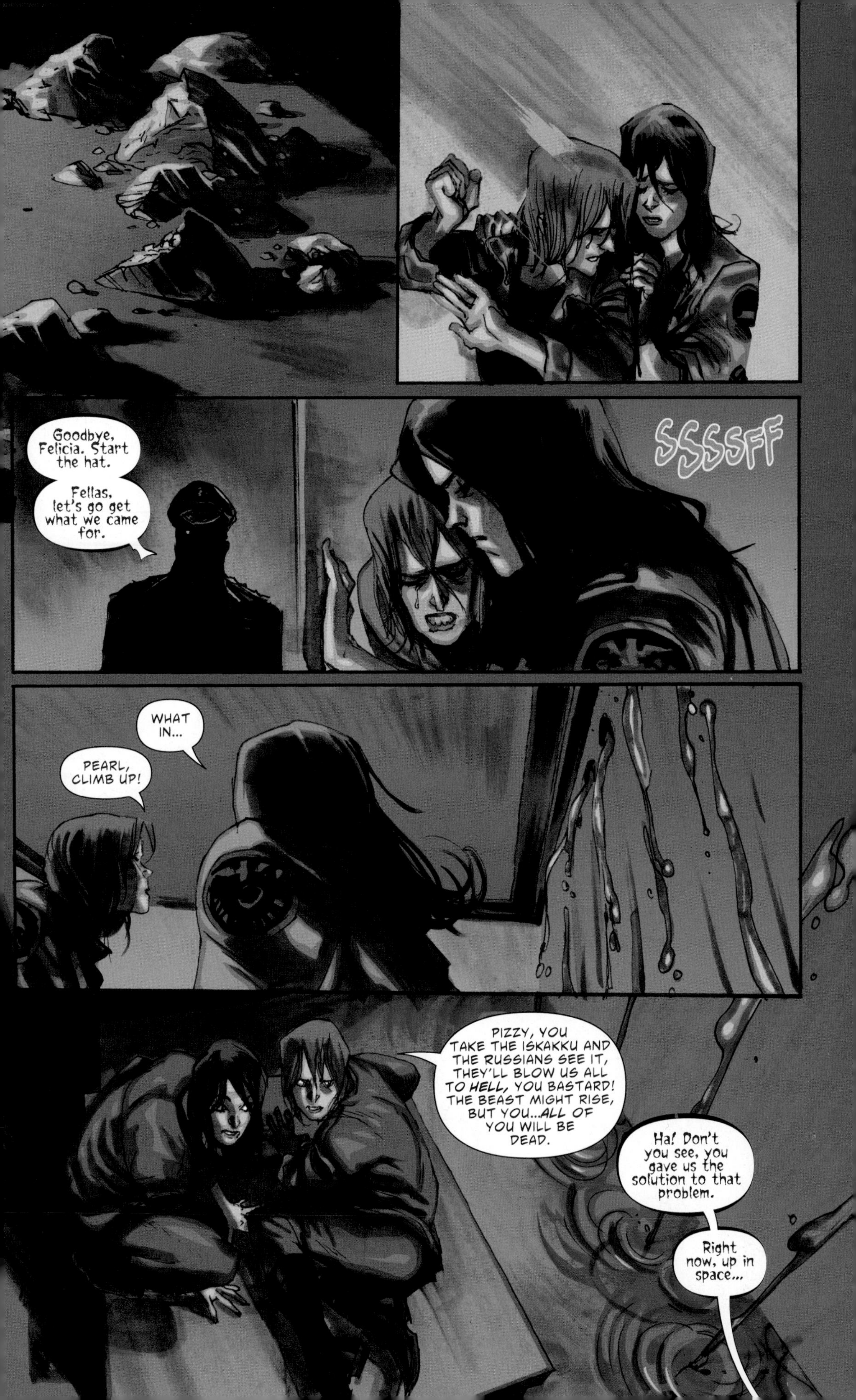

Goodbye, Felicia. Start the hat.
Fellas, let's go get what we came for.
SSSSFF
WHAT IN...
PEARL, CLIMB UP!
PIZZY, YOU TAKE THE ISKAKKU AND THE RUSSIANS SEE IT, THEY'LL BLOW US ALL TO HELL, YOU BASTARD! THE BEAST MIGHT RISE, BUT YOU...ALL OF YOU WILL BE DEAD.
Ha! Don't you see, you gave us the solution to that problem.
Right now, up in space...

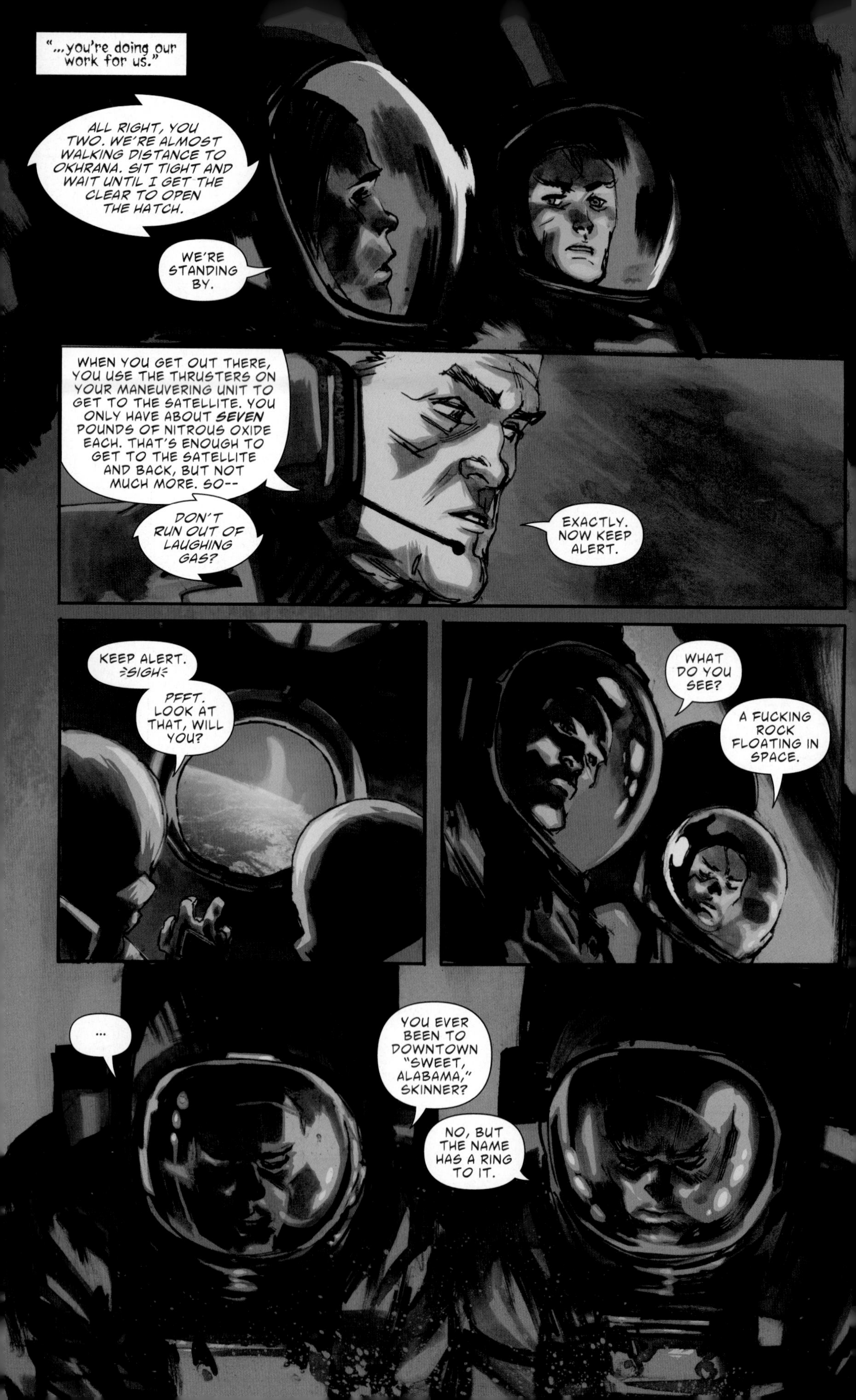
"...you're doing our work for us."
ALL RIGHT, YOU TWO. WE'RE ALMOST WALKING DISTANCE TO OKHRANA. SIT TIGHT AND WAIT UNTIL I GET THE CLEAR TO OPEN THE HATCH.
WE'RE STANDING BY.
WHEN YOU GET OUT THERE, YOU USE THE THRUSTERS ON YOUR MANEUVERING UNIT TO GET TO THE SATELLITE. YOU ONLY HAVE ABOUT SEVEN POUNDS OF NITROUS OXIDE EACH. THAT'S ENOUGH TO GET TO THE SATELLITE AND BACK, BUT NOT MUCH MORE. SO--
DON'T RUN OUT OF LAUGHING GAS?
EXACTLY. NOW KEEP ALERT.
KEEP ALERT. SIGH
PFFT. LOOK AT THAT, WILL YOU?
WHAT DO YOU SEE?
A FUCKING ROCK FLOATING IN SPACE.
...
YOU EVER BEEN TO DOWNTOWN "SWEET, ALABAMA," SKINNER?
NO, BUT THE NAME HAS A RING TO IT.

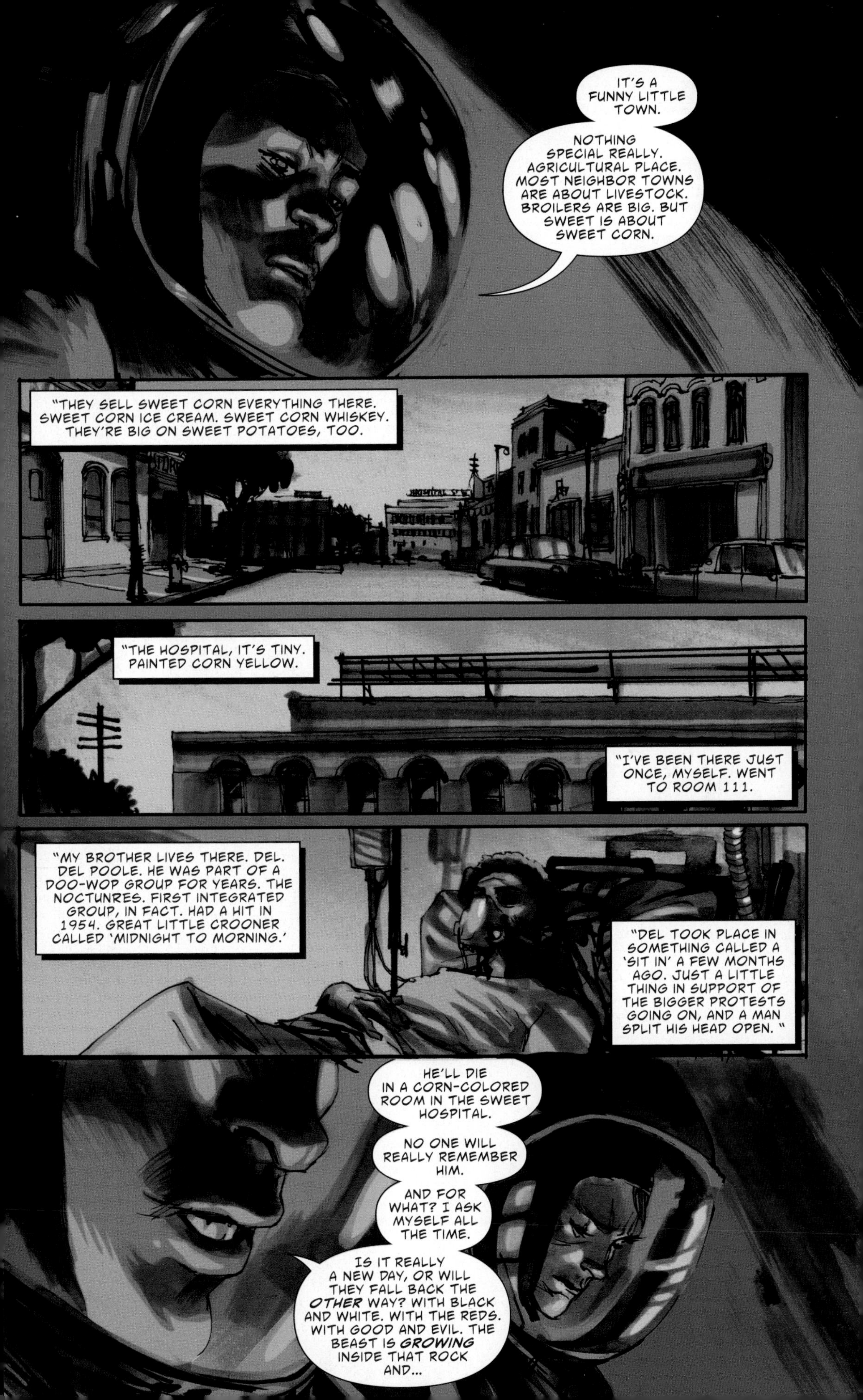
IT'S A FUNNY LITTLE TOWN.
NOTHING SPECIAL REALLY. AGRICULTURAL PLACE. MOST NEIGHBOR TOWNS ARE ABOUT LIVESTOCK. BROILERS ARE BIG. BUT SWEET IS ABOUT SWEET CORN.
"THEY SELL SWEET CORN EVERYTHING THERE. SWEET CORN ICE CREAM. SWEET CORN WHISKEY. THEY'RE BIG ON SWEET POTATOES, TOO.
"THE HOSPITAL, IT'S TINY. PAINTED CORN YELLOW.
"I'VE BEEN THERE JUST ONCE, MYSELF. WENT TO ROOM 111.
"MY BROTHER LIVES THERE. DEL. DEL POOLE. HE WAS PART OF A DOO-WOP GROUP FOR YEARS. THE NOCTUNRES. FIRST INTEGRATED GROUP, IN FACT. HAD A HIT IN 1954. GREAT LITTLE CROONER CALLED 'MIDNIGHT TO MORNING.'
"DEL TOOK PLACE IN SOMETHING CALLED A 'SIT IN' A FEW MONTHS AGO. JUST A LITTLE THING IN SUPPORT OF THE BIGGER PROTESTS GOING ON, AND A MAN SPLIT HIS HEAD OPEN."
HE'LL DIE IN A CORN-COLORED ROOM IN THE SWEET HOSPITAL.
NO ONE WILL REALLY REMEMBER HIM.
AND FOR WHAT? I ASK MYSELF ALL THE TIME.
IS IT REALLY A NEW DAY, OR WILL THEY FALL BACK THE *OTHER* WAY? WITH BLACK AND WHITE. WITH THE REDS. WITH GOOD AND EVIL. THE BEAST IS *GROWING* INSIDE THAT ROCK AND...

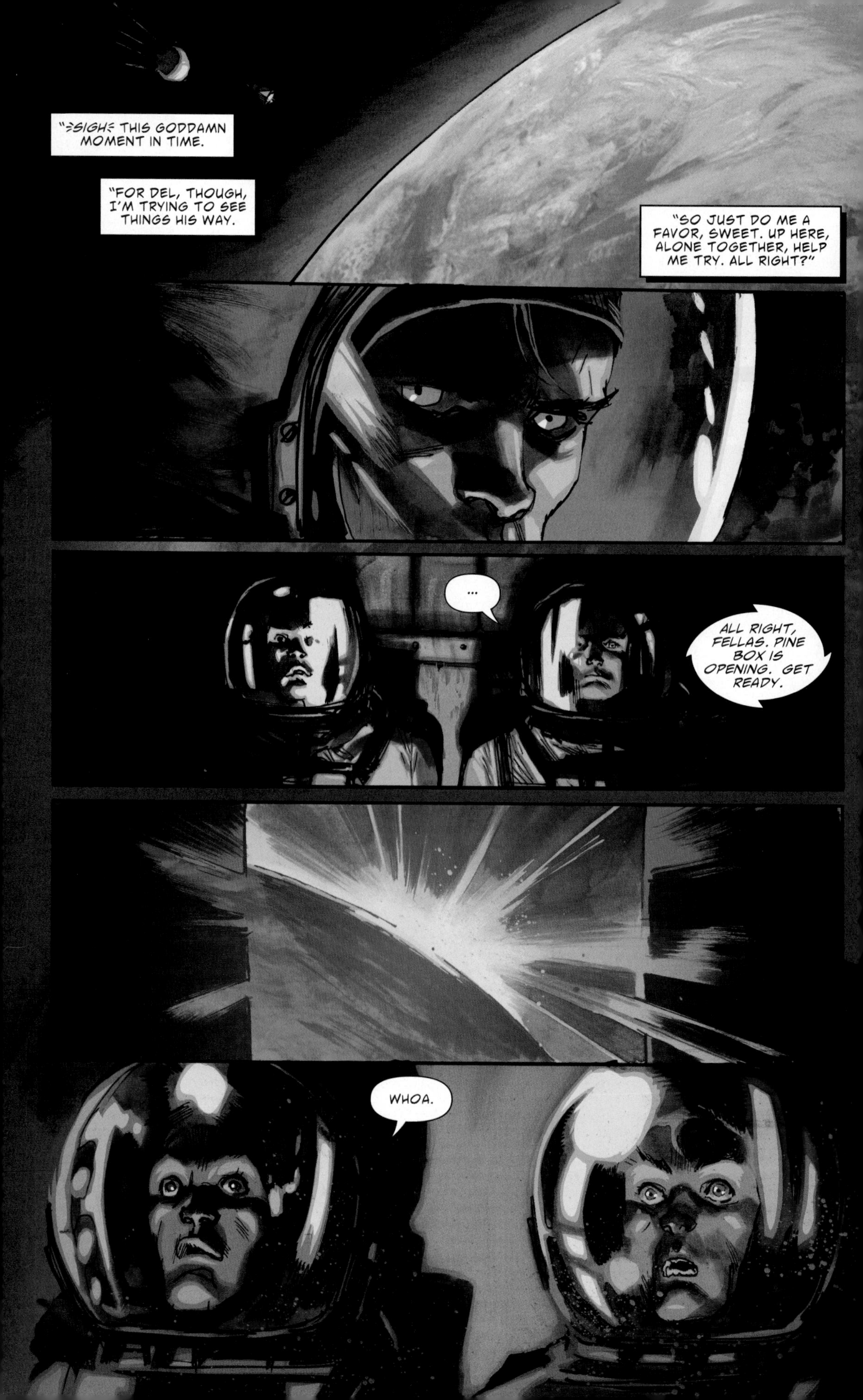
"≶SIGH≶ THIS GODDAMN MOMENT IN TIME.
"FOR DEL, THOUGH, I'M TRYING TO SEE THINGS HIS WAY.
"SO JUST DO ME A FAVOR, SWEET. UP HERE, ALONE TOGETHER, HELP ME TRY. ALL RIGHT?"
...
ALL RIGHT, FELLAS. PINE BOX IS OPENING. GET READY.
WHOA.

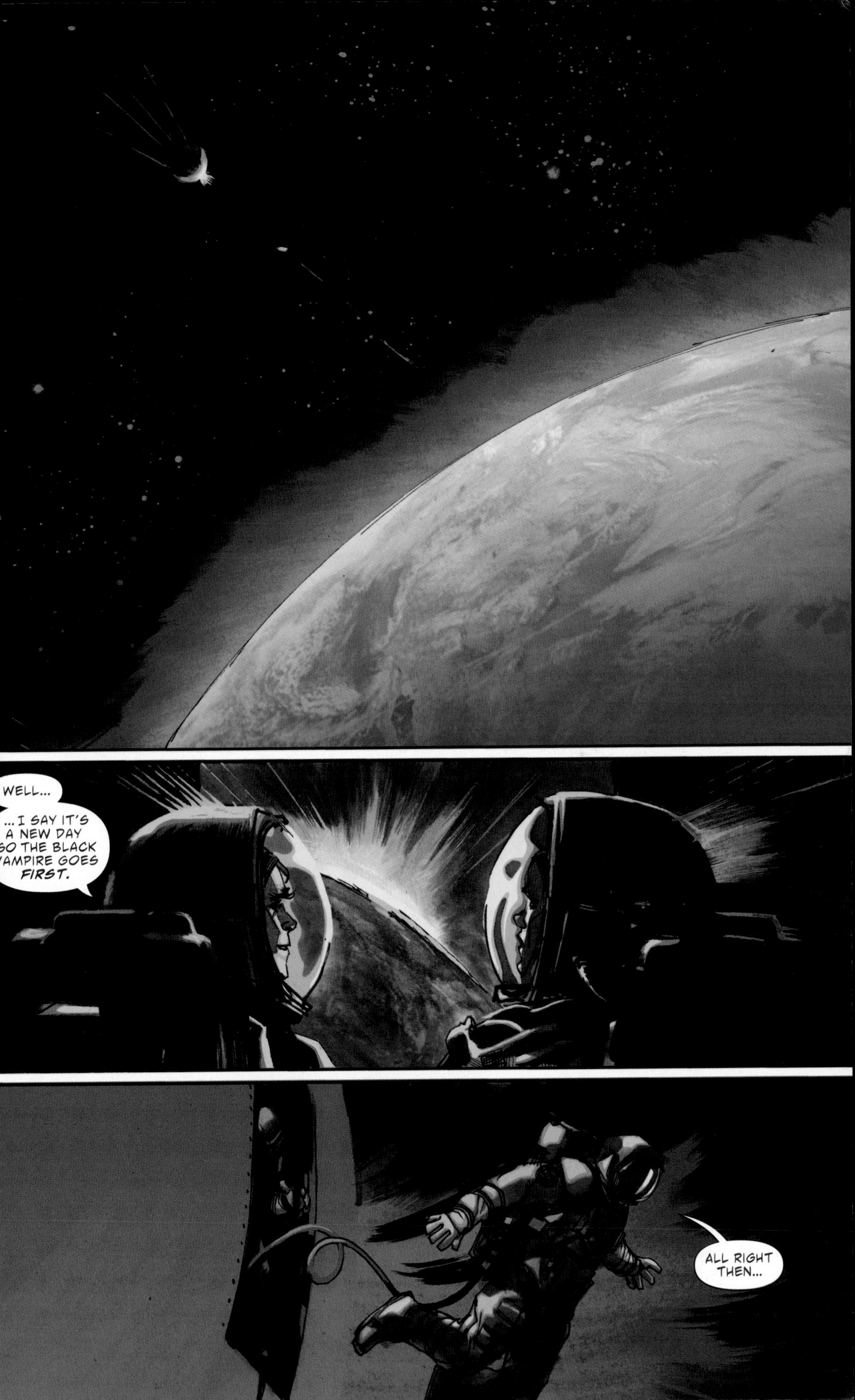

WELL...
...I SAY IT'S A NEW DAY SO THE BLACK VAMPIRE GOES FIRST.
ALL RIGHT THEN...

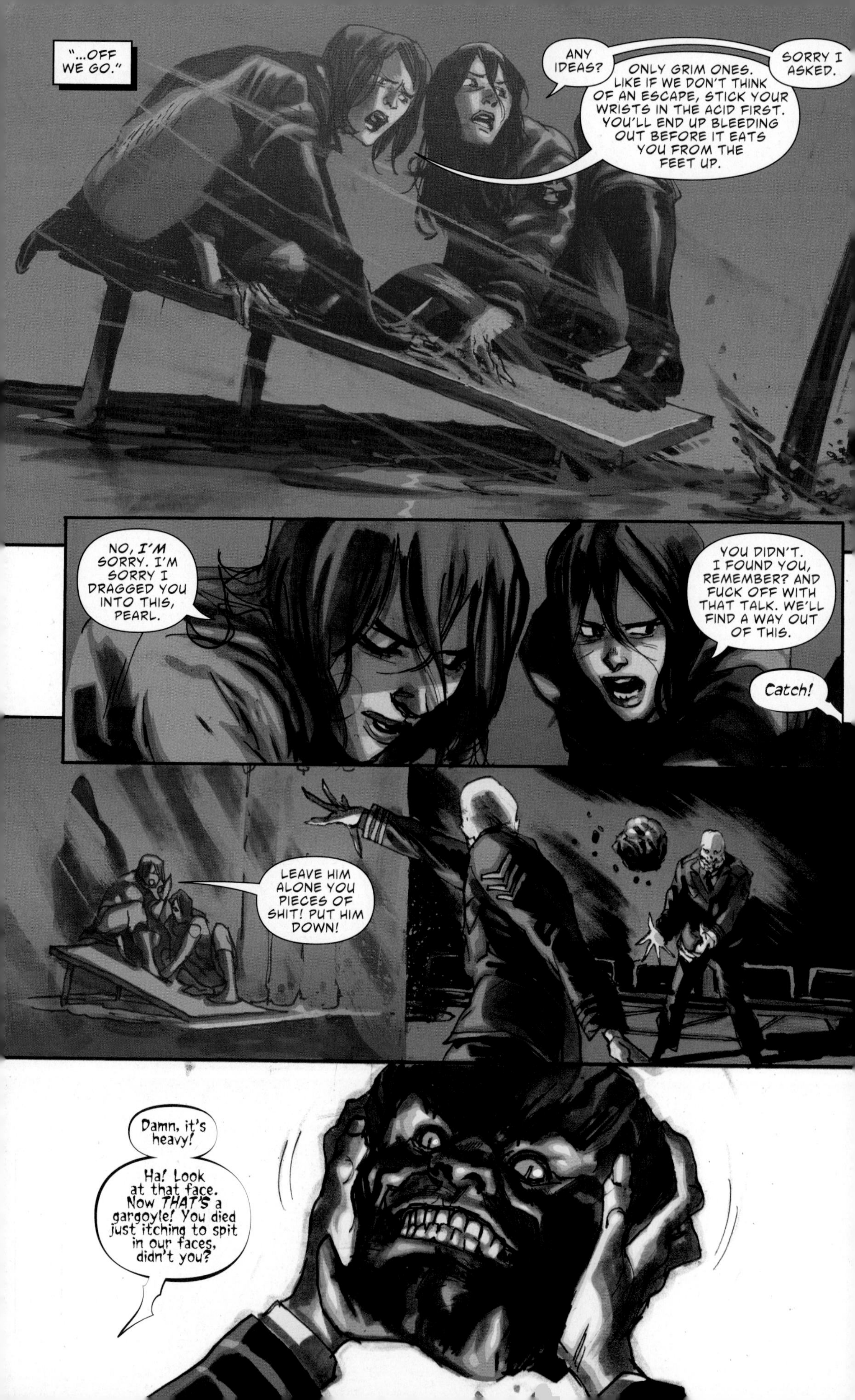
"...OFF WE GO."
ANY IDEAS?
ONLY GRIM ONES. LIKE IF WE DON'T THINK OF AN ESCAPE, STICK YOUR WRISTS IN THE ACID FIRST. YOU'LL END UP BLEEDING OUT BEFORE IT EATS YOU FROM THE FEET UP.
SORRY I ASKED.
NO, I'M SORRY. I'M SORRY I DRAGGED YOU INTO THIS, PEARL.
YOU DIDN'T. I FOUND YOU, REMEMBER? AND FUCK OFF WITH THAT TALK. WE'LL FIND A WAY OUT OF THIS.
Catch!
LEAVE HIM ALONE YOU PIECES OF SHIT! PUT HIM DOWN!
Damn, it's heavy!
Ha! Look at that face. Now THAT'S a gargoyle! You died just itching to spit in our faces, didn't you?

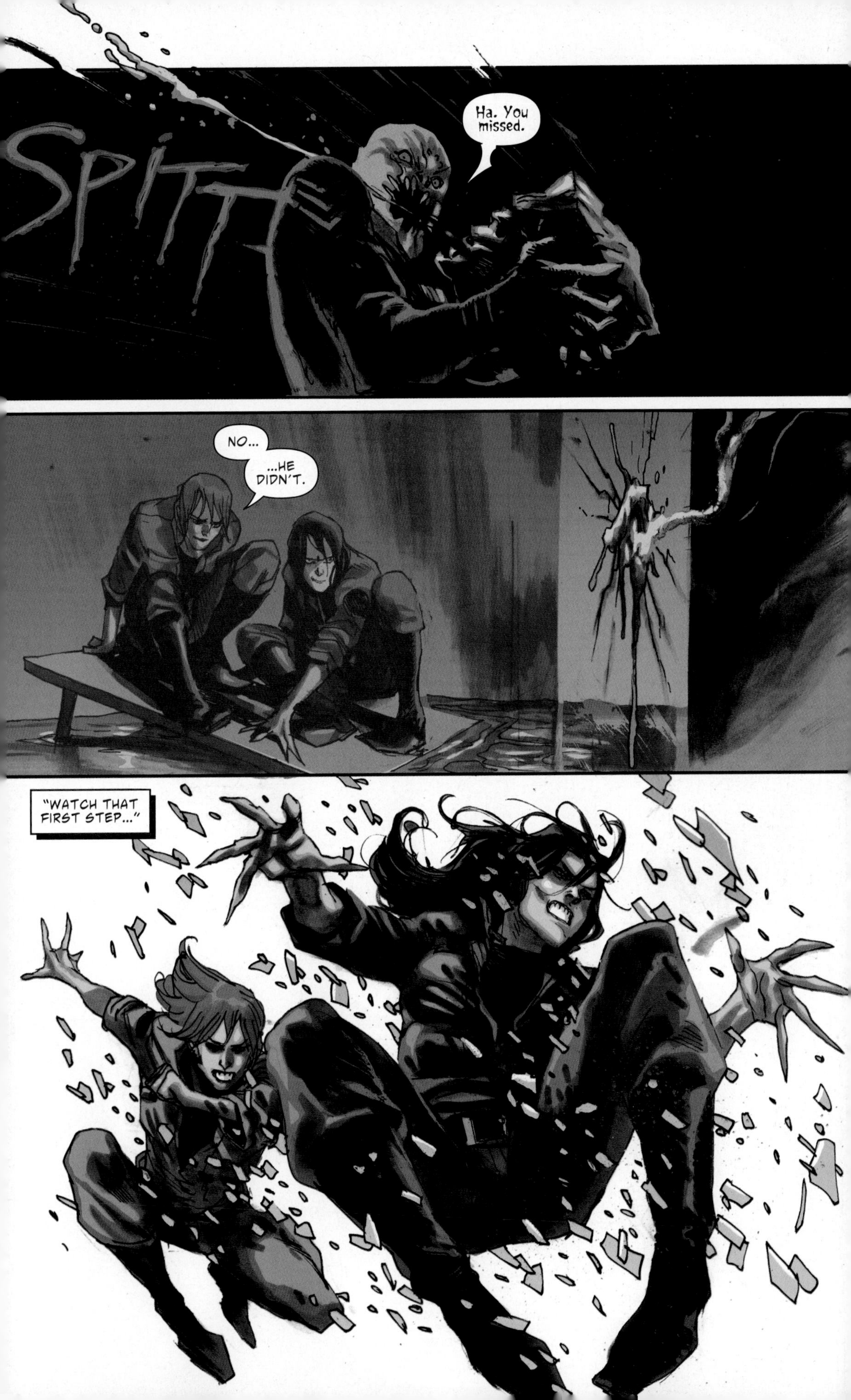
SPITT
Ha. You missed.
NO...
...HE DIDN'T.
"WATCH THAT FIRST STEP..."

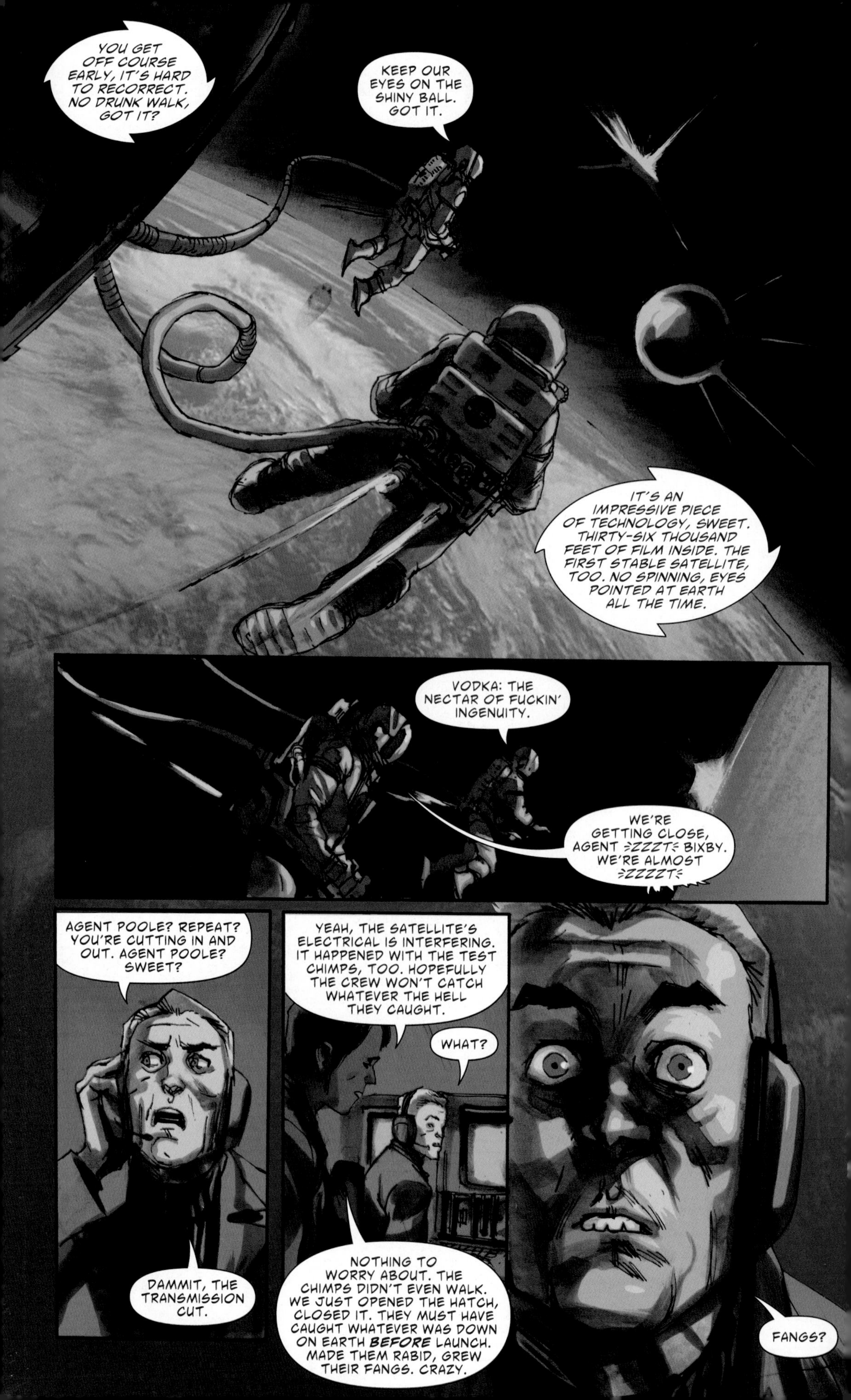
YOU GET OFF COURSE EARLY, IT'S HARD TO RECORRECT. NO DRUNK WALK, GOT IT?
KEEP OUR EYES ON THE SHINY BALL. GOT IT.
IT'S AN IMPRESSIVE PIECE OF TECHNOLOGY, SWEET. THIRTY-SIX THOUSAND FEET OF FILM INSIDE. THE FIRST STABLE SATELLITE, TOO. NO SPINNING, EYES POINTED AT EARTH ALL THE TIME.
VODKA: THE NECTAR OF FUCKIN' INGENUITY.
WE'RE GETTING CLOSE, AGENT ≠ZZZT≠ BIXBY. WE'RE ALMOST ≠ZZZZT≠
AGENT POOLE? REPEAT? YOU'RE CUTTING IN AND OUT. AGENT POOLE? SWEET?
DAMMIT, THE TRANSMISSION CUT.
YEAH, THE SATELLITE'S ELECTRICAL IS INTERFERING. IT HAPPENED WITH THE TEST CHIMPS, TOO. HOPEFULLY THE CREW WON'T CATCH WHATEVER THE HELL THEY CAUGHT.
WHAT?
NOTHING TO WORRY ABOUT. THE CHIMPS DIDN'T EVEN WALK. WE JUST OPENED THE HATCH, CLOSED IT. THEY MUST HAVE CAUGHT WHATEVER WAS DOWN ON EARTH **BEFORE** LAUNCH. MADE THEM RABID, GREW THEIR FANGS. CRAZY.
FANGS?

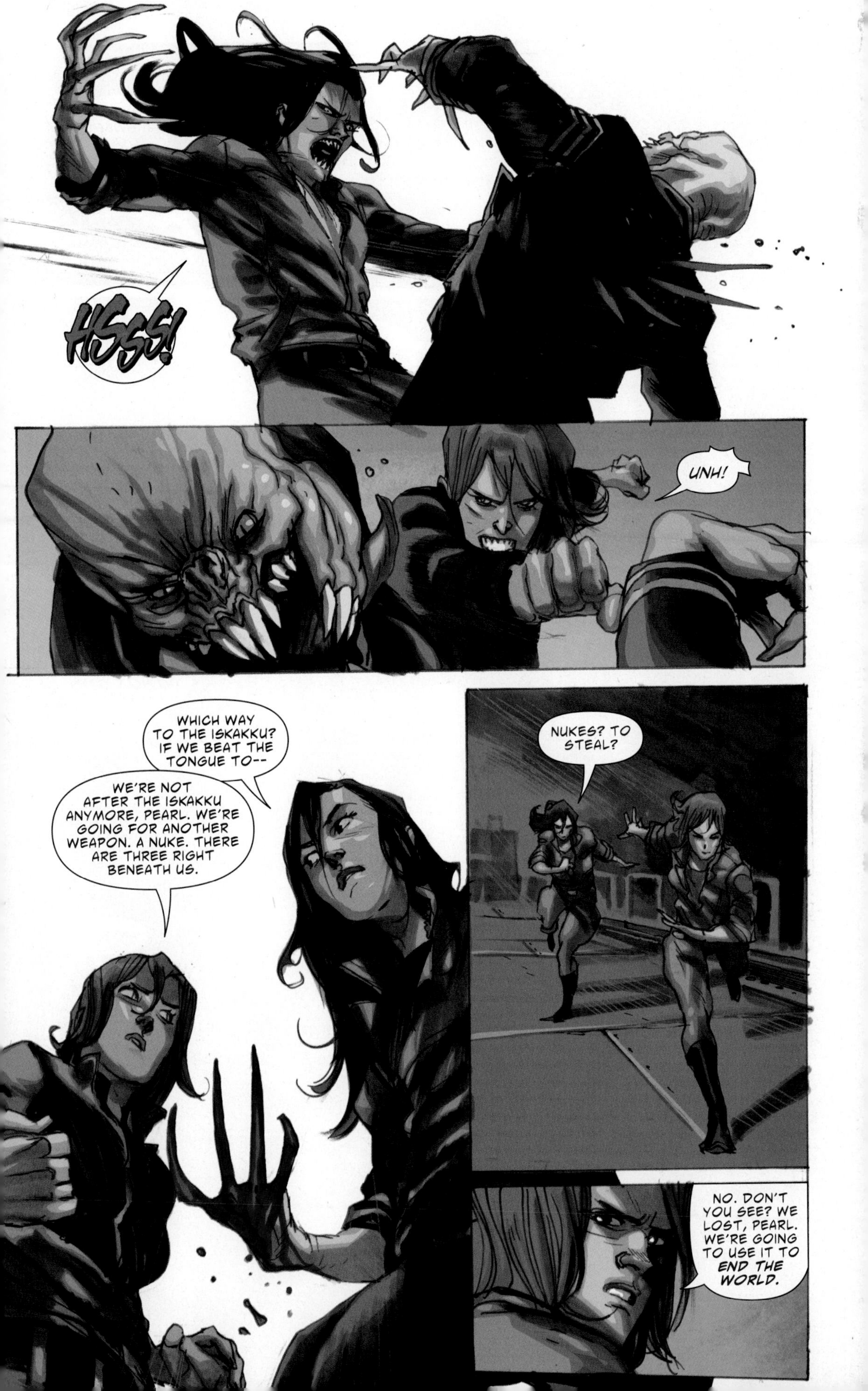
HISSS!
UNH!
WHICH WAY TO THE ISKAKKU? IF WE BEAT THE TONGUE TO--
WE'RE NOT AFTER THE ISKAKKU ANYMORE, PEARL. WE'RE GOING FOR ANOTHER WEAPON. A NUKE. THERE ARE THREE RIGHT BENEATH US.
NUKES? TO STEAL?
NO. DON'T YOU SEE? WE LOST, PEARL. WE'RE GOING TO USE IT TO END THE WORLD.

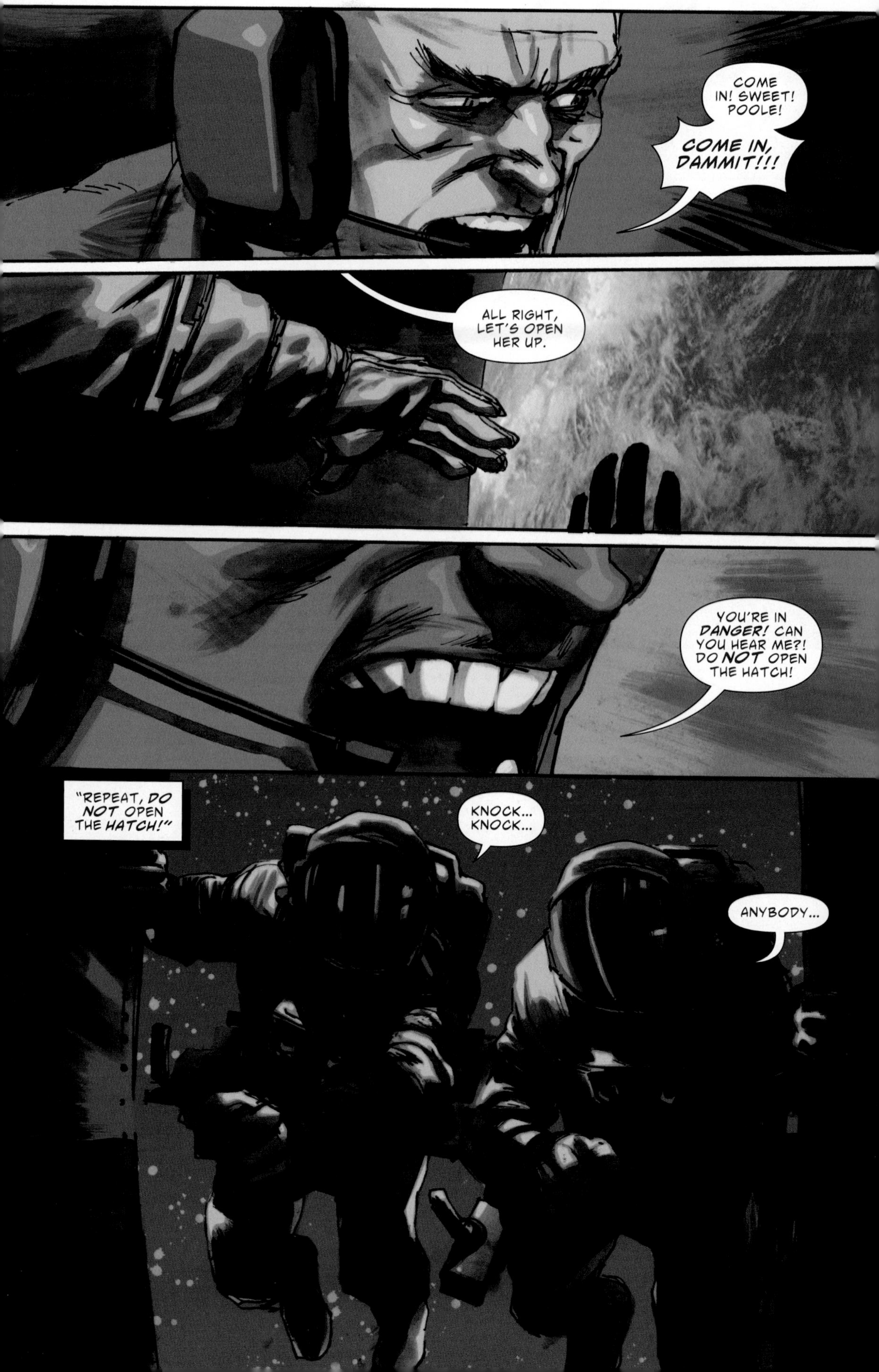
COME IN! SWEET! POOLE!
COME IN, DAMMIT!!!
ALL RIGHT, LET'S OPEN HER UP.
YOU'RE IN DANGER! CAN YOU HEAR ME?! DO NOT OPEN THE HATCH!
"REPEAT, DO NOT OPEN THE HATCH!"
KNOCK... KNOCK...
ANYBODY...

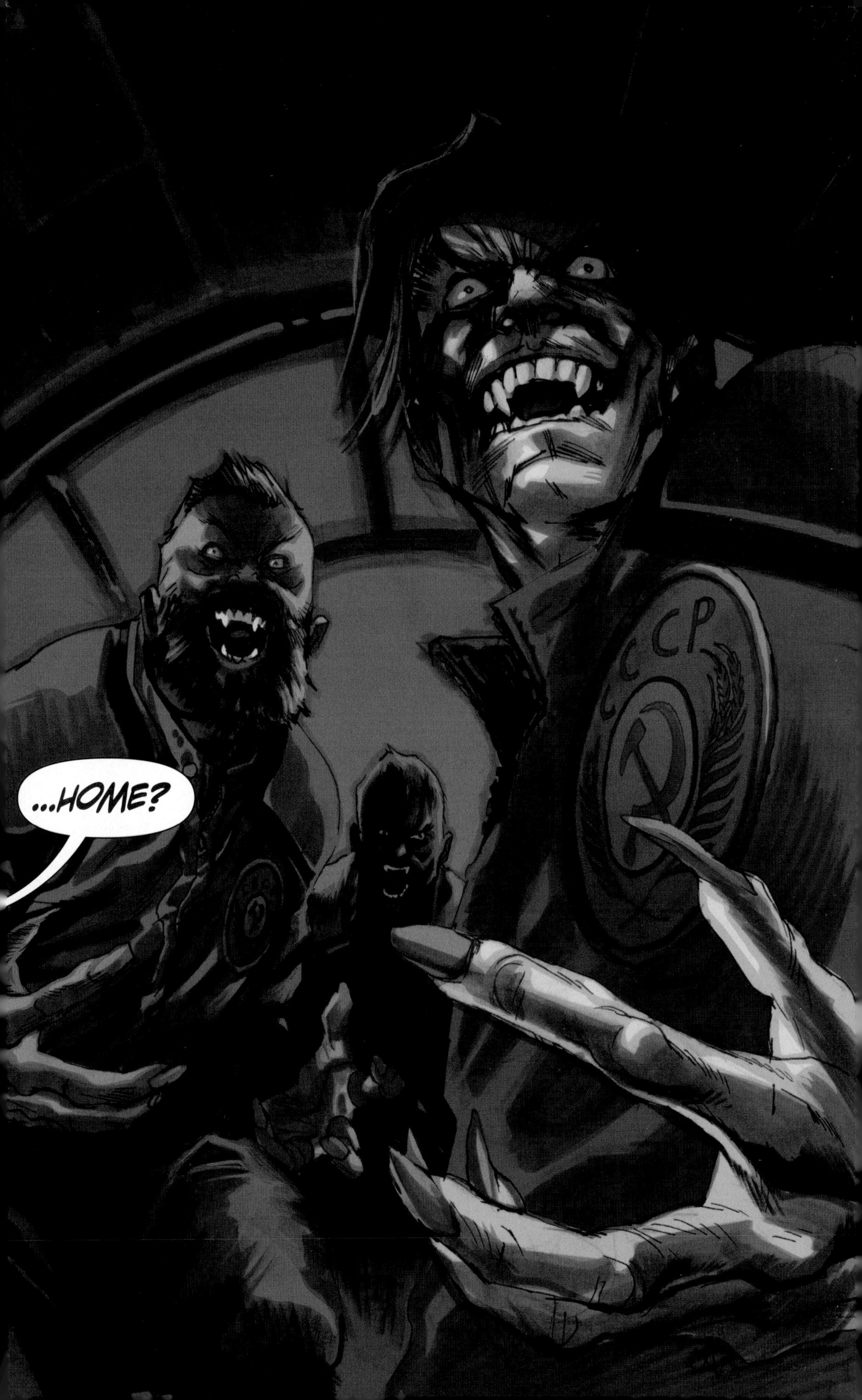
...HOME?
CCCP

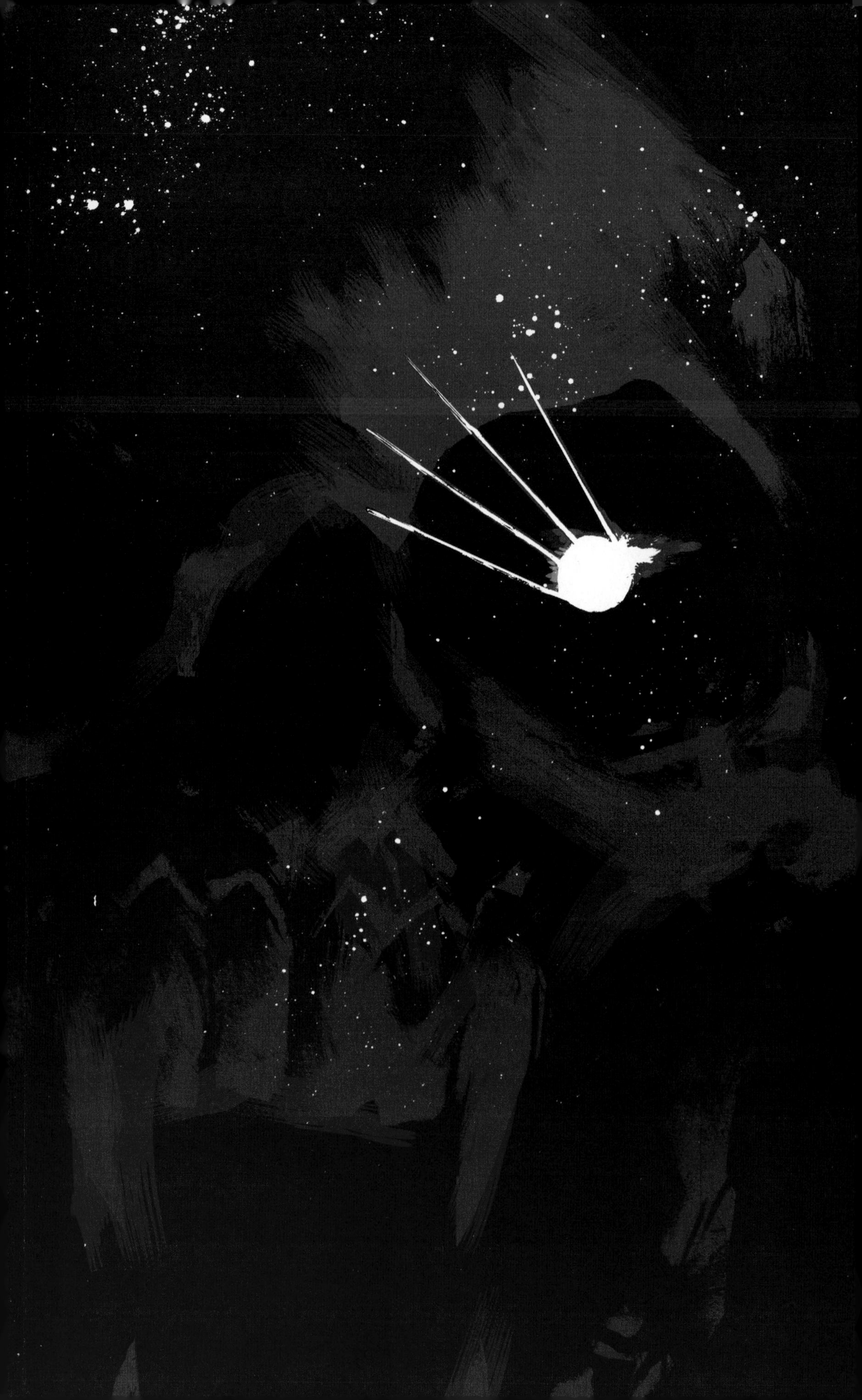

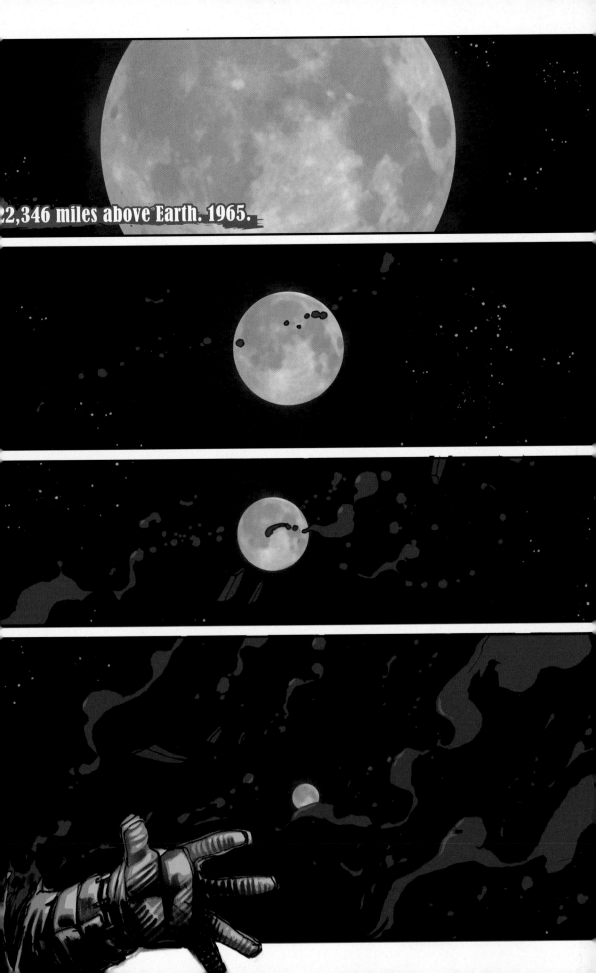

22,346 miles above Earth. 1965.

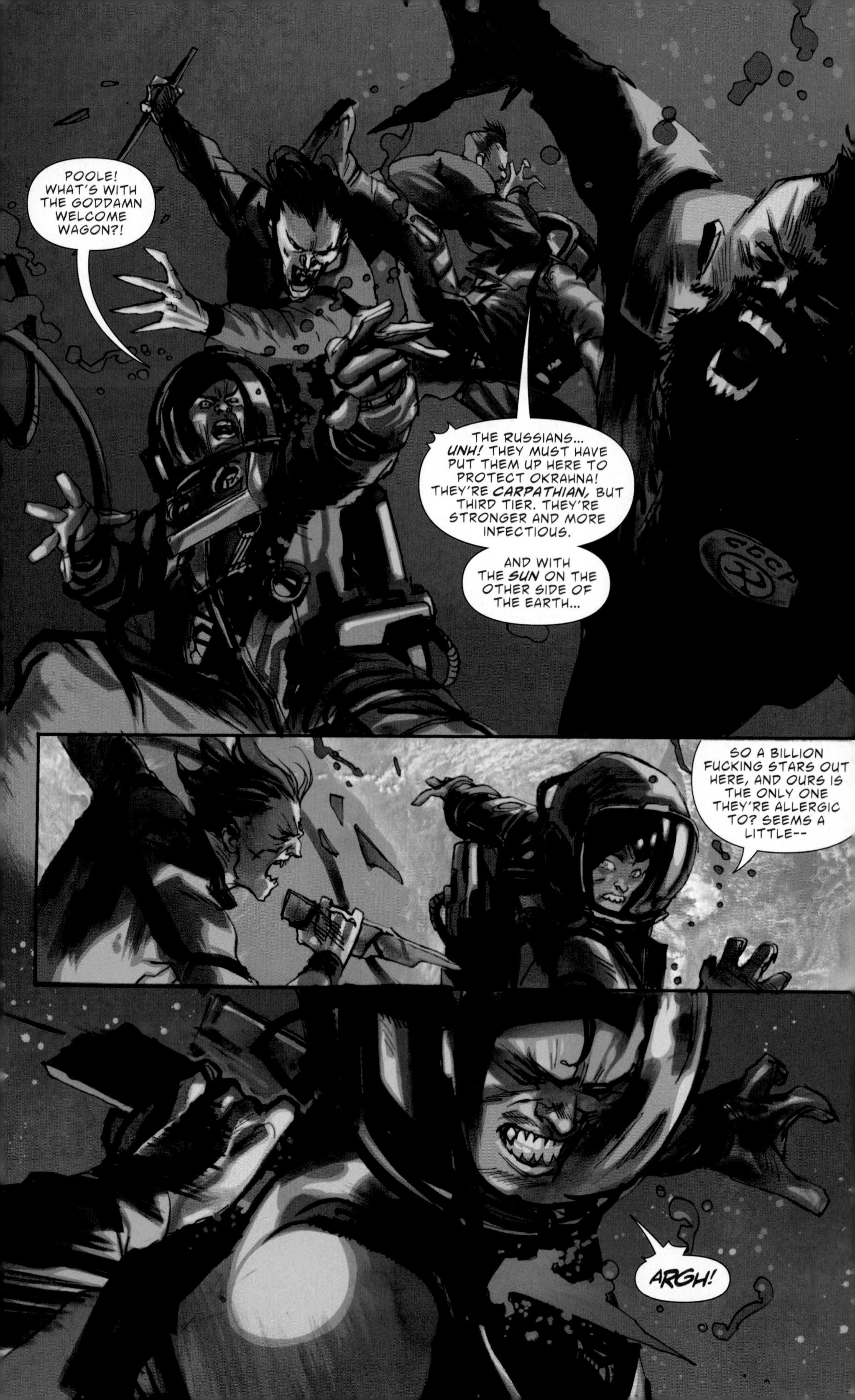

POOLE! WHAT'S WITH THE GODDAMN WELCOME WAGON?!
THE RUSSIANS... UNH! THEY MUST HAVE PUT THEM UP HERE TO PROTECT OKRAHNA! THEY'RE CARPATHIAN, BUT THIRD TIER. THEY'RE STRONGER AND MORE INFECTIOUS.
AND WITH THE SUN ON THE OTHER SIDE OF THE EARTH...
CCCP
SO A BILLION FUCKING STARS OUT HERE, AND OURS IS THE ONLY ONE THEY'RE ALLERGIC TO? SEEMS A LITTLE--
ARGH!

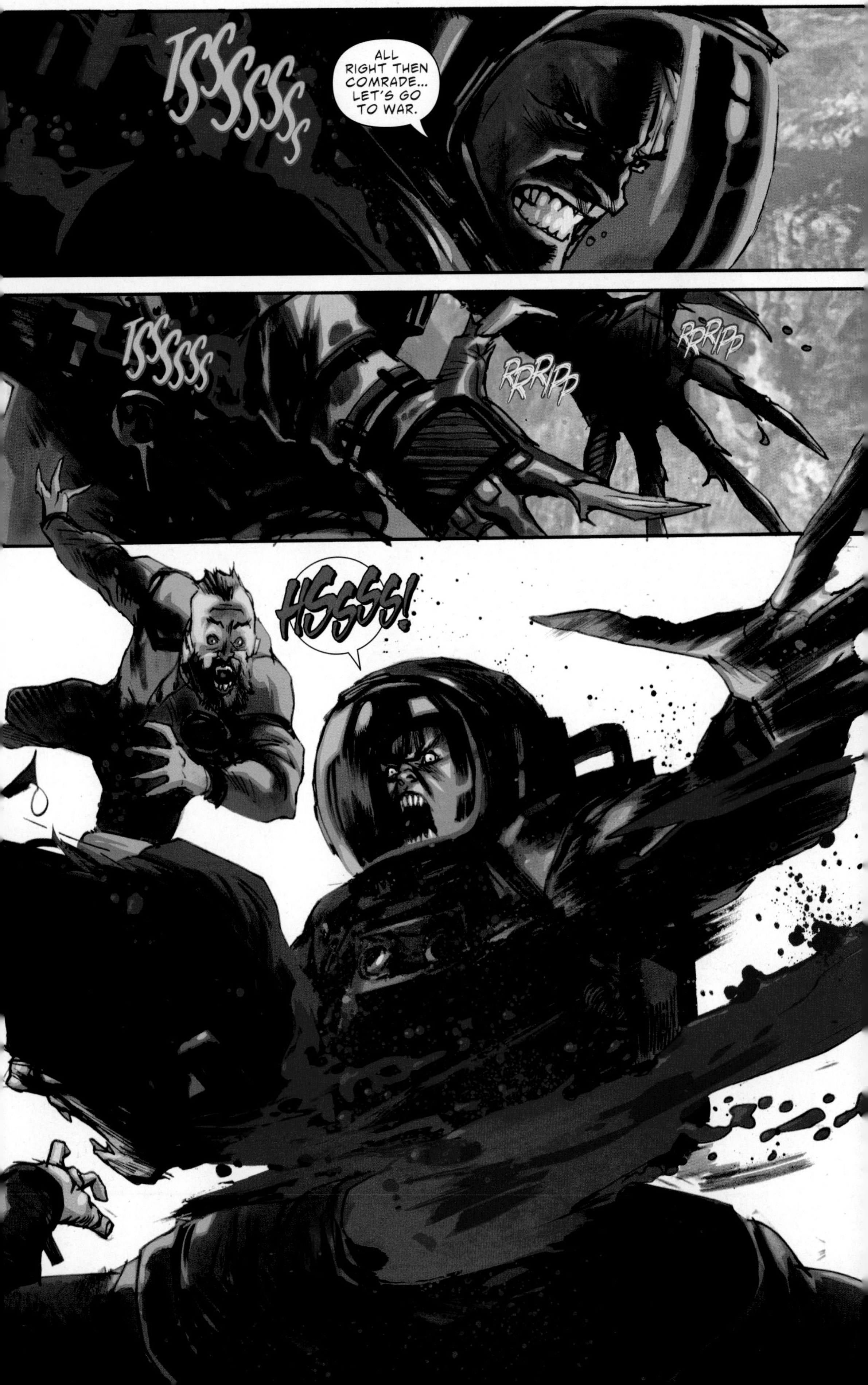
TSSSSSSS
ALL RIGHT THEN COMRADE... LET'S GO TO WAR.
TSSSSS
RRRIPP
RRRIPP
HSSSS!

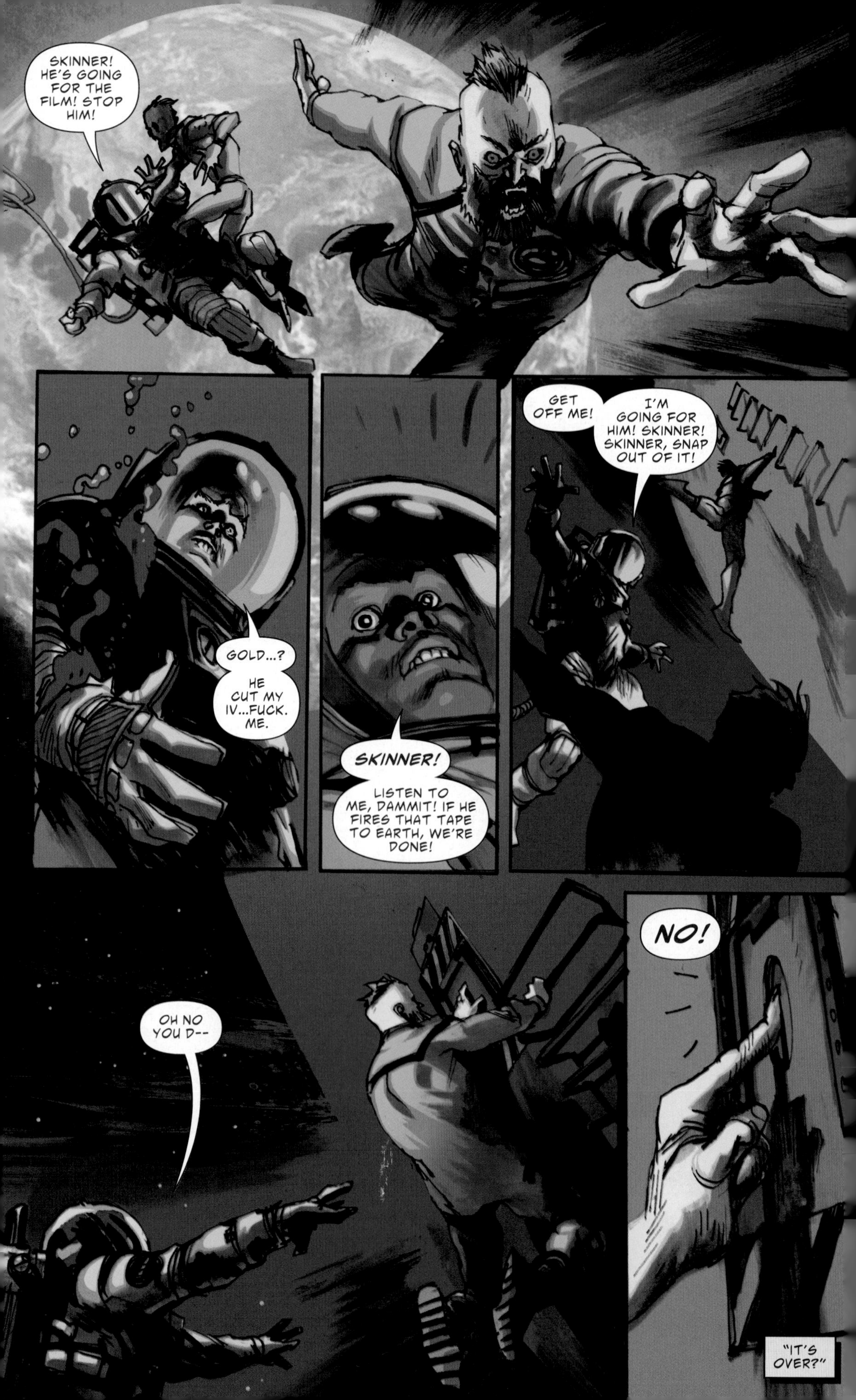
SKINNER! HE'S GOING FOR THE FILM! STOP HIM!
GOLD...?
HE CUT MY IV...FUCK. ME.
SKINNER!
LISTEN TO ME, DAMMIT! IF HE FIRES THAT TAPE TO EARTH, WE'RE DONE!
GET OFF ME!
I'M GOING FOR HIM! SKINNER! SKINNER, SNAP OUT OF IT!
OH NO YOU D--
NO!
"IT'S OVER?"

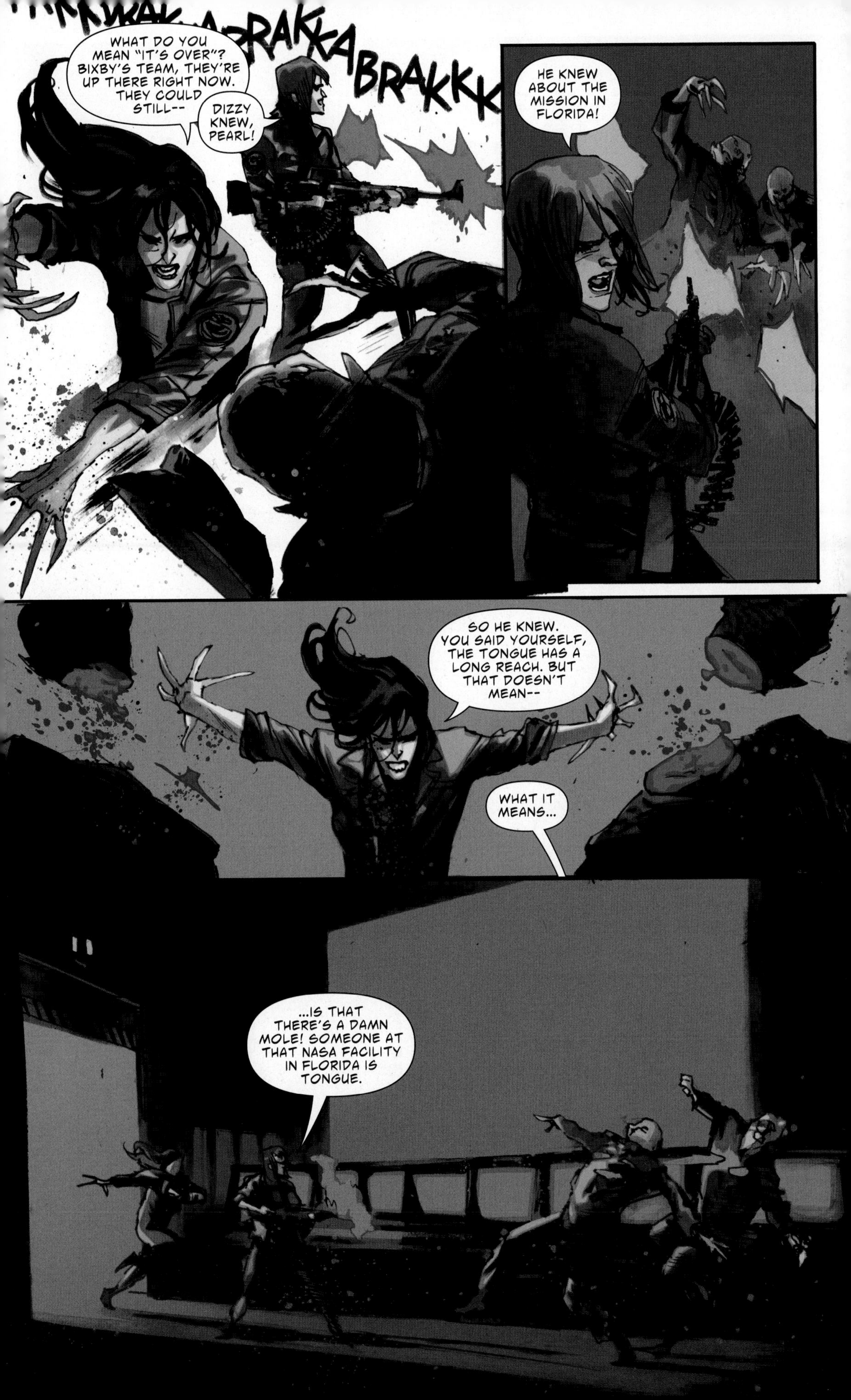
RAKKABRAKKK
WHAT DO YOU MEAN "IT'S OVER"? BIXBY'S TEAM, THEY'RE UP THERE RIGHT NOW. THEY COULD STILL--
DIZZY KNEW, PEARL!
HE KNEW ABOUT THE MISSION IN FLORIDA!
SO HE KNEW. YOU SAID YOURSELF, THE TONGUE HAS A LONG REACH. BUT THAT DOESN'T MEAN--
WHAT IT MEANS...
...IS THAT THERE'S A DAMN MOLE! SOMEONE AT THAT NASA FACILITY IN FLORIDA IS TONGUE.

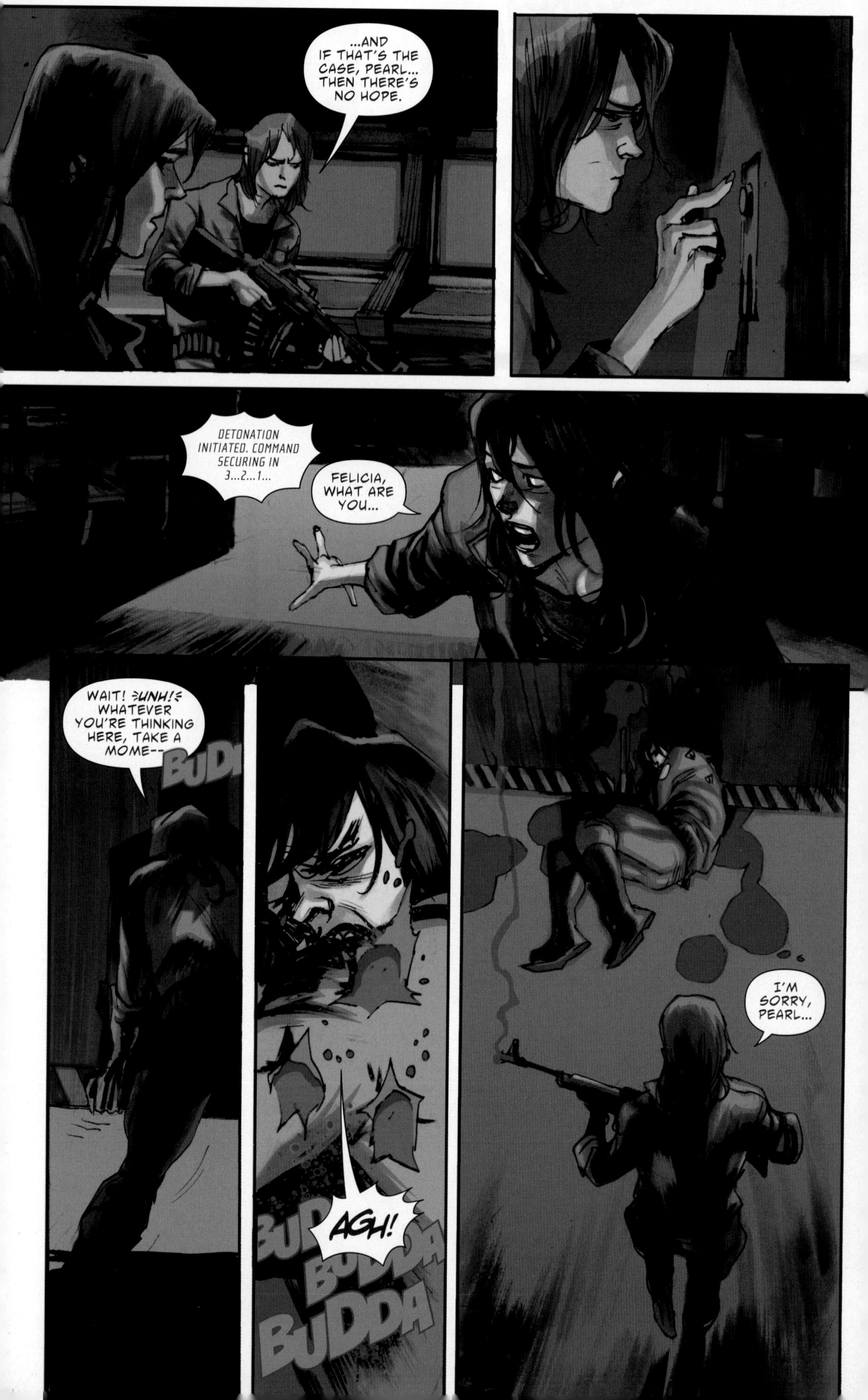
...AND IF THAT'S THE CASE, PEARL... THEN THERE'S NO HOPE.
DETONATION INITIATED. COMMAND SECURING IN 3...2...1...
FELICIA, WHAT ARE YOU...
WAIT! UNH! WHATEVER YOU'RE THINKING HERE, TAKE A MOME--
BUDD
BUDDA BUDDA BUDDA
AGH!
I'M SORRY, PEARL...

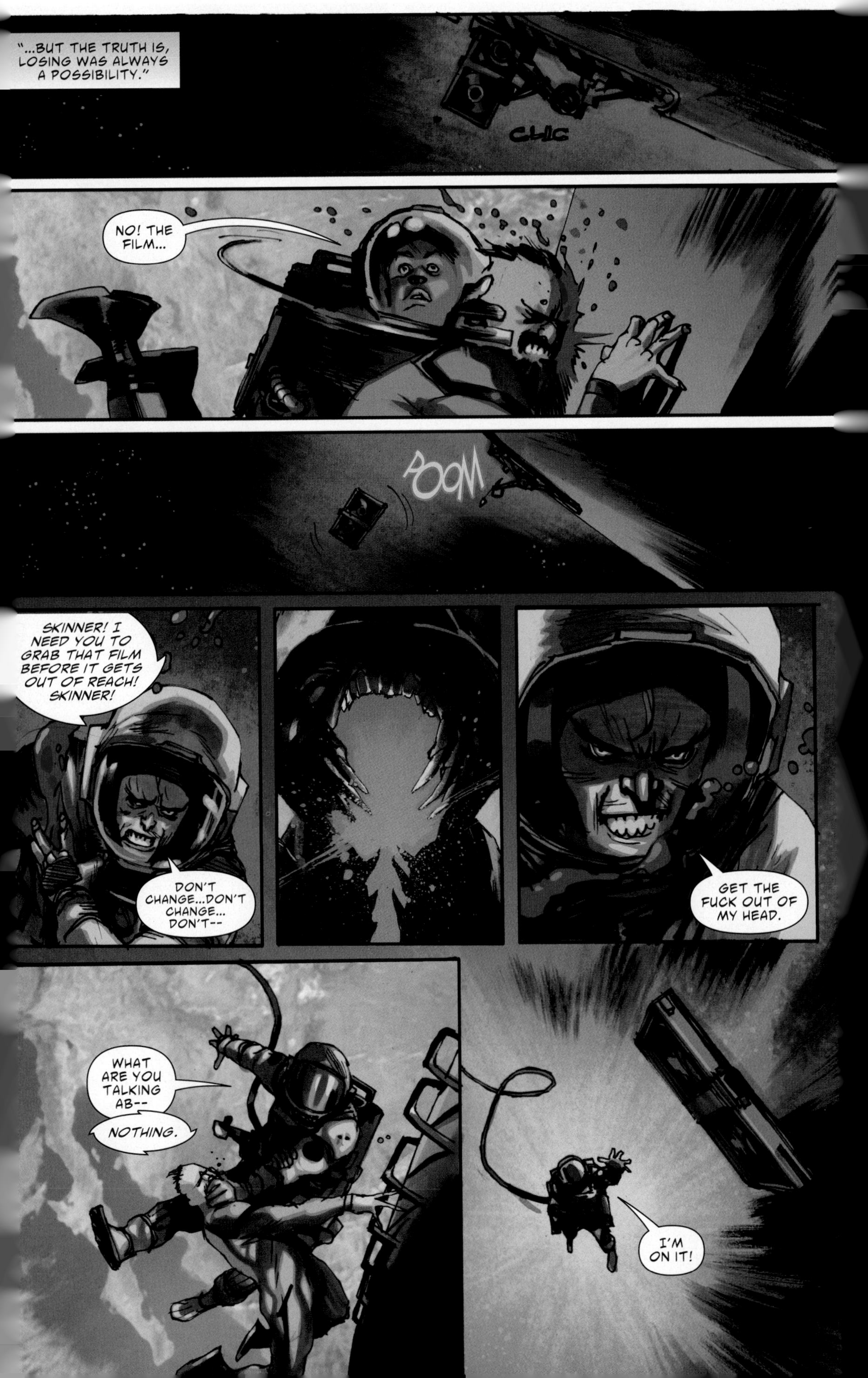
"...BUT THE TRUTH IS, LOSING WAS ALWAYS A POSSIBILITY."
CLIC
NO! THE FILM...
BOOM
SKINNER! I NEED YOU TO GRAB THAT FILM BEFORE IT GETS OUT OF REACH! SKINNER!
DON'T CHANGE...DON'T CHANGE... DON'T--
GET THE FUCK OUT OF MY HEAD.
WHAT ARE YOU TALKING AB--
NOTHING.
I'M ON IT!

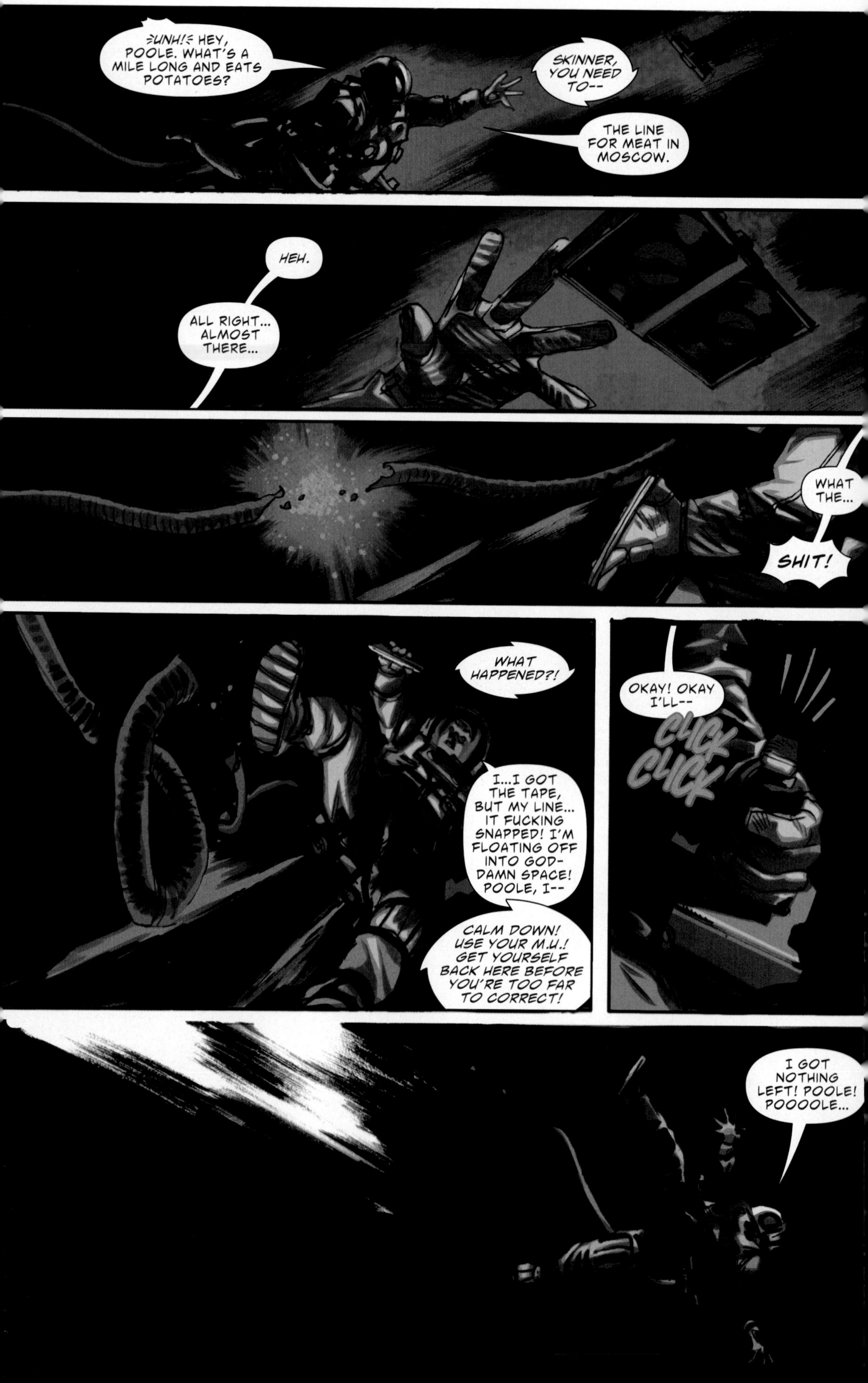

=UNH!= HEY, POOLE. WHAT'S A MILE LONG AND EATS POTATOES?
SKINNER, YOU NEED TO--
THE LINE FOR MEAT IN MOSCOW.
HEH.
ALL RIGHT... ALMOST THERE...
WHAT THE...
SHIT!
WHAT HAPPENED?!
I...I GOT THE TAPE, BUT MY LINE... IT FUCKING SNAPPED! I'M FLOATING OFF INTO GOD-DAMN SPACE! POOLE, I--
CALM DOWN! USE YOUR M.U.! GET YOURSELF BACK HERE BEFORE YOU'RE TOO FAR TO CORRECT!
OKAY! OKAY I'LL--
CLICK CLICK
I GOT NOTHING LEFT! POOLE! POOOOLE...

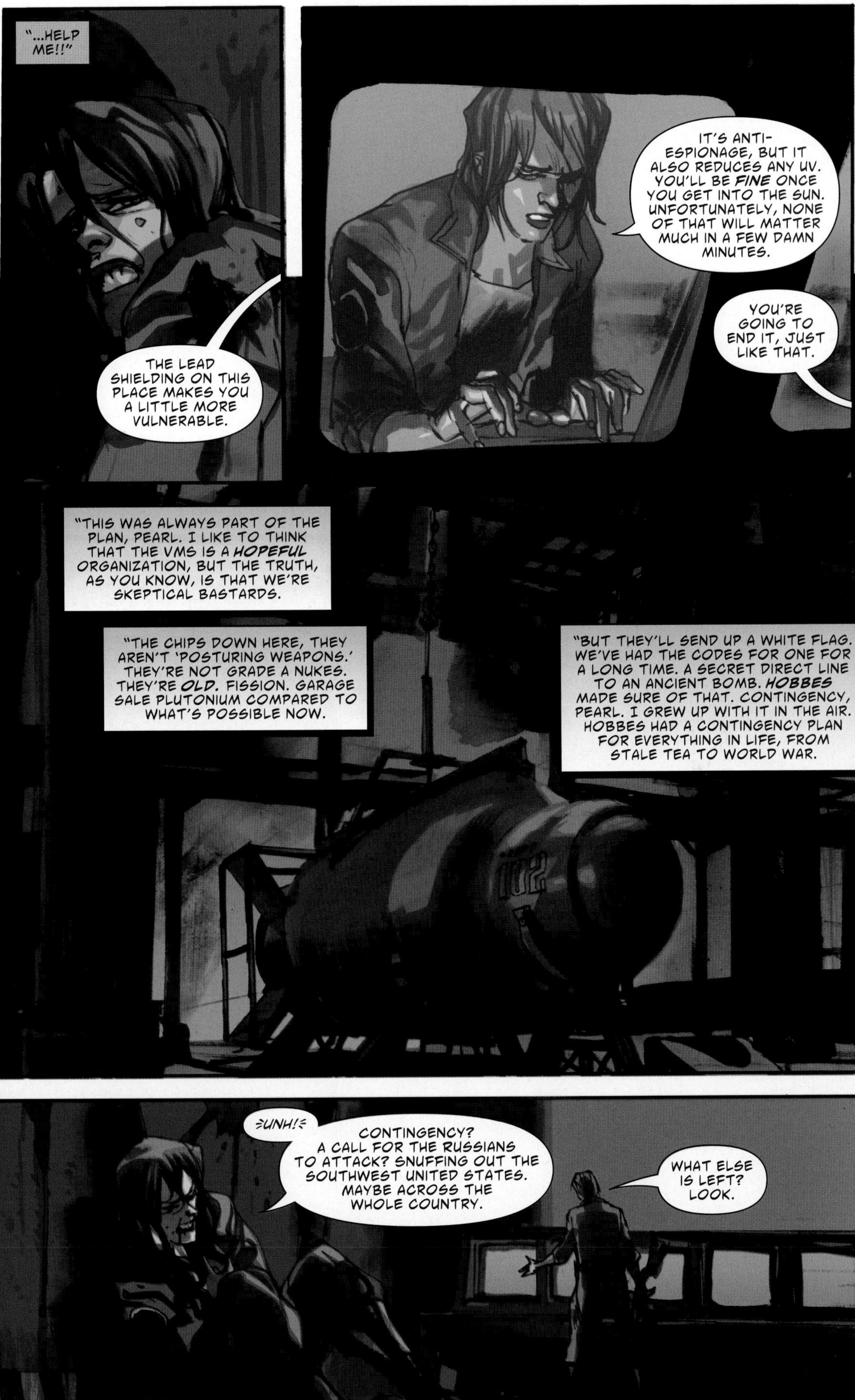
"...HELP ME!!"
THE LEAD SHIELDING ON THIS PLACE MAKES YOU A LITTLE MORE VULNERABLE.
IT'S ANTI-ESPIONAGE, BUT IT ALSO REDUCES ANY UV. YOU'LL BE FINE ONCE YOU GET INTO THE SUN. UNFORTUNATELY, NONE OF THAT WILL MATTER MUCH IN A FEW DAMN MINUTES.
YOU'RE GOING TO END IT, JUST LIKE THAT.
"THIS WAS ALWAYS PART OF THE PLAN, PEARL. I LIKE TO THINK THAT THE VMS IS A HOPEFUL ORGANIZATION, BUT THE TRUTH, AS YOU KNOW, IS THAT WE'RE SKEPTICAL BASTARDS.
"THE CHIPS DOWN HERE, THEY AREN'T 'POSTURING WEAPONS.' THEY'RE NOT GRADE A NUKES. THEY'RE OLD. FISSION. GARAGE SALE PLUTONIUM COMPARED TO WHAT'S POSSIBLE NOW.
"BUT THEY'LL SEND UP A WHITE FLAG. WE'VE HAD THE CODES FOR ONE FOR A LONG TIME. A SECRET DIRECT LINE TO AN ANCIENT BOMB. HOBBES MADE SURE OF THAT. CONTINGENCY, PEARL. I GREW UP WITH IT IN THE AIR. HOBBES HAD A CONTINGENCY PLAN FOR EVERYTHING IN LIFE, FROM STALE TEA TO WORLD WAR.
UNH!
CONTINGENCY? A CALL FOR THE RUSSIANS TO ATTACK? SNUFFING OUT THE SOUTHWEST UNITED STATES. MAYBE ACROSS THE WHOLE COUNTRY.
WHAT ELSE IS LEFT? LOOK.

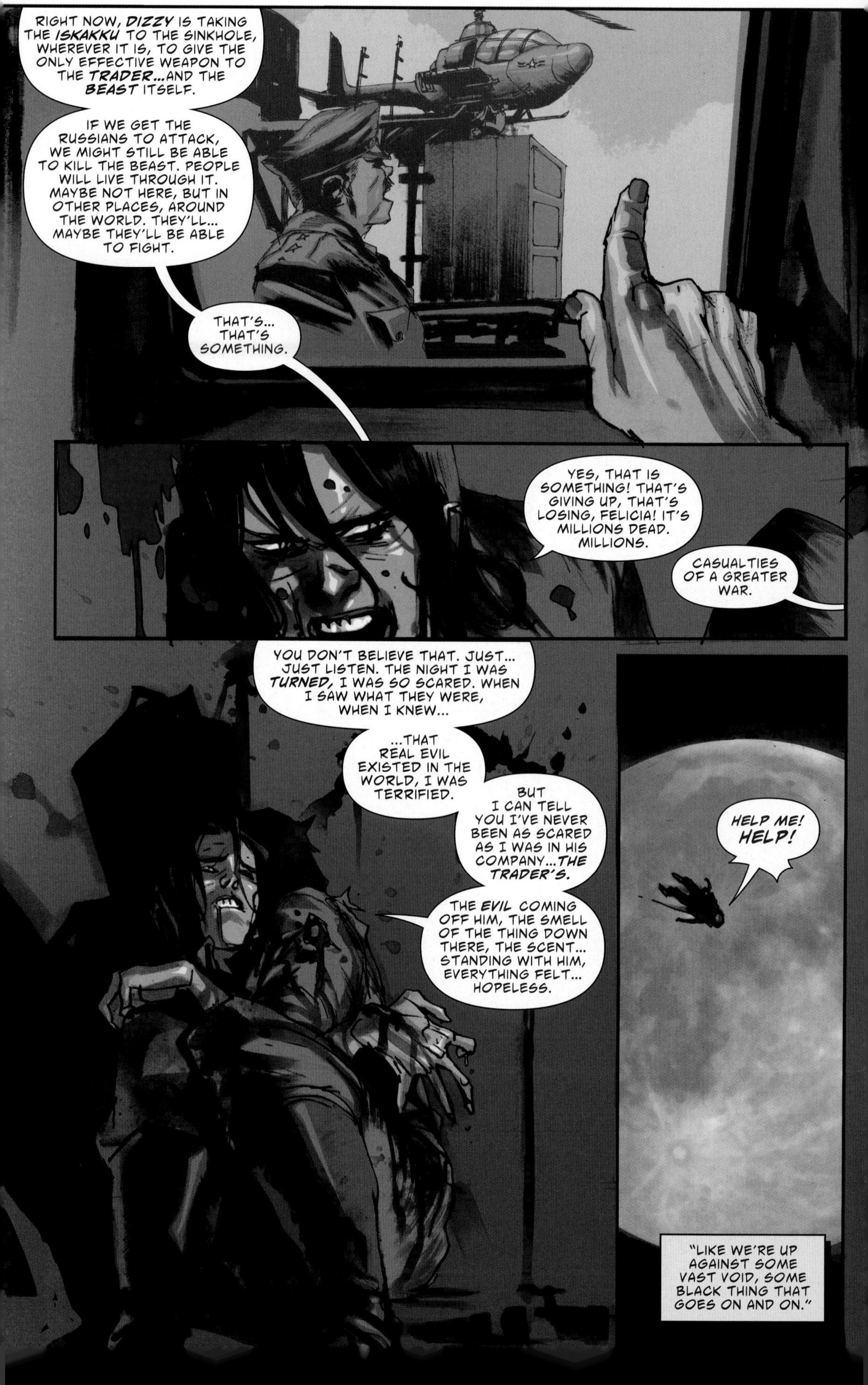
RIGHT NOW, DIZZY IS TAKING THE ISKAKKU TO THE SINKHOLE, WHEREVER IT IS, TO GIVE THE ONLY EFFECTIVE WEAPON TO THE TRADER...AND THE BEAST ITSELF.
IF WE GET THE RUSSIANS TO ATTACK, WE MIGHT STILL BE ABLE TO KILL THE BEAST. PEOPLE WILL LIVE THROUGH IT. MAYBE NOT HERE, BUT IN OTHER PLACES, AROUND THE WORLD. THEY'LL... MAYBE THEY'LL BE ABLE TO FIGHT.
THAT'S... THAT'S SOMETHING.
YES, THAT IS SOMETHING! THAT'S GIVING UP, THAT'S LOSING, FELICIA! IT'S MILLIONS DEAD. MILLIONS.
CASUALTIES OF A GREATER WAR.
YOU DON'T BELIEVE THAT. JUST... JUST LISTEN. THE NIGHT I WAS TURNED, I WAS SO SCARED. WHEN I SAW WHAT THEY WERE, WHEN I KNEW...
...THAT REAL EVIL EXISTED IN THE WORLD, I WAS TERRIFIED.
BUT I CAN TELL YOU I'VE NEVER BEEN AS SCARED AS I WAS IN HIS COMPANY...THE TRADER'S.
THE EVIL COMING OFF HIM, THE SMELL OF THE THING DOWN THERE, THE SCENT... STANDING WITH HIM, EVERYTHING FELT... HOPELESS.
HELP ME! HELP!
"LIKE WE'RE UP AGAINST SOME VAST VOID, SOME BLACK THING THAT GOES ON AND ON."

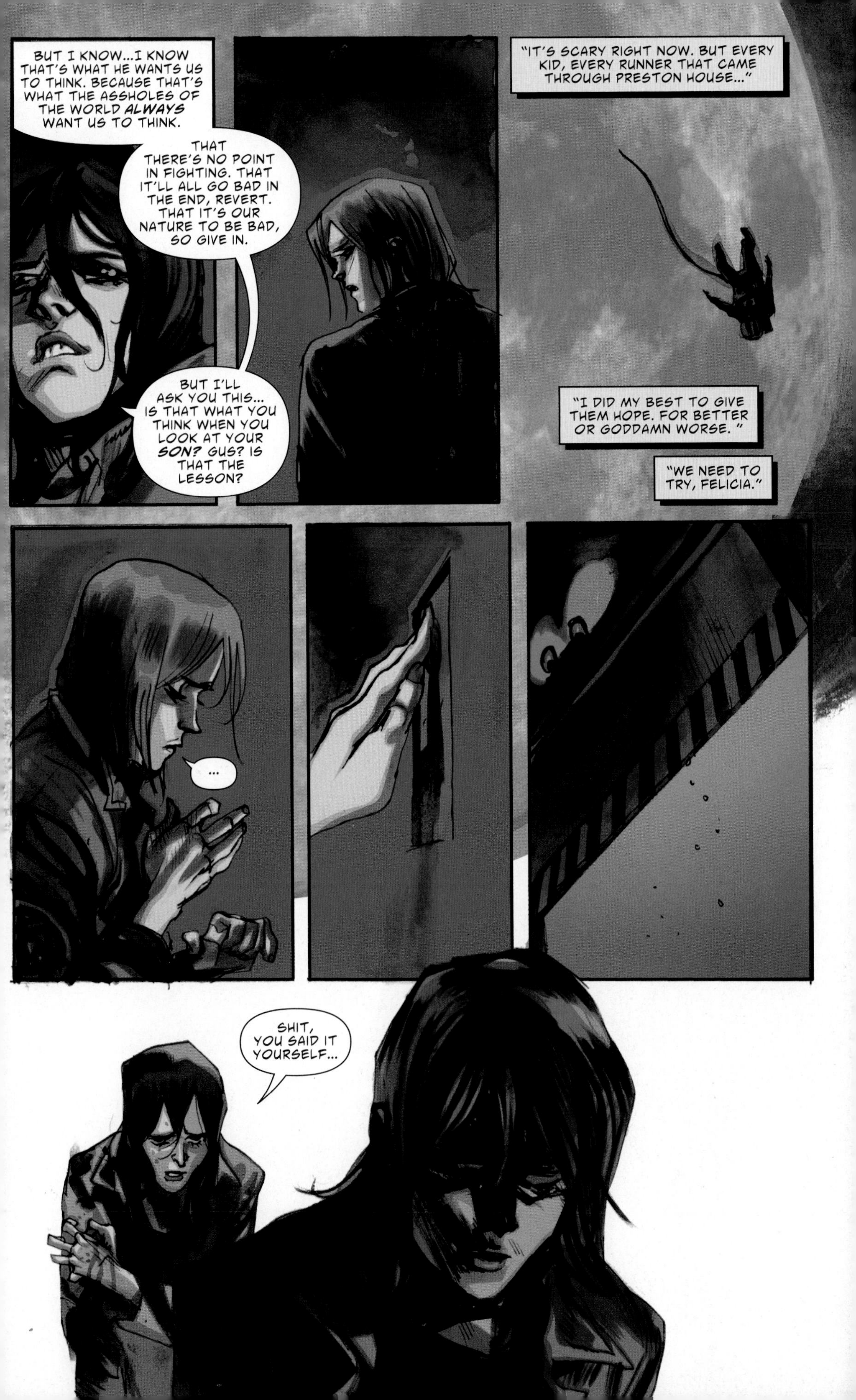
BUT I KNOW...I KNOW THAT'S WHAT HE WANTS US TO THINK. BECAUSE THAT'S WHAT THE ASSHOLES OF THE WORLD ALWAYS WANT US TO THINK.
THAT THERE'S NO POINT IN FIGHTING. THAT IT'LL ALL GO BAD IN THE END, REVERT. THAT IT'S OUR NATURE TO BE BAD, SO GIVE IN.
BUT I'LL ASK YOU THIS... IS THAT WHAT YOU THINK WHEN YOU LOOK AT YOUR SON? GUS? IS THAT THE LESSON?
"IT'S SCARY RIGHT NOW. BUT EVERY KID, EVERY RUNNER THAT CAME THROUGH PRESTON HOUSE..."
"I DID MY BEST TO GIVE THEM HOPE. FOR BETTER OR GODDAMN WORSE."
"WE NEED TO TRY, FELICIA."
...
SHIT, YOU SAID IT YOURSELF...

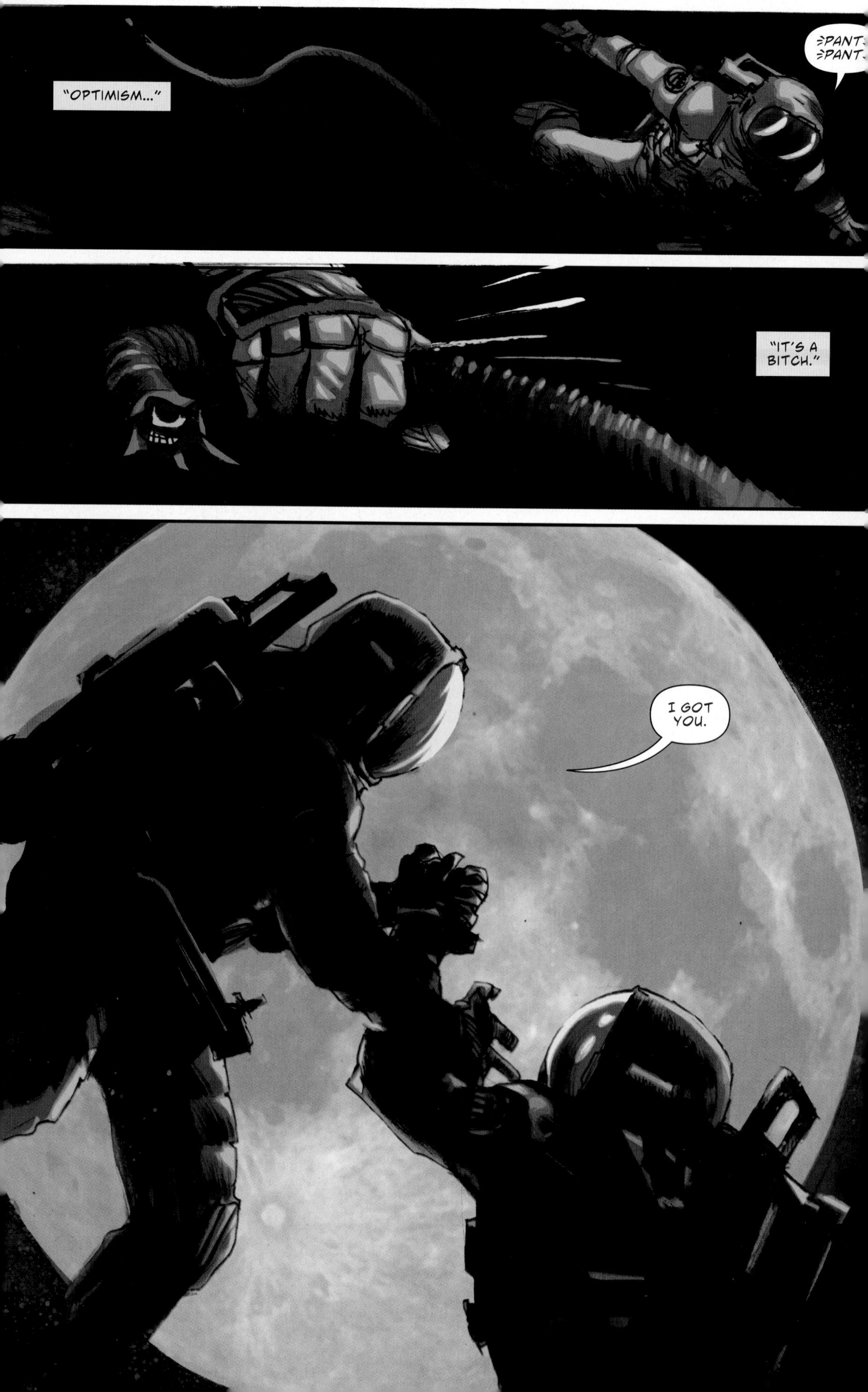
"OPTIMISM..."
=PANT=
=PANT=
"IT'S A BITCH."
I GOT YOU.

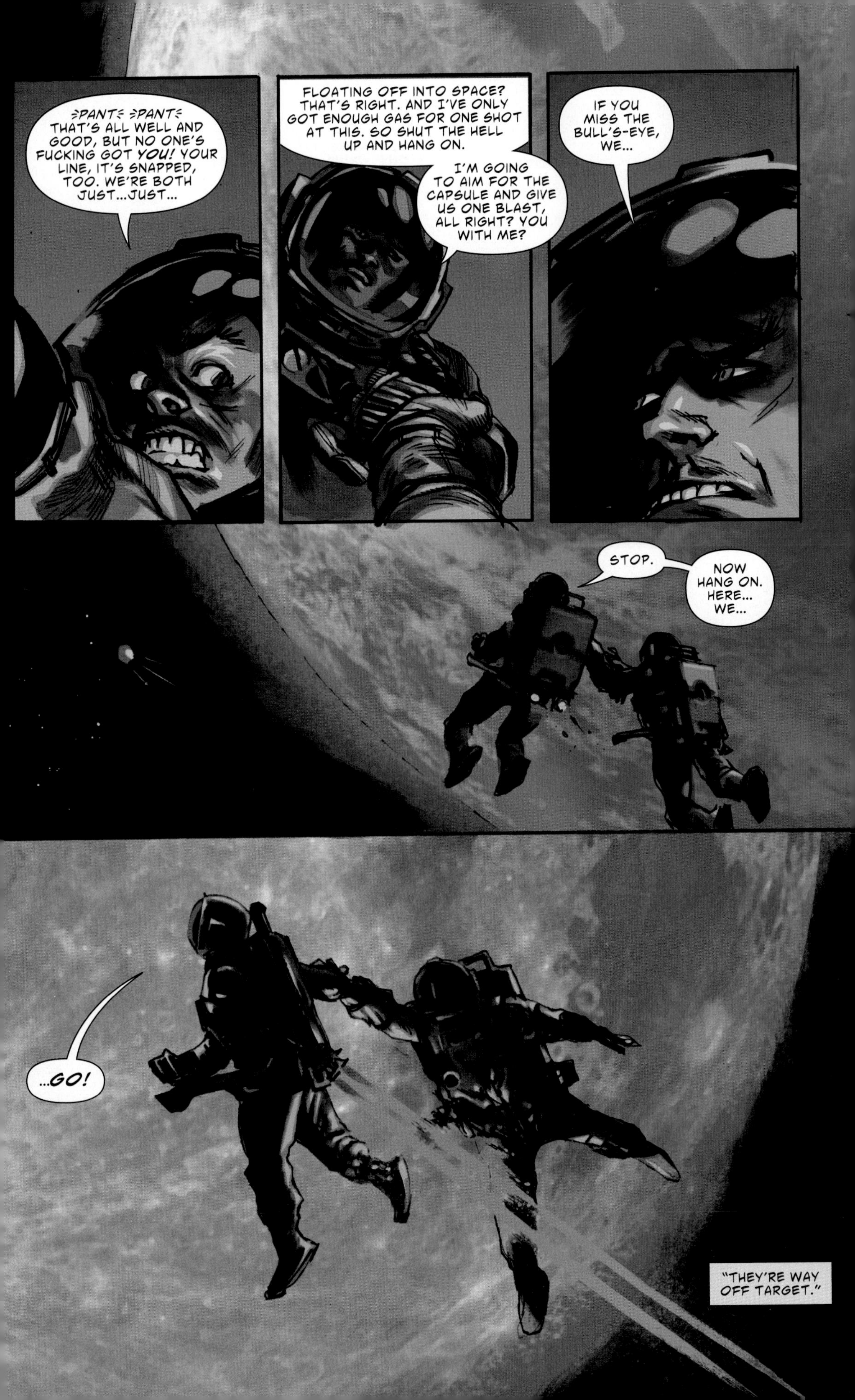

≈PANT≈ ≈PANT≈
THAT'S ALL WELL AND GOOD, BUT NO ONE'S FUCKING GOT *YOU!* YOUR LINE, IT'S SNAPPED, TOO. WE'RE BOTH JUST...JUST...
FLOATING OFF INTO SPACE? THAT'S RIGHT. AND I'VE ONLY GOT ENOUGH GAS FOR ONE SHOT AT THIS. SO SHUT THE HELL UP AND HANG ON.
I'M GOING TO AIM FOR THE CAPSULE AND GIVE US ONE BLAST, ALL RIGHT? YOU WITH ME?
IF YOU MISS THE BULL'S-EYE, WE...
STOP.
NOW HANG ON. HERE... WE...
...*GO!*
"THEY'RE WAY OFF TARGET."

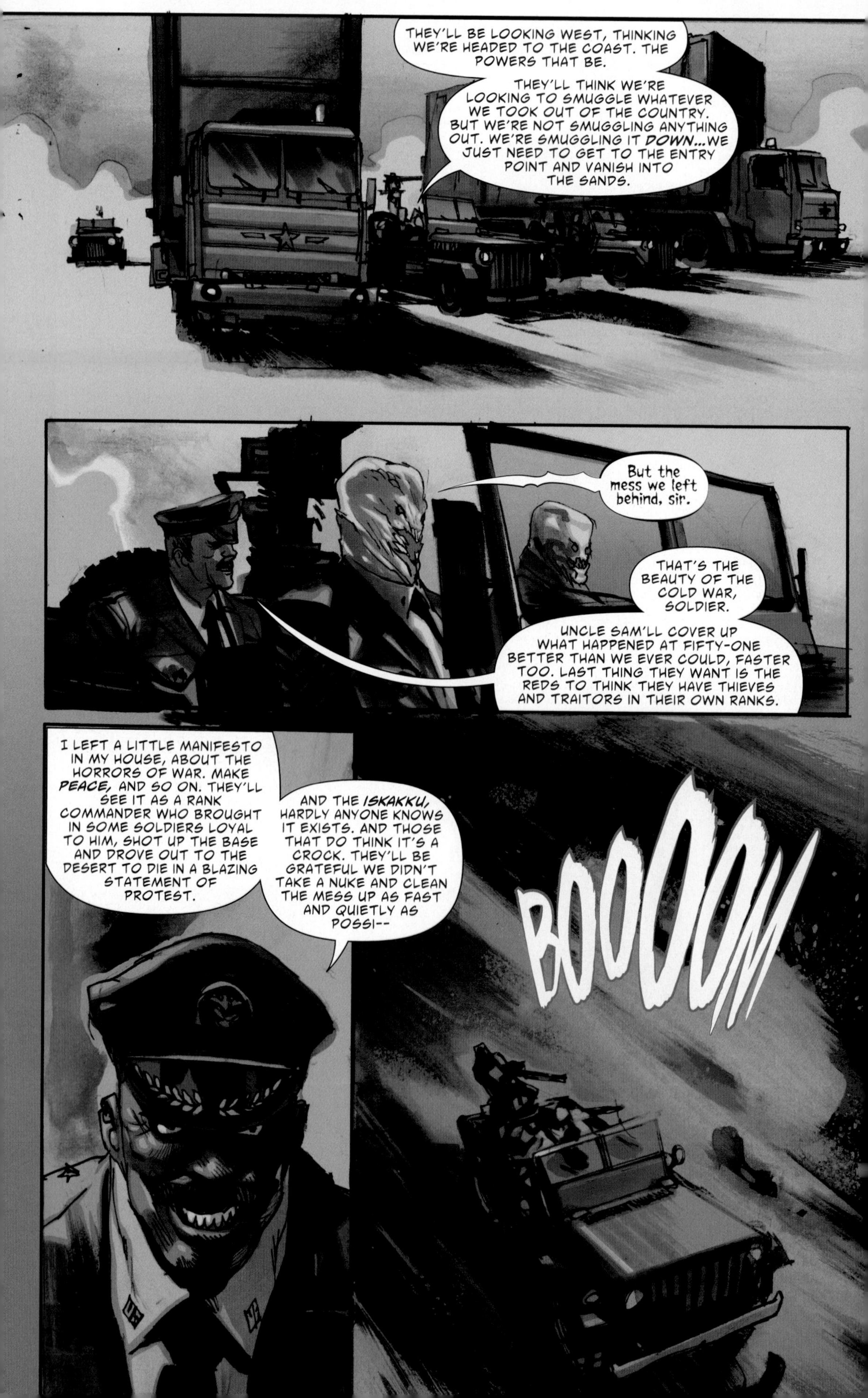
THEY'LL BE LOOKING WEST, THINKING WE'RE HEADED TO THE COAST. THE POWERS THAT BE.
THEY'LL THINK WE'RE LOOKING TO SMUGGLE WHATEVER WE TOOK OUT OF THE COUNTRY. BUT WE'RE NOT SMUGGLING ANYTHING OUT. WE'RE SMUGGLING IT *DOWN*...WE JUST NEED TO GET TO THE ENTRY POINT AND VANISH INTO THE SANDS.
But the mess we left behind, sir.
THAT'S THE BEAUTY OF THE COLD WAR, SOLDIER.
UNCLE SAM'LL COVER UP WHAT HAPPENED AT FIFTY-ONE BETTER THAN WE EVER COULD, FASTER TOO. LAST THING THEY WANT IS THE REDS TO THINK THEY HAVE THIEVES AND TRAITORS IN THEIR OWN RANKS.
I LEFT A LITTLE MANIFESTO IN MY HOUSE, ABOUT THE HORRORS OF WAR. MAKE *PEACE,* AND SO ON. THEY'LL SEE IT AS A RANK COMMANDER WHO BROUGHT IN SOME SOLDIERS LOYAL TO HIM, SHOT UP THE BASE AND DROVE OUT TO THE DESERT TO DIE IN A BLAZING STATEMENT OF PROTEST.
AND THE *ISKAKKU,* HARDLY ANYONE KNOWS IT EXISTS. AND THOSE THAT DO THINK IT'S A CROCK. THEY'LL BE GRATEFUL WE DIDN'T TAKE A NUKE AND CLEAN THE MESS UP AS FAST AND QUIETLY AS POSSI--
BOOOOM

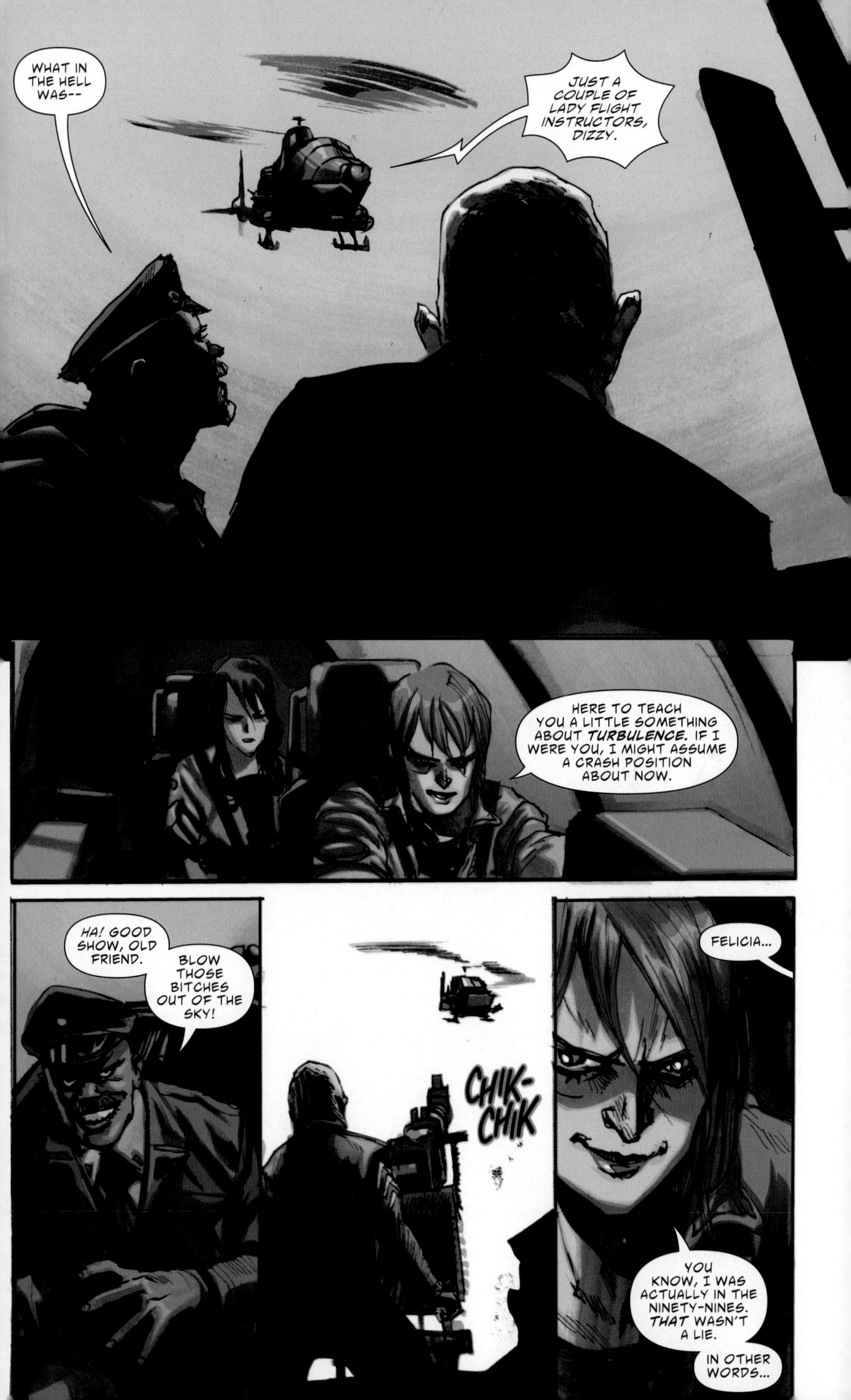
WHAT IN THE HELL WAS--
JUST A COUPLE OF LADY FLIGHT INSTRUCTORS, DIZZY.
HERE TO TEACH YOU A LITTLE SOMETHING ABOUT TURBULENCE. IF I WERE YOU, I MIGHT ASSUME A CRASH POSITION ABOUT NOW.
HA! GOOD SHOW, OLD FRIEND.
BLOW THOSE BITCHES OUT OF THE SKY!
CHIK-CHIK
FELICIA...
YOU KNOW, I WAS ACTUALLY IN THE NINETY-NINES. THAT WASN'T A LIE.
IN OTHER WORDS...

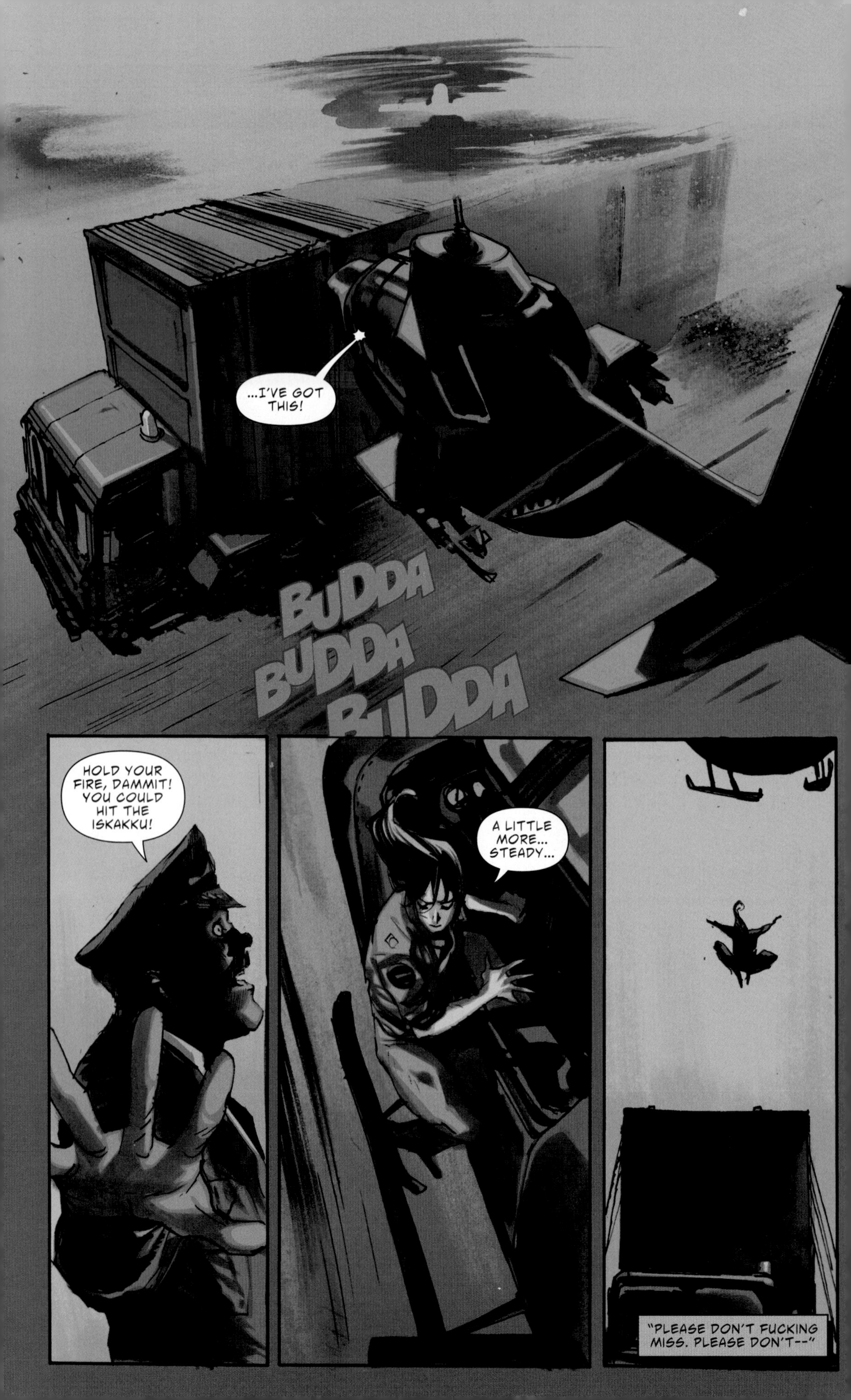
...I'VE GOT THIS!
BUDDA BUDDA BUDDA
HOLD YOUR FIRE, DAMMIT! YOU COULD HIT THE ISKAKKU!
A LITTLE MORE... STEADY...
"PLEASE DON'T FUCKING MISS. PLEASE DON'T--"

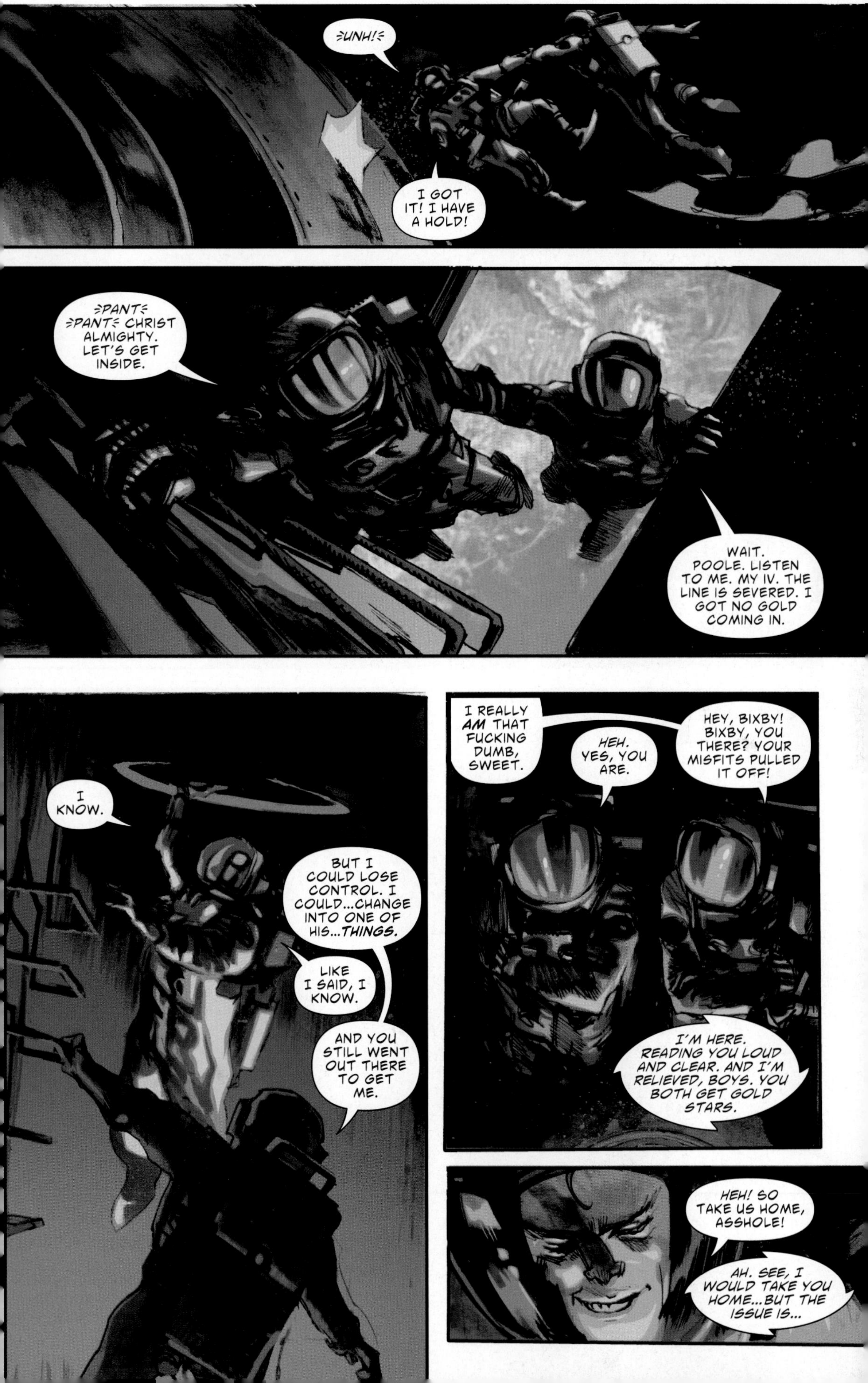

=UNH!=
I GOT IT! I HAVE A HOLD!
=PANT= =PANT= CHRIST ALMIGHTY. LET'S GET INSIDE.
WAIT. POOLE. LISTEN TO ME. MY IV. THE LINE IS SEVERED. I GOT NO GOLD COMING IN.
I KNOW.
BUT I COULD LOSE CONTROL. I COULD...CHANGE INTO ONE OF HIS...*THINGS.*
LIKE I SAID, I KNOW.
AND YOU STILL WENT OUT THERE TO GET ME.
I REALLY *AM* THAT FUCKING DUMB, SWEET.
HEH. YES, YOU ARE.
HEY, BIXBY! BIXBY, YOU THERE? YOUR MISFITS PULLED IT OFF!
I'M HERE. READING YOU LOUD AND CLEAR. AND I'M RELIEVED, BOYS. YOU BOTH GET GOLD STARS.
HEH! SO TAKE US HOME, ASSHOLE!
AH. SEE, I WOULD TAKE YOU HOME...BUT THE ISSUE IS...

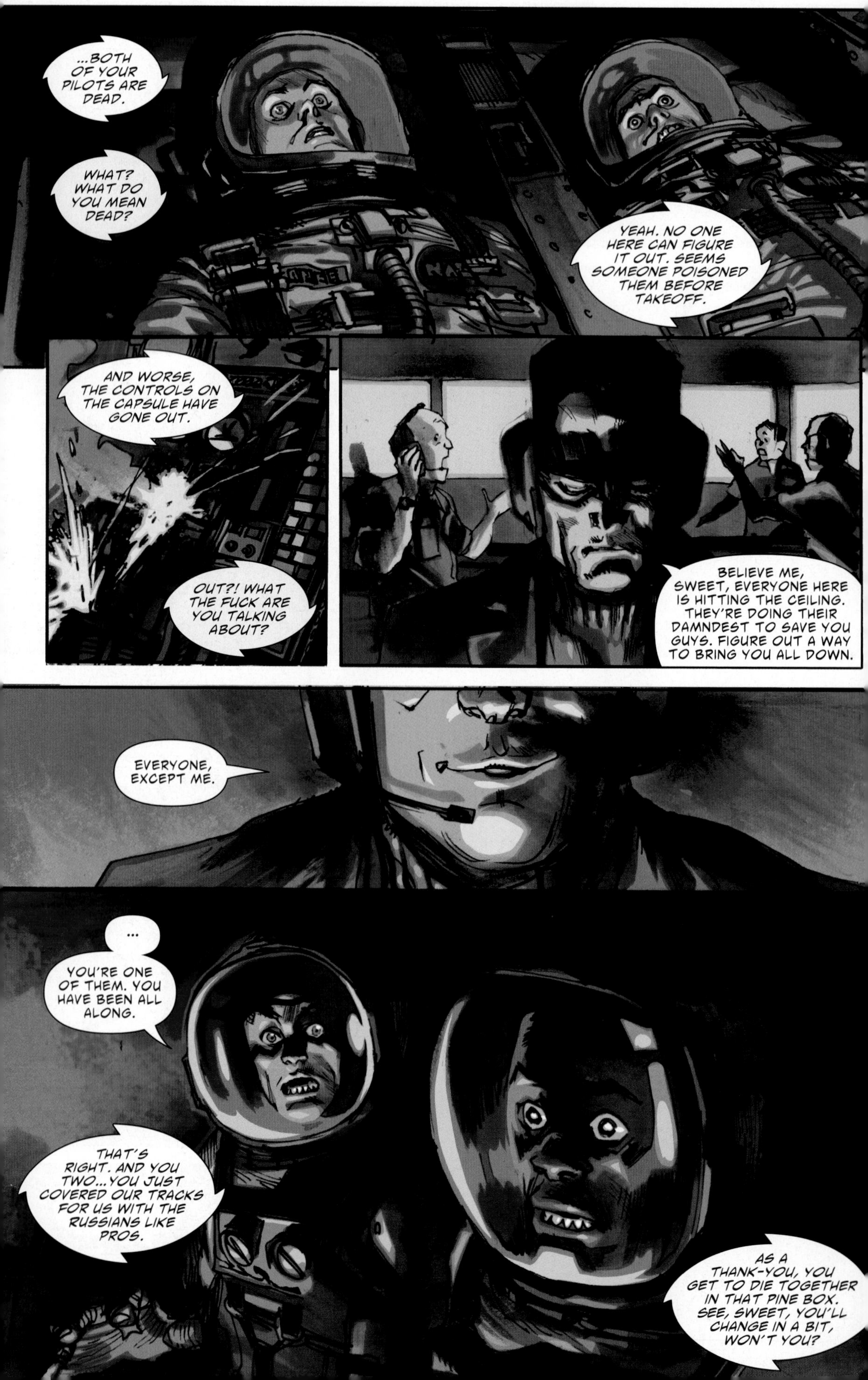
...BOTH OF YOUR PILOTS ARE DEAD.
WHAT? WHAT DO YOU MEAN DEAD?
YEAH. NO ONE HERE CAN FIGURE IT OUT. SEEMS SOMEONE POISONED THEM BEFORE TAKEOFF.
AND WORSE, THE CONTROLS ON THE CAPSULE HAVE GONE OUT.
OUT?! WHAT THE FUCK ARE YOU TALKING ABOUT?
BELIEVE ME, SWEET, EVERYONE HERE IS HITTING THE CEILING. THEY'RE DOING THEIR DAMNDEST TO SAVE YOU GUYS. FIGURE OUT A WAY TO BRING YOU ALL DOWN.
EVERYONE, EXCEPT ME.
...
YOU'RE ONE OF THEM. YOU HAVE BEEN ALL ALONG.
THAT'S RIGHT. AND YOU TWO...YOU JUST COVERED OUR TRACKS FOR US WITH THE RUSSIANS LIKE PROS.
AS A THANK-YOU, YOU GET TO DIE TOGETHER IN THAT PINE BOX. SEE, SWEET, YOU'LL CHANGE IN A BIT, WON'T YOU?

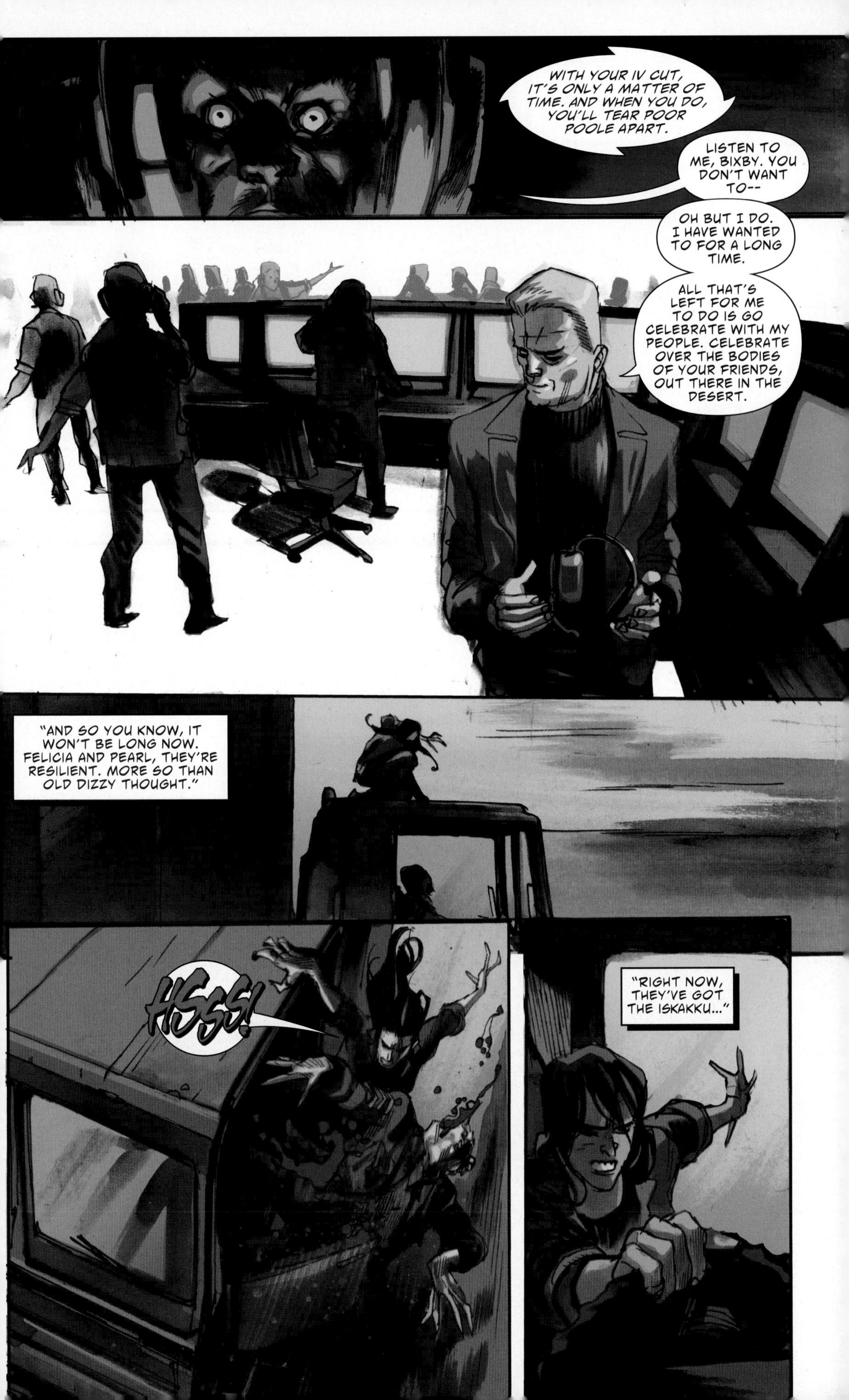
WITH YOUR IV CUT, IT'S ONLY A MATTER OF TIME. AND WHEN YOU DO, YOU'LL TEAR POOR POOLE APART.
LISTEN TO ME, BIXBY. YOU DON'T WANT TO--
OH BUT I DO. I HAVE WANTED TO FOR A LONG TIME.
ALL THAT'S LEFT FOR ME TO DO IS GO CELEBRATE WITH MY PEOPLE. CELEBRATE OVER THE BODIES OF YOUR FRIENDS, OUT THERE IN THE DESERT.
"AND SO YOU KNOW, IT WON'T BE LONG NOW. FELICIA AND PEARL, THEY'RE RESILIENT. MORE SO THAN OLD DIZZY THOUGHT."
HSSS!
"RIGHT NOW, THEY'VE GOT THE ISKAKKU..."

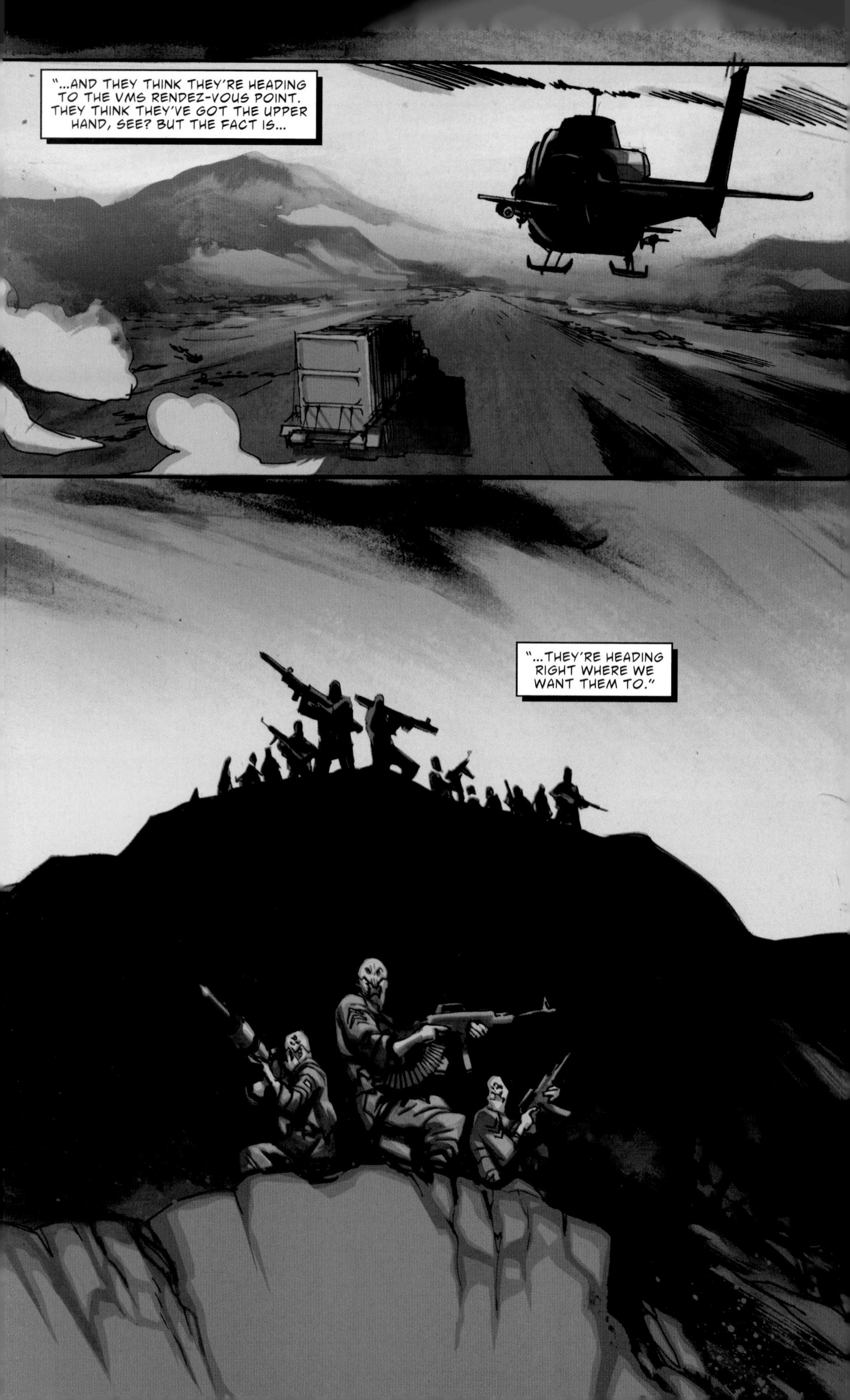
"...AND THEY THINK THEY'RE HEADING TO THE VMS RENDEZ-VOUS POINT. THEY THINK THEY'VE GOT THE UPPER HAND, SEE? BUT THE FACT IS...
"...THEY'RE HEADING RIGHT WHERE WE WANT THEM TO."

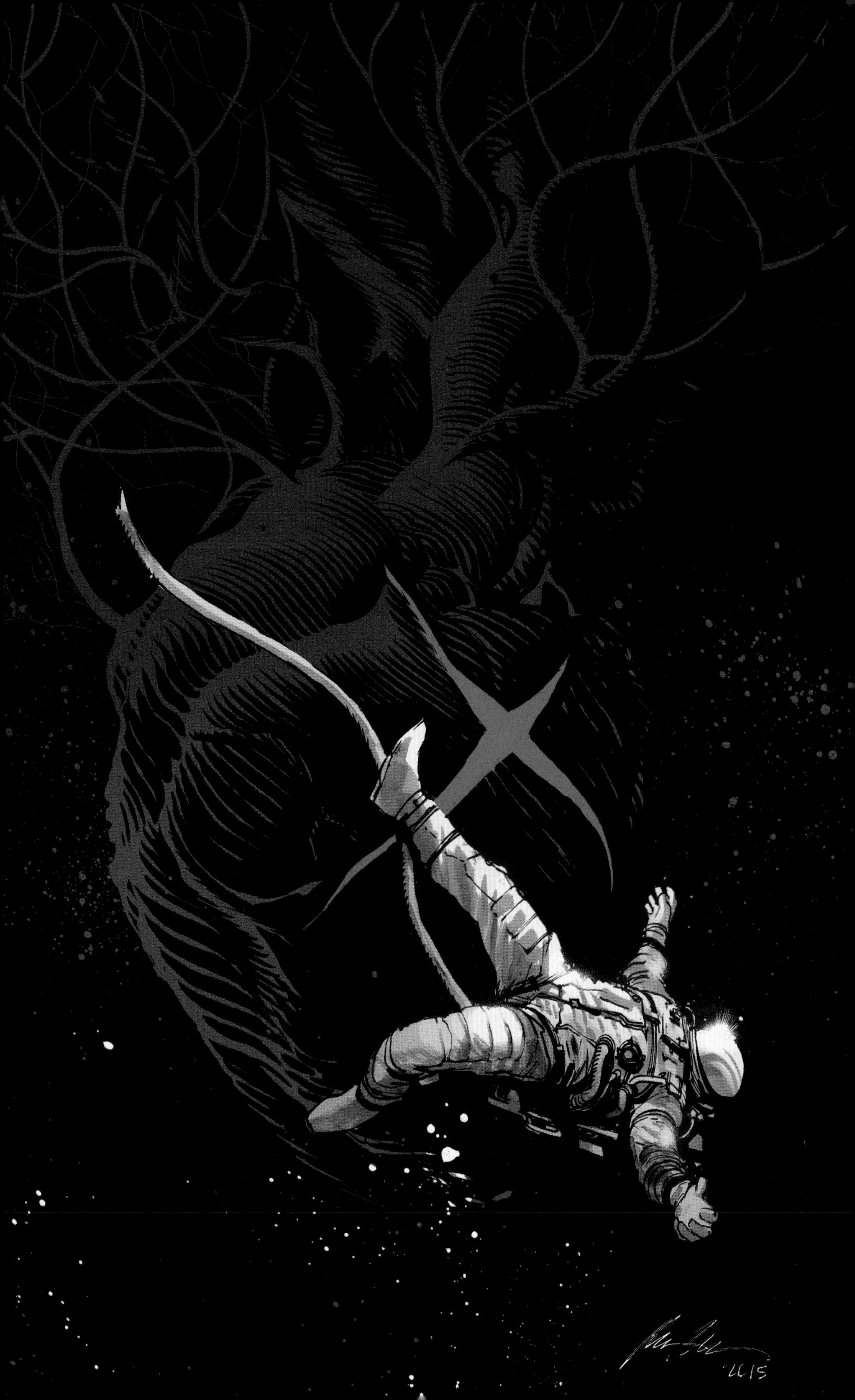

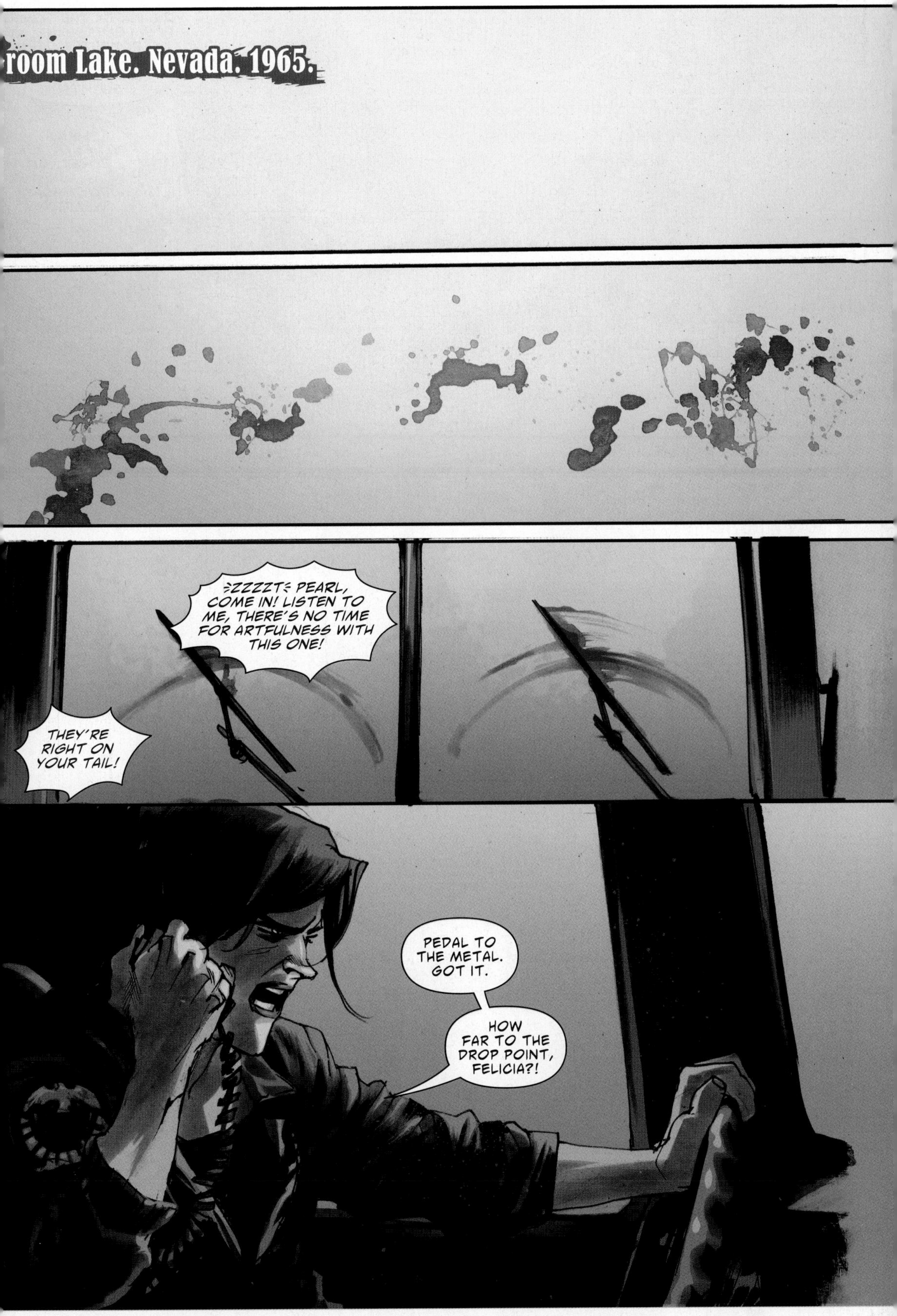

room Lake. Nevada. 1965.
=ZZZZT= PEARL, COME IN! LISTEN TO ME, THERE'S NO TIME FOR ARTFULNESS WITH THIS ONE!
THEY'RE RIGHT ON YOUR TAIL!
PEDAL TO THE METAL. GOT IT.
HOW FAR TO THE DROP POINT, FELICIA?!

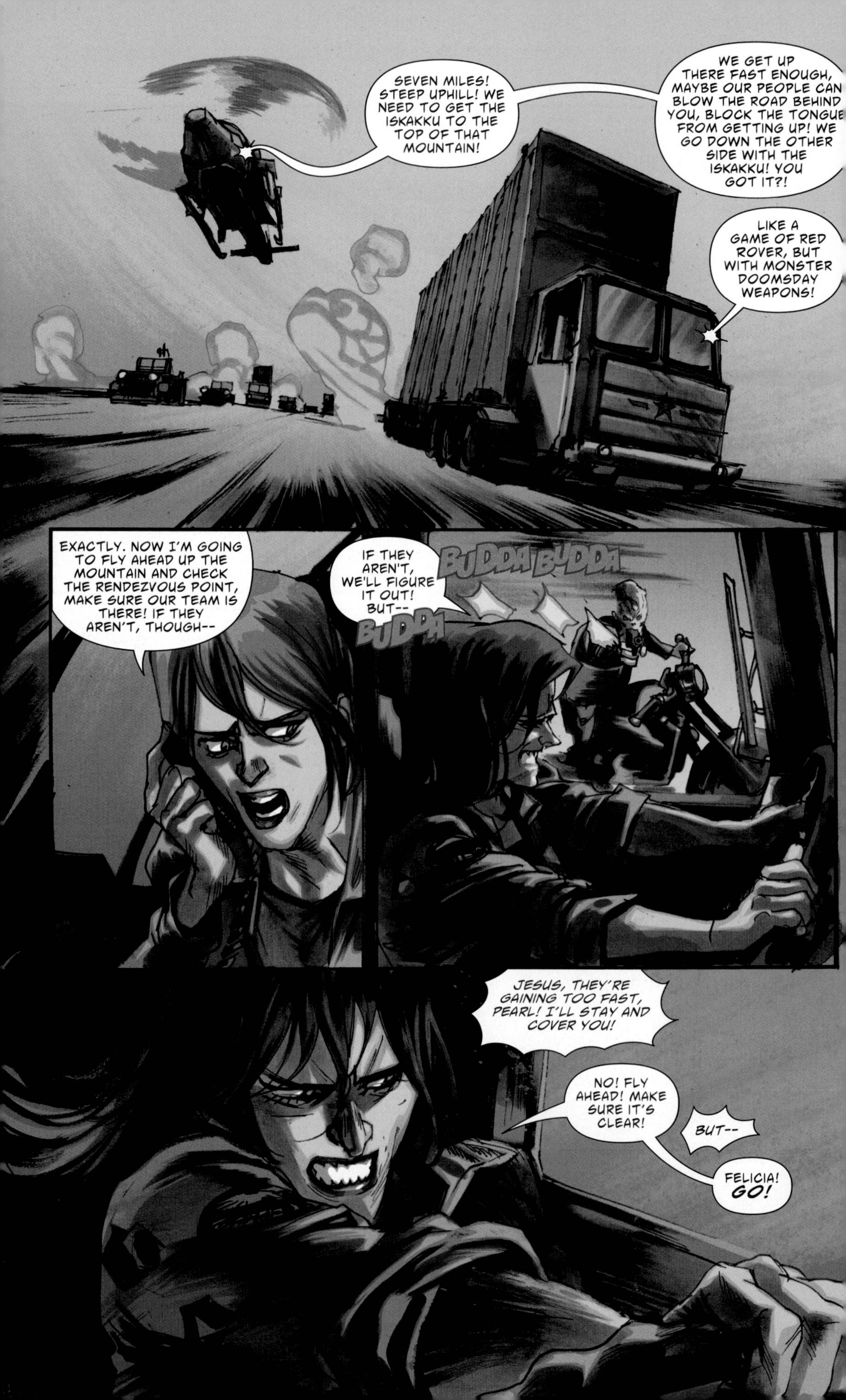
SEVEN MILES! STEEP UPHILL! WE NEED TO GET THE ISKAKKU TO THE TOP OF THAT MOUNTAIN!
WE GET UP THERE FAST ENOUGH, MAYBE OUR PEOPLE CAN BLOW THE ROAD BEHIND YOU, BLOCK THE TONGUE FROM GETTING UP! WE GO DOWN THE OTHER SIDE WITH THE ISKAKKU! YOU GOT IT?!
LIKE A GAME OF RED ROVER, BUT WITH MONSTER DOOMSDAY WEAPONS!
EXACTLY. NOW I'M GOING TO FLY AHEAD UP THE MOUNTAIN AND CHECK THE RENDEZVOUS POINT, MAKE SURE OUR TEAM IS THERE! IF THEY AREN'T, THOUGH--
IF THEY AREN'T, WE'LL FIGURE IT OUT! BUT--
BUDDA BUDDA
BUDDA
JESUS, THEY'RE GAINING TOO FAST, PEARL! I'LL STAY AND COVER YOU!
NO! FLY AHEAD! MAKE SURE IT'S CLEAR!
BUT--
FELICIA! GO!

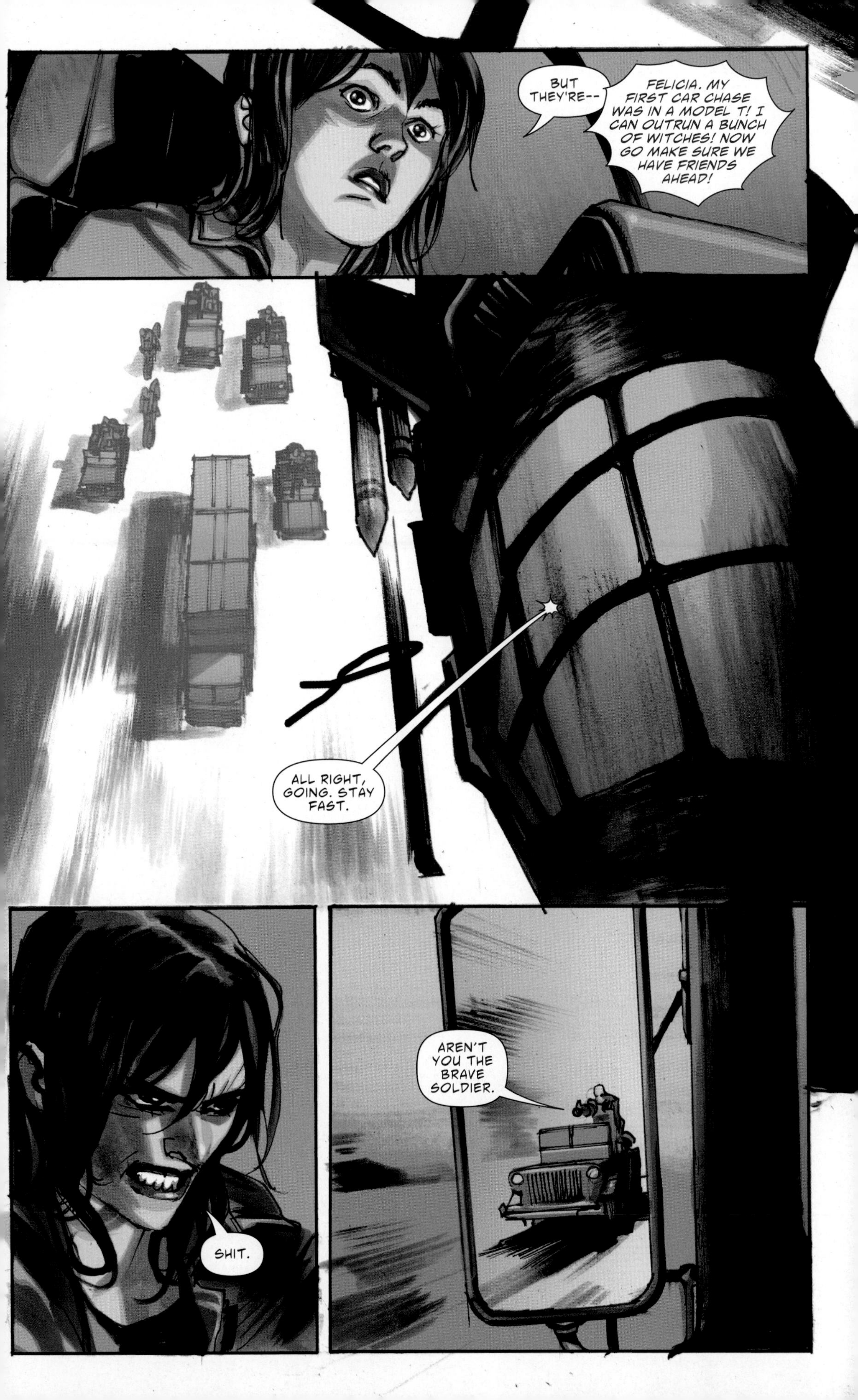
BUT THEY'RE--
FELICIA. MY FIRST CAR CHASE WAS IN A MODEL T! I CAN OUTRUN A BUNCH OF WITCHES! NOW GO MAKE SURE WE HAVE FRIENDS AHEAD!
ALL RIGHT, GOING. STAY FAST.
SHIT.
AREN'T YOU THE BRAVE SOLDIER.

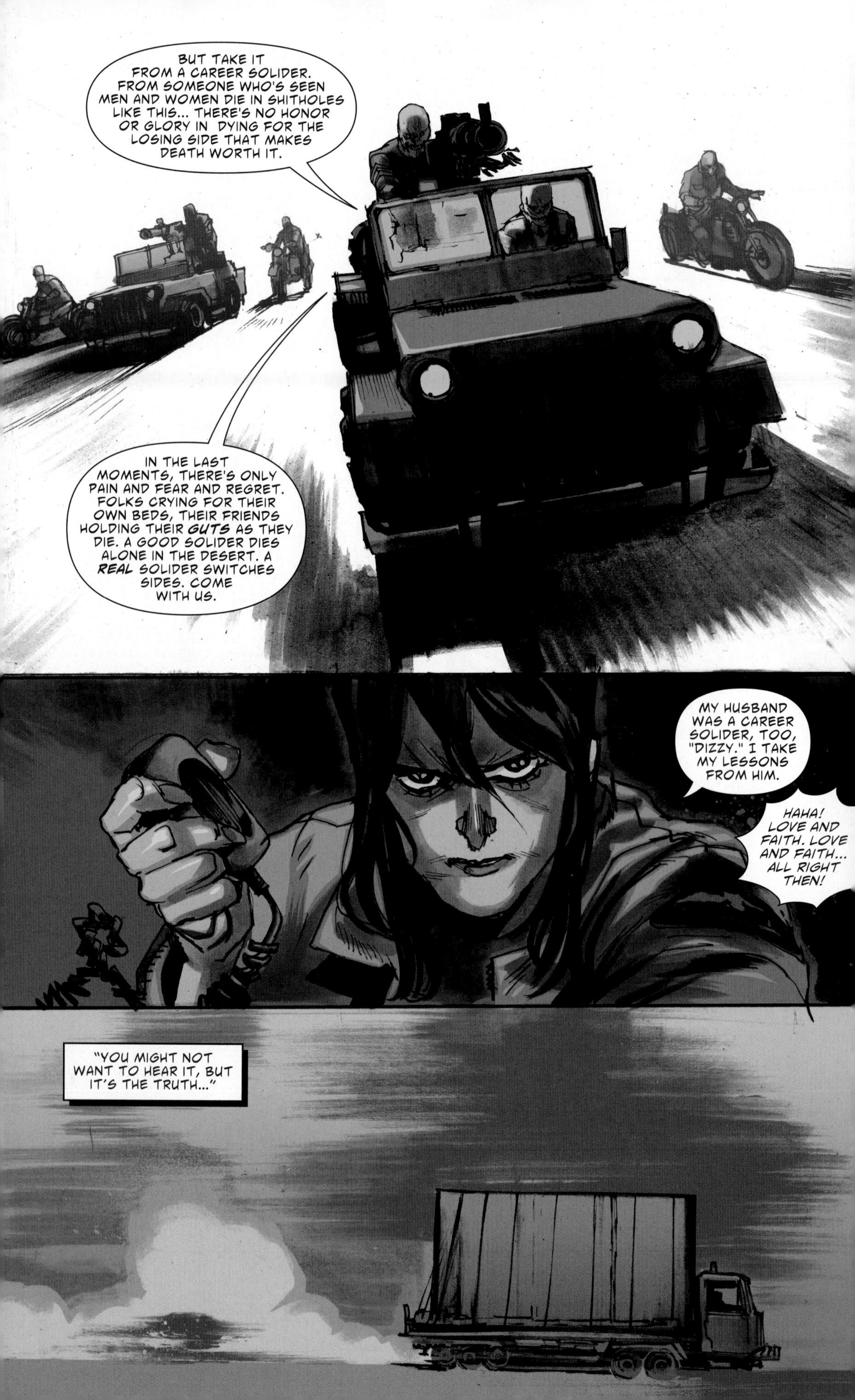
BUT TAKE IT FROM A CAREER SOLIDER. FROM SOMEONE WHO'S SEEN MEN AND WOMEN DIE IN SHITHOLES LIKE THIS... THERE'S NO HONOR OR GLORY IN DYING FOR THE LOSING SIDE THAT MAKES DEATH WORTH IT.
IN THE LAST MOMENTS, THERE'S ONLY PAIN AND FEAR AND REGRET. FOLKS CRYING FOR THEIR OWN BEDS, THEIR FRIENDS HOLDING THEIR GUTS AS THEY DIE. A GOOD SOLIDER DIES ALONE IN THE DESERT. A REAL SOLIDER SWITCHES SIDES. COME WITH US.
MY HUSBAND WAS A CAREER SOLIDER, TOO, "DIZZY." I TAKE MY LESSONS FROM HIM.
HAHA! LOVE AND FAITH. LOVE AND FAITH... ALL RIGHT THEN!
"YOU MIGHT NOT WANT TO HEAR IT, BUT IT'S THE TRUTH..."

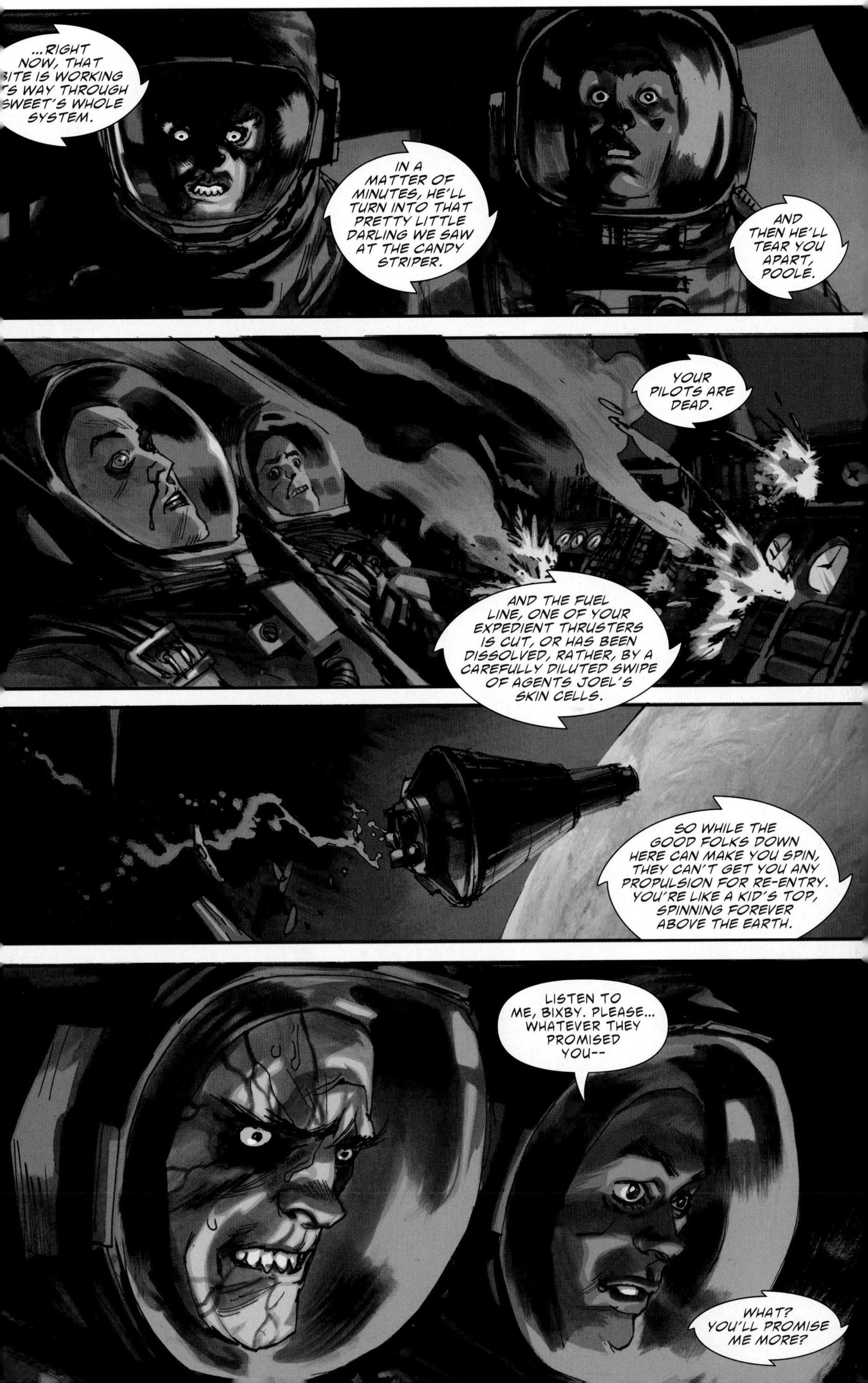
...RIGHT NOW, THAT BITE IS WORKING 'S WAY THROUGH SWEET'S WHOLE SYSTEM.
IN A MATTER OF MINUTES, HE'LL TURN INTO THAT PRETTY LITTLE DARLING WE SAW AT THE CANDY STRIPER.
AND THEN HE'LL TEAR YOU APART, POOLE.
YOUR PILOTS ARE DEAD.
AND THE FUEL LINE, ONE OF YOUR EXPEDIENT THRUSTERS IS CUT, OR HAS BEEN DISSOLVED, RATHER, BY A CAREFULLY DILUTED SWIPE OF AGENTS JOEL'S SKIN CELLS.
SO WHILE THE GOOD FOLKS DOWN HERE CAN MAKE YOU SPIN, THEY CAN'T GET YOU ANY PROPULSION FOR RE-ENTRY. YOU'RE LIKE A KID'S TOP, SPINNING FOREVER ABOVE THE EARTH.
LISTEN TO ME, BIXBY. PLEASE... WHATEVER THEY PROMISED YOU--
WHAT? YOU'LL PROMISE ME MORE?

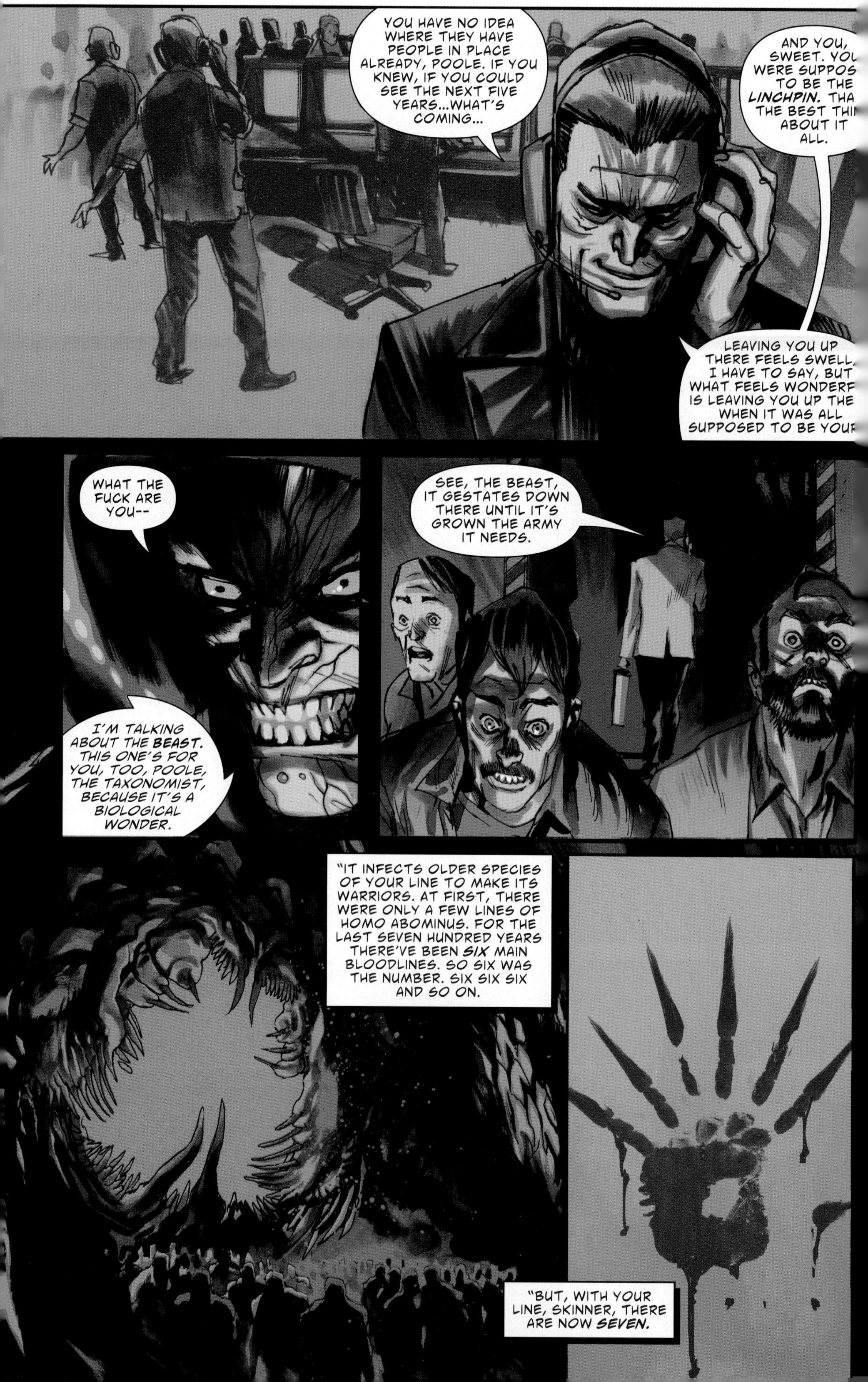
YOU HAVE NO IDEA WHERE THEY HAVE PEOPLE IN PLACE ALREADY, POOLE. IF YOU KNEW, IF YOU COULD SEE THE NEXT FIVE YEARS...WHAT'S COMING...
AND YOU, SWEET. YOU WERE SUPPOS TO BE THE LINCHPIN. THA THE BEST THI ABOUT IT ALL.
LEAVING YOU UP THERE FEELS SWELL, I HAVE TO SAY, BUT WHAT FEELS WONDERF IS LEAVING YOU UP THE WHEN IT WAS ALL SUPPOSED TO BE YOUR
WHAT THE FUCK ARE YOU--
I'M TALKING ABOUT THE BEAST. THIS ONE'S FOR YOU, TOO, POOLE, THE TAXONOMIST, BECAUSE IT'S A BIOLOGICAL WONDER.
SEE, THE BEAST, IT GESTATES DOWN THERE UNTIL IT'S GROWN THE ARMY IT NEEDS.
"IT INFECTS OLDER SPECIES OF YOUR LINE TO MAKE ITS WARRIORS. AT FIRST, THERE WERE ONLY A FEW LINES OF HOMO ABOMINUS. FOR THE LAST SEVEN HUNDRED YEARS THERE'VE BEEN SIX MAIN BLOODLINES. SO SIX WAS THE NUMBER. SIX SIX SIX AND SO ON.
"BUT, WITH YOUR LINE, SKINNER, THERE ARE NOW SEVEN.

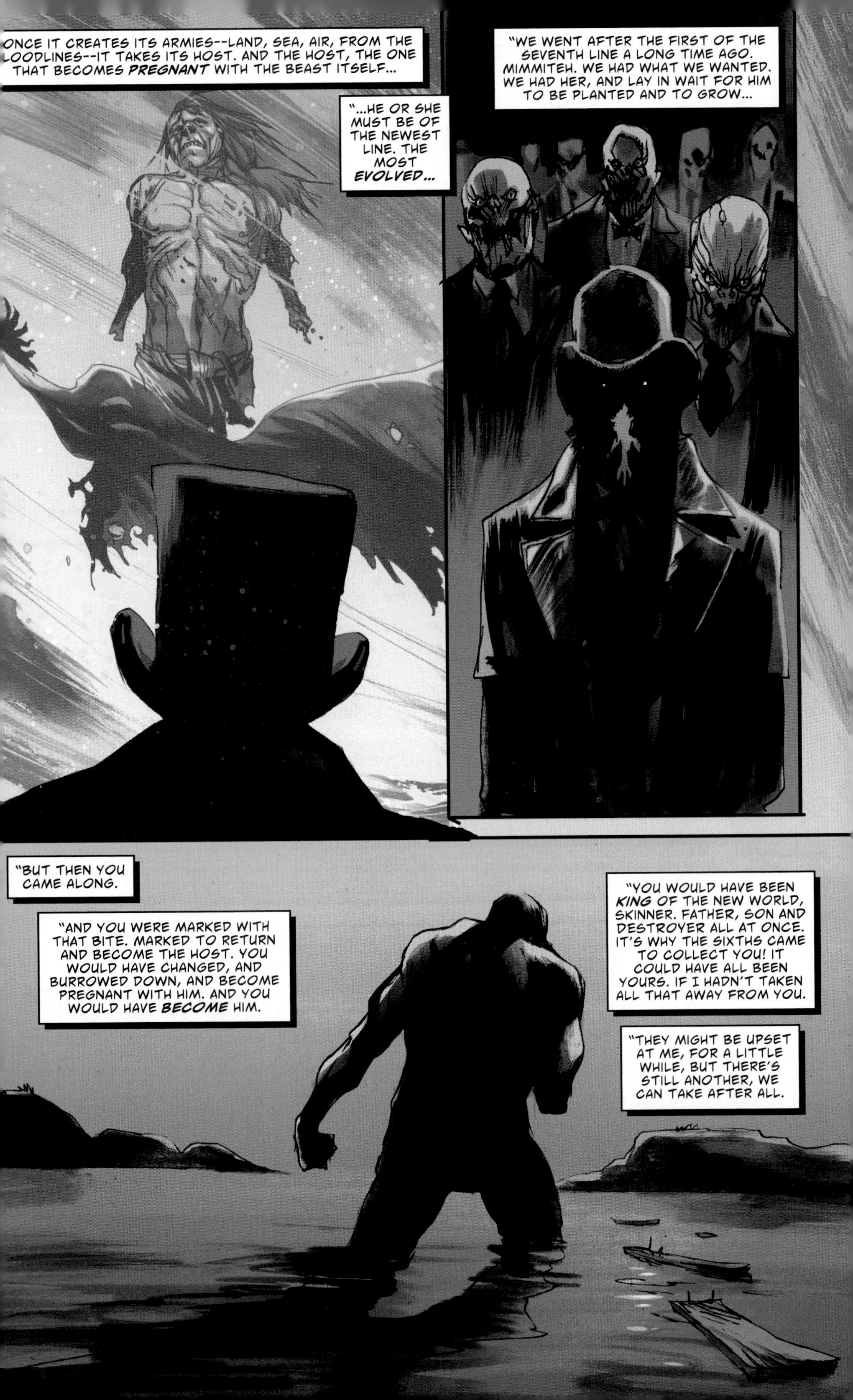

ONCE IT CREATES ITS ARMIES--LAND, SEA, AIR, FROM THE LOODLINES--IT TAKES ITS HOST. AND THE HOST, THE ONE THAT BECOMES PREGNANT WITH THE BEAST ITSELF...
"...HE OR SHE MUST BE OF THE NEWEST LINE. THE MOST EVOLVED...
"WE WENT AFTER THE FIRST OF THE SEVENTH LINE A LONG TIME AGO. MIMMITEH. WE HAD WHAT WE WANTED. WE HAD HER, AND LAY IN WAIT FOR HIM TO BE PLANTED AND TO GROW...
"BUT THEN YOU CAME ALONG.
"AND YOU WERE MARKED WITH THAT BITE. MARKED TO RETURN AND BECOME THE HOST. YOU WOULD HAVE CHANGED, AND BURROWED DOWN, AND BECOME PREGNANT WITH HIM. AND YOU WOULD HAVE BECOME HIM.
"YOU WOULD HAVE BEEN KING OF THE NEW WORLD, SKINNER. FATHER, SON AND DESTROYER ALL AT ONCE. IT'S WHY THE SIXTHS CAME TO COLLECT YOU! IT COULD HAVE ALL BEEN YOURS. IF I HADN'T TAKEN ALL THAT AWAY FROM YOU.
"THEY MIGHT BE UPSET AT ME, FOR A LITTLE WHILE, BUT THERE'S STILL ANOTHER, WE CAN TAKE AFTER ALL.

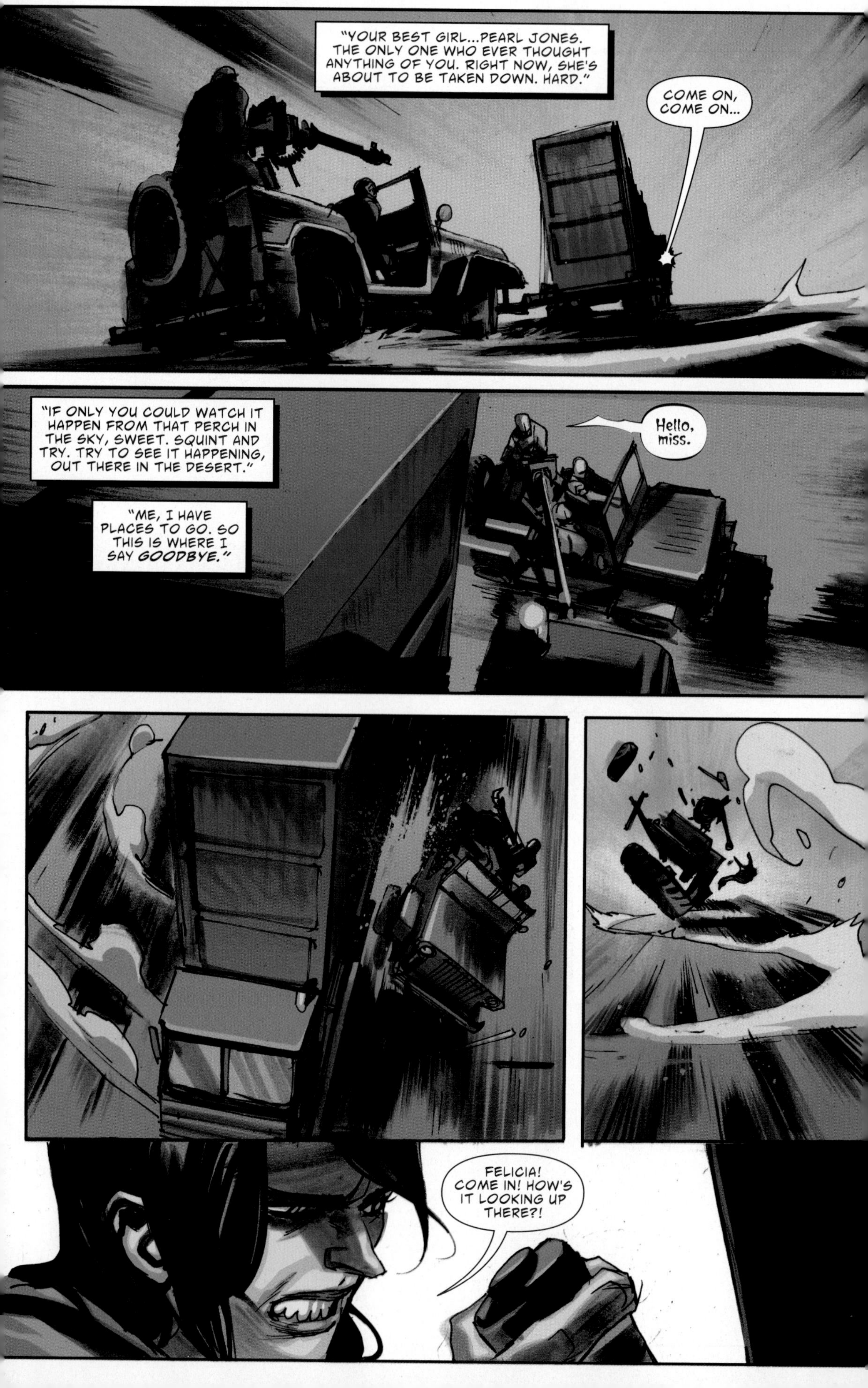
"YOUR BEST GIRL...PEARL JONES. THE ONLY ONE WHO EVER THOUGHT ANYTHING OF YOU. RIGHT NOW, SHE'S ABOUT TO BE TAKEN DOWN. HARD."
COME ON, COME ON...
"IF ONLY YOU COULD WATCH IT HAPPEN FROM THAT PERCH IN THE SKY, SWEET. SQUINT AND TRY. TRY TO SEE IT HAPPENING, OUT THERE IN THE DESERT."
"ME, I HAVE PLACES TO GO. SO THIS IS WHERE I SAY GOODBYE."
Hello, miss.
FELICIA! COME IN! HOW'S IT LOOKING UP THERE?!

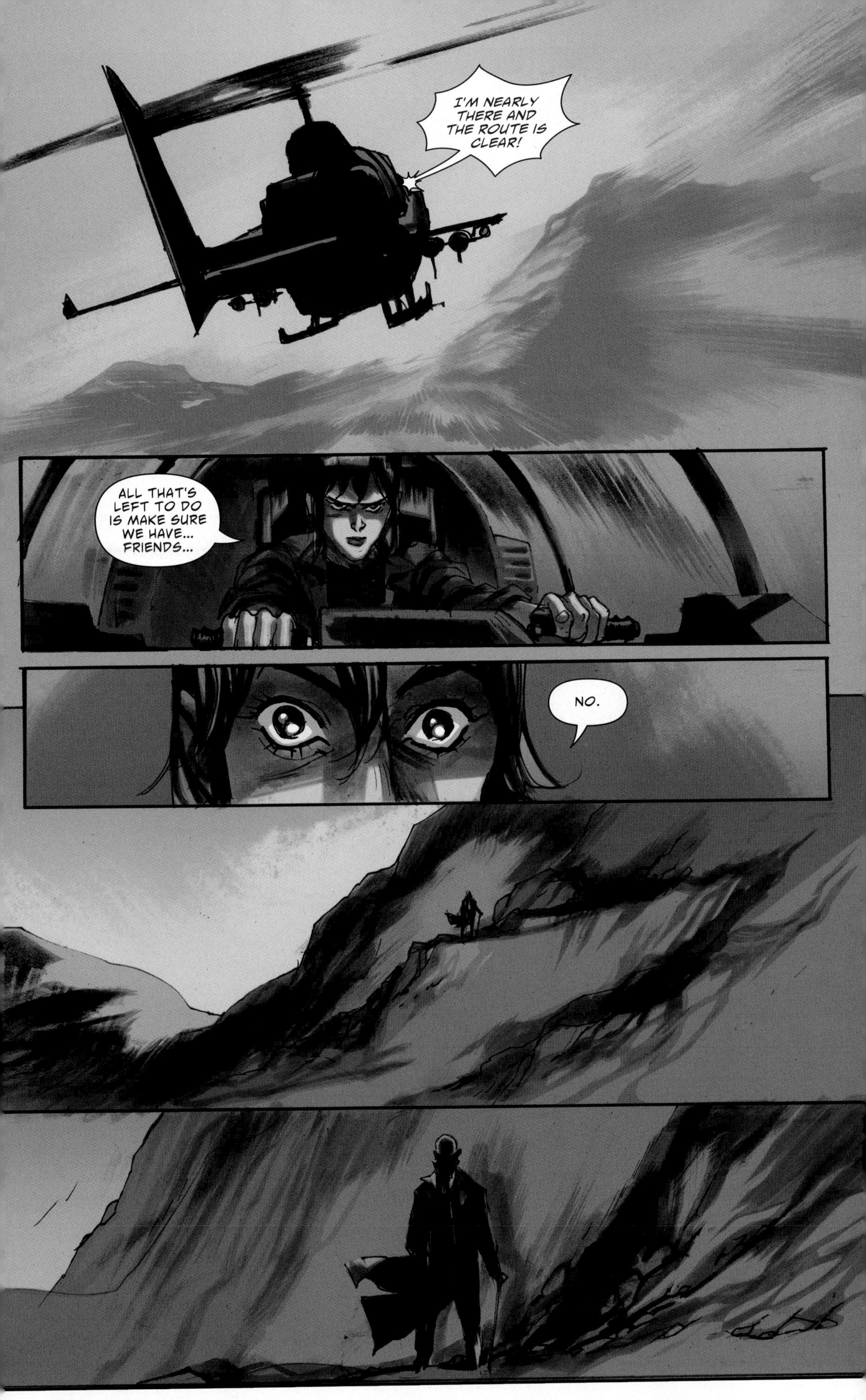
I'M NEARLY THERE AND THE ROUTE IS CLEAR!
ALL THAT'S LEFT TO DO IS MAKE SURE WE HAVE... FRIENDS...
NO.

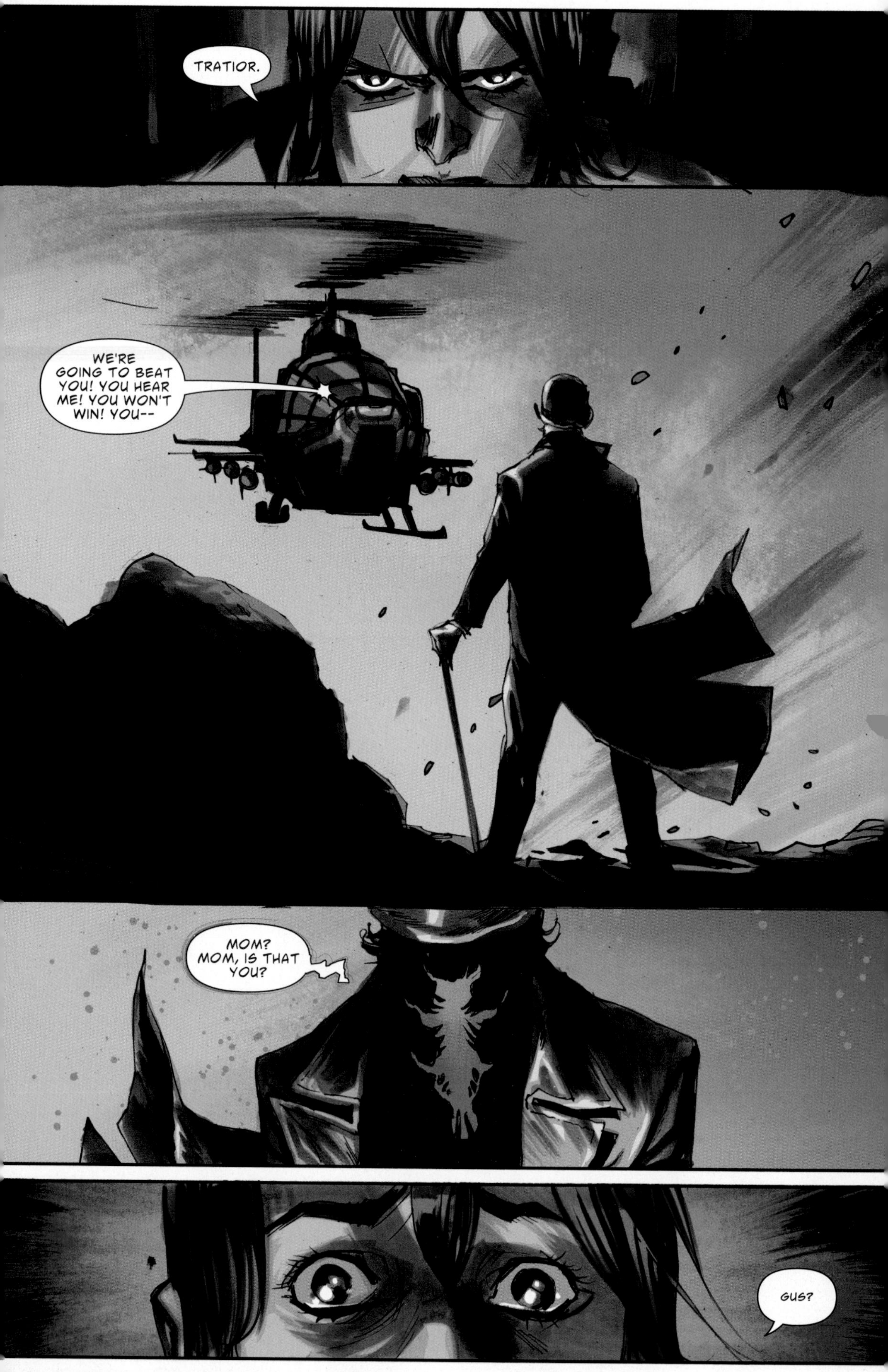
TRATIOR.
WE'RE GOING TO BEAT YOU! YOU HEAR ME! YOU WON'T WIN! YOU--
MOM? MOM, IS THAT YOU?
GUS?

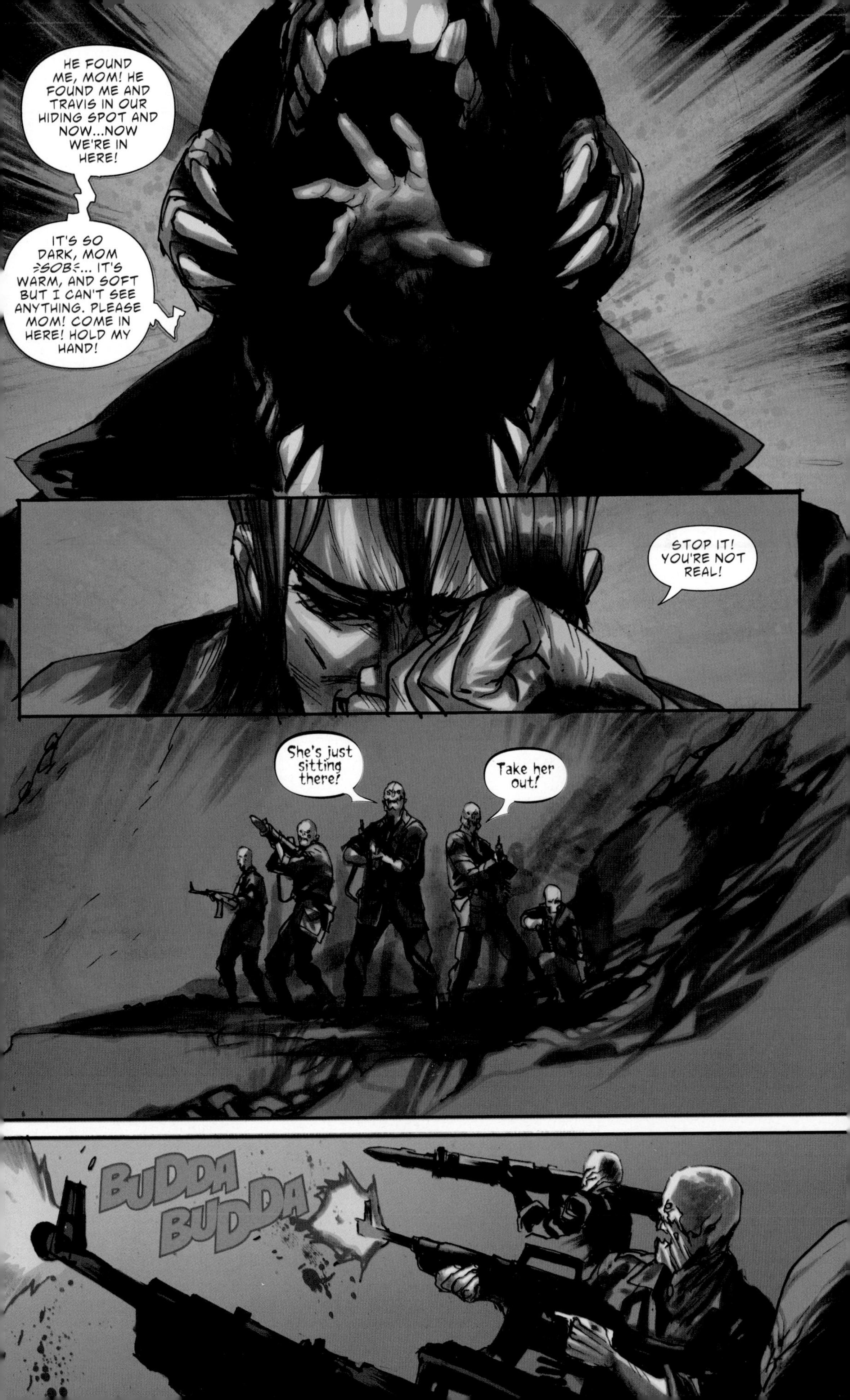
HE FOUND ME, MOM! HE FOUND ME AND TRAVIS IN OUR HIDING SPOT AND NOW...NOW WE'RE IN HERE!
IT'S SO DARK, MOM ⇒SOB⇐... IT'S WARM, AND SOFT BUT I CAN'T SEE ANYTHING. PLEASE MOM! COME IN HERE! HOLD MY HAND!
STOP IT! YOU'RE NOT REAL!
She's just sitting there!
Take her out!
BUDDA BUDDA

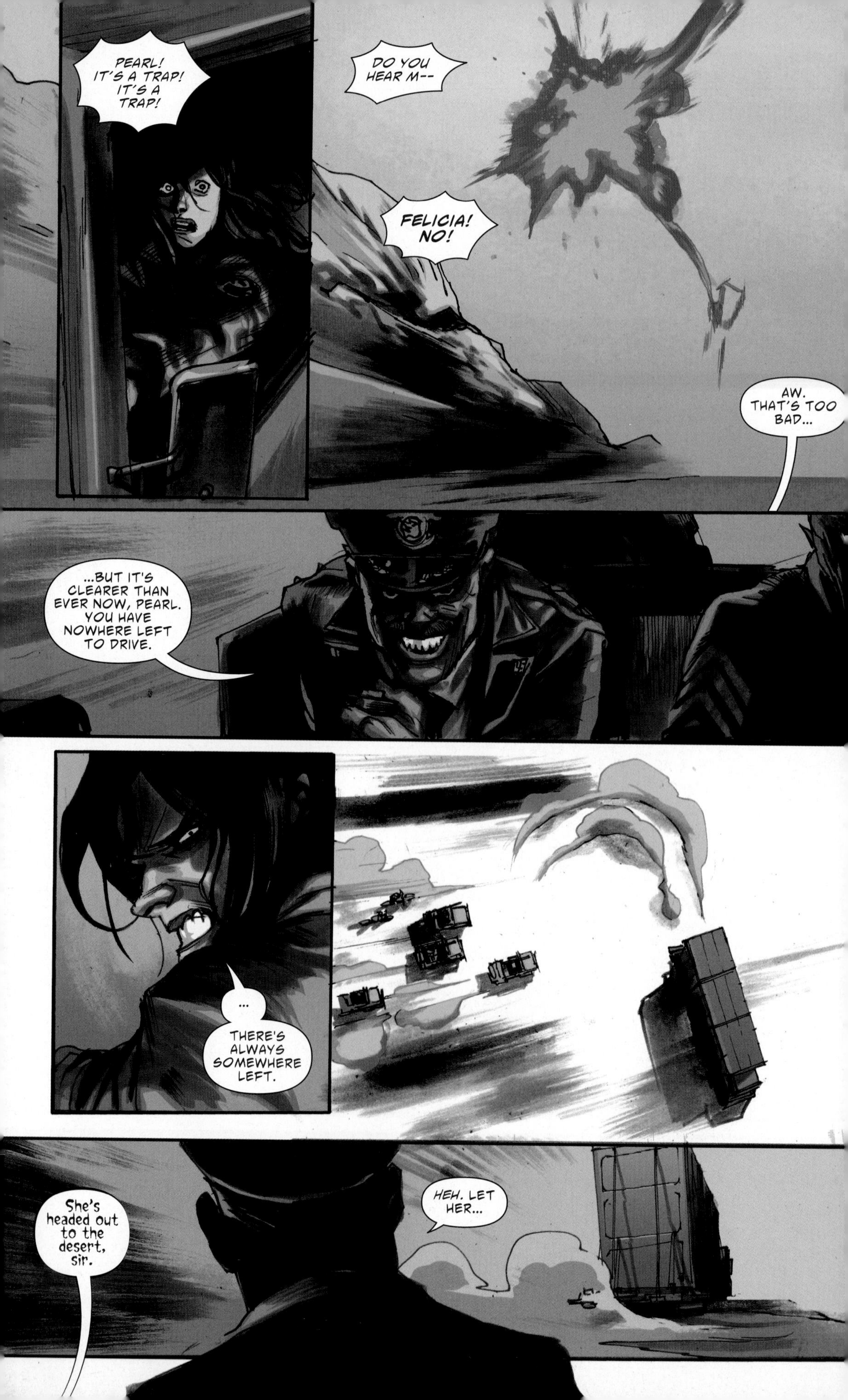
PEARL! IT'S A TRAP! IT'S A TRAP!
DO YOU HEAR M--
FELICIA! NO!
AW. THAT'S TOO BAD...
...BUT IT'S CLEARER THAN EVER NOW, PEARL. YOU HAVE NOWHERE LEFT TO DRIVE.
...
THERE'S ALWAYS SOMEWHERE LEFT.
She's headed out to the desert, sir.
HEH. LET HER...

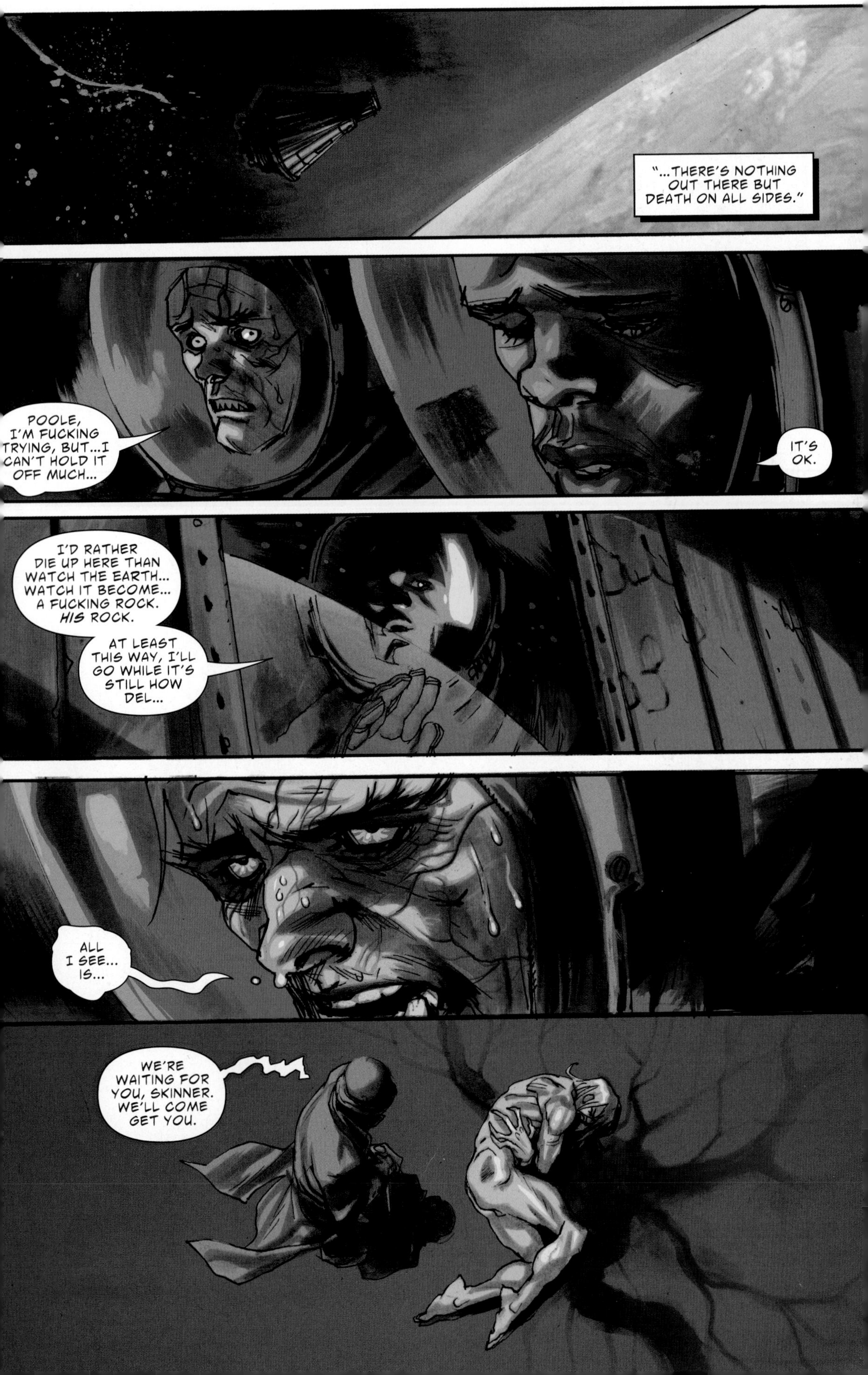
"...THERE'S NOTHING OUT THERE BUT DEATH ON ALL SIDES."
POOLE, I'M FUCKING TRYING, BUT...I CAN'T HOLD IT OFF MUCH...
IT'S OK.
I'D RATHER DIE UP HERE THAN WATCH THE EARTH... WATCH IT BECOME... A FUCKING ROCK. HIS ROCK.
AT LEAST THIS WAY, I'LL GO WHILE IT'S STILL HOW DEL...
ALL I SEE... IS...
WE'RE WAITING FOR YOU, SKINNER. WE'LL COME GET YOU.

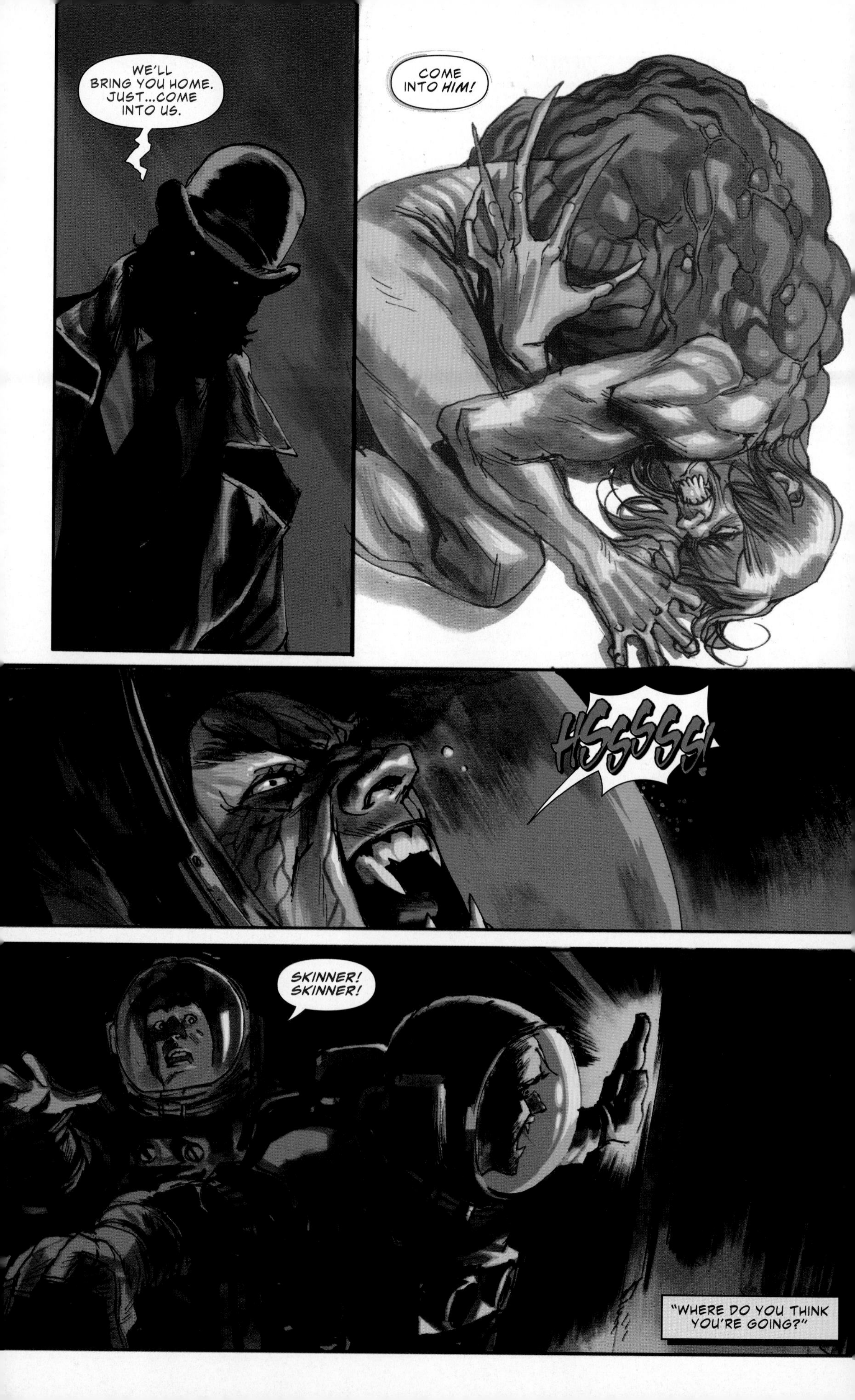
WE'LL BRING YOU HOME. JUST...COME INTO US.
COME INTO HIM!
HSSSSS!
SKINNER! SKINNER!
"WHERE DO YOU THINK YOU'RE GOING?"

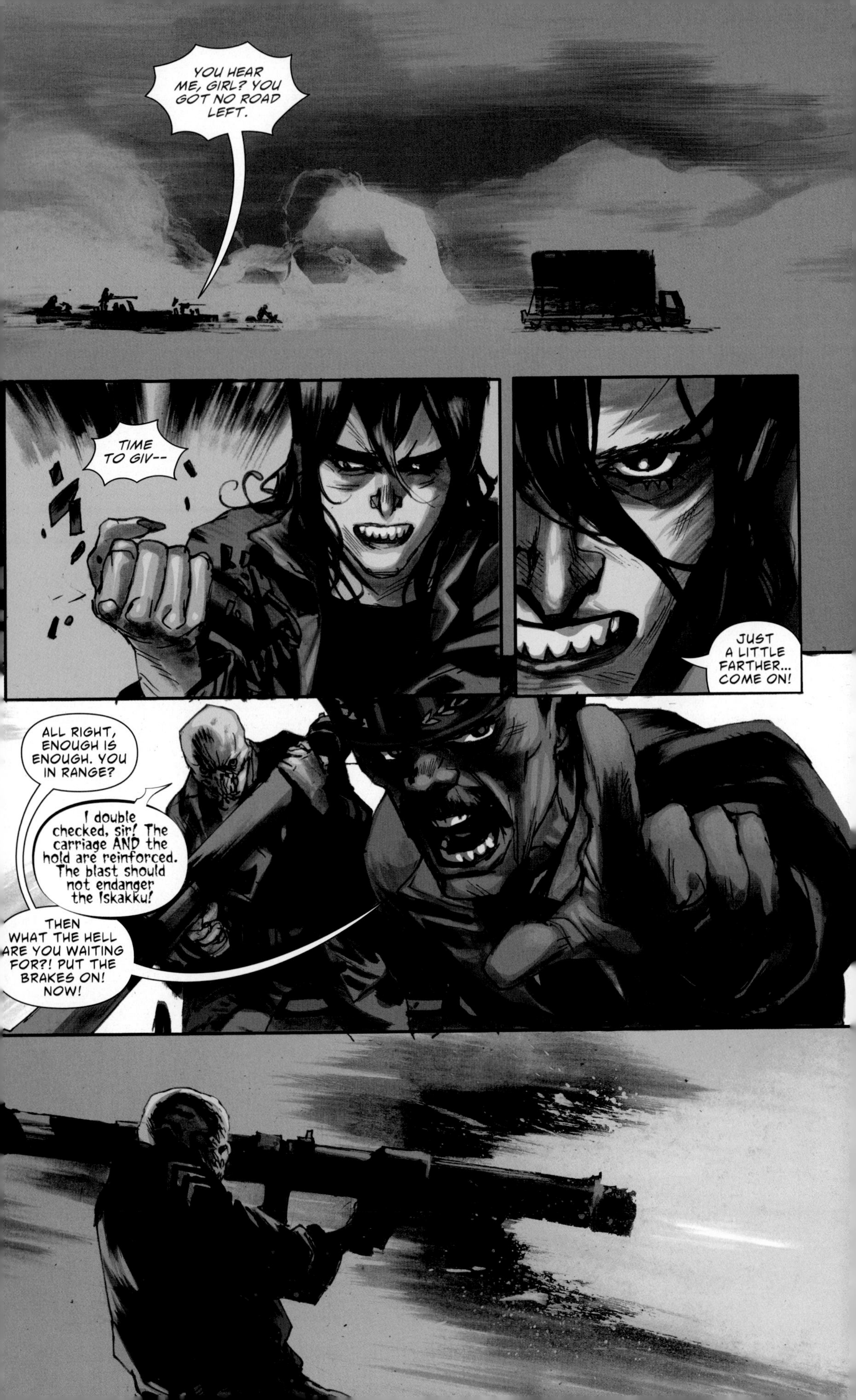
YOU HEAR ME, GIRL? YOU GOT NO ROAD LEFT.
TIME TO GIV--
JUST A LITTLE FARTHER... COME ON!
ALL RIGHT, ENOUGH IS ENOUGH. YOU IN RANGE?
I double checked, sir! The carriage AND the hold are reinforced. The blast should not endanger the Iskakku!
THEN WHAT THE HELL ARE YOU WAITING FOR?! PUT THE BRAKES ON! NOW!

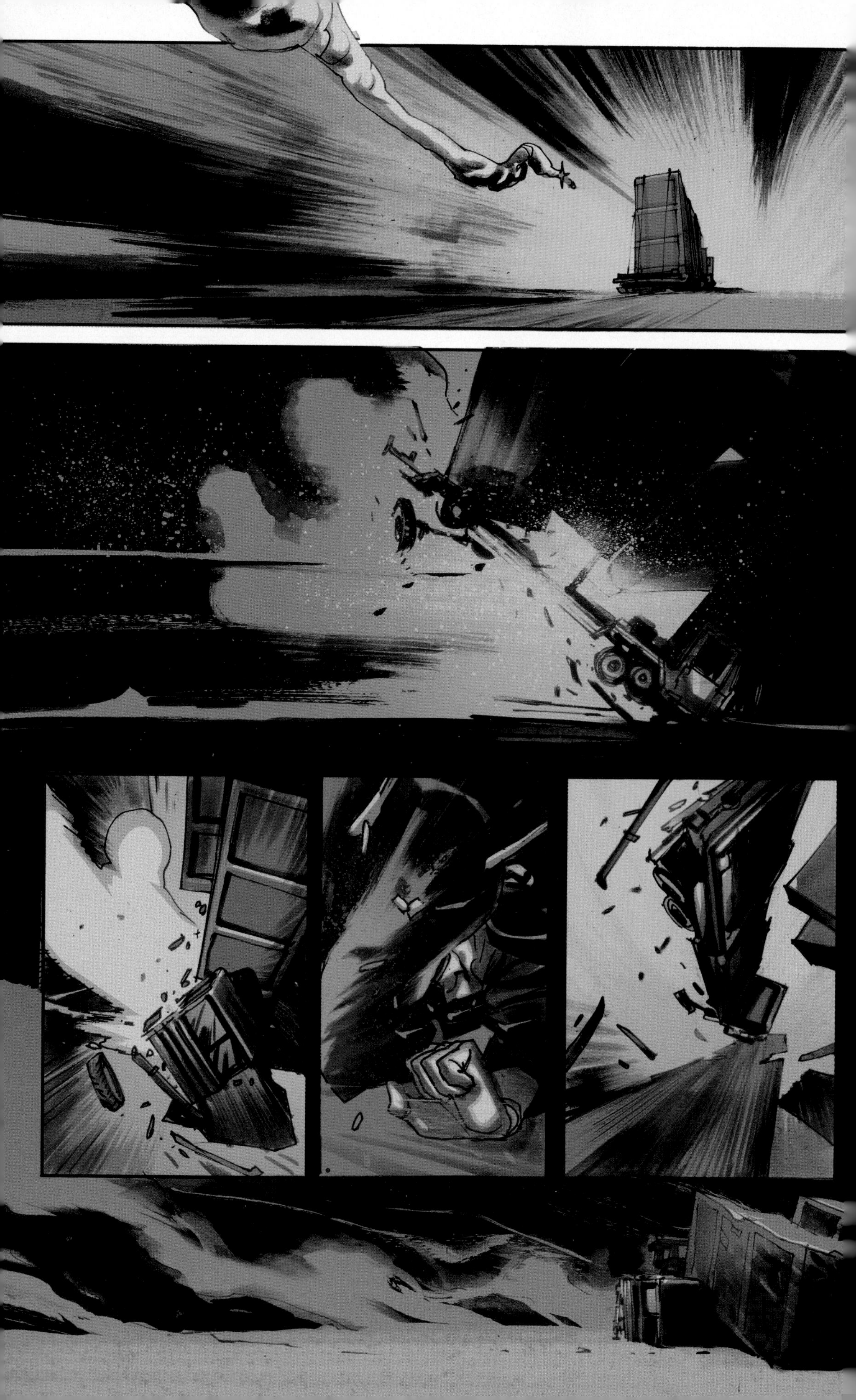

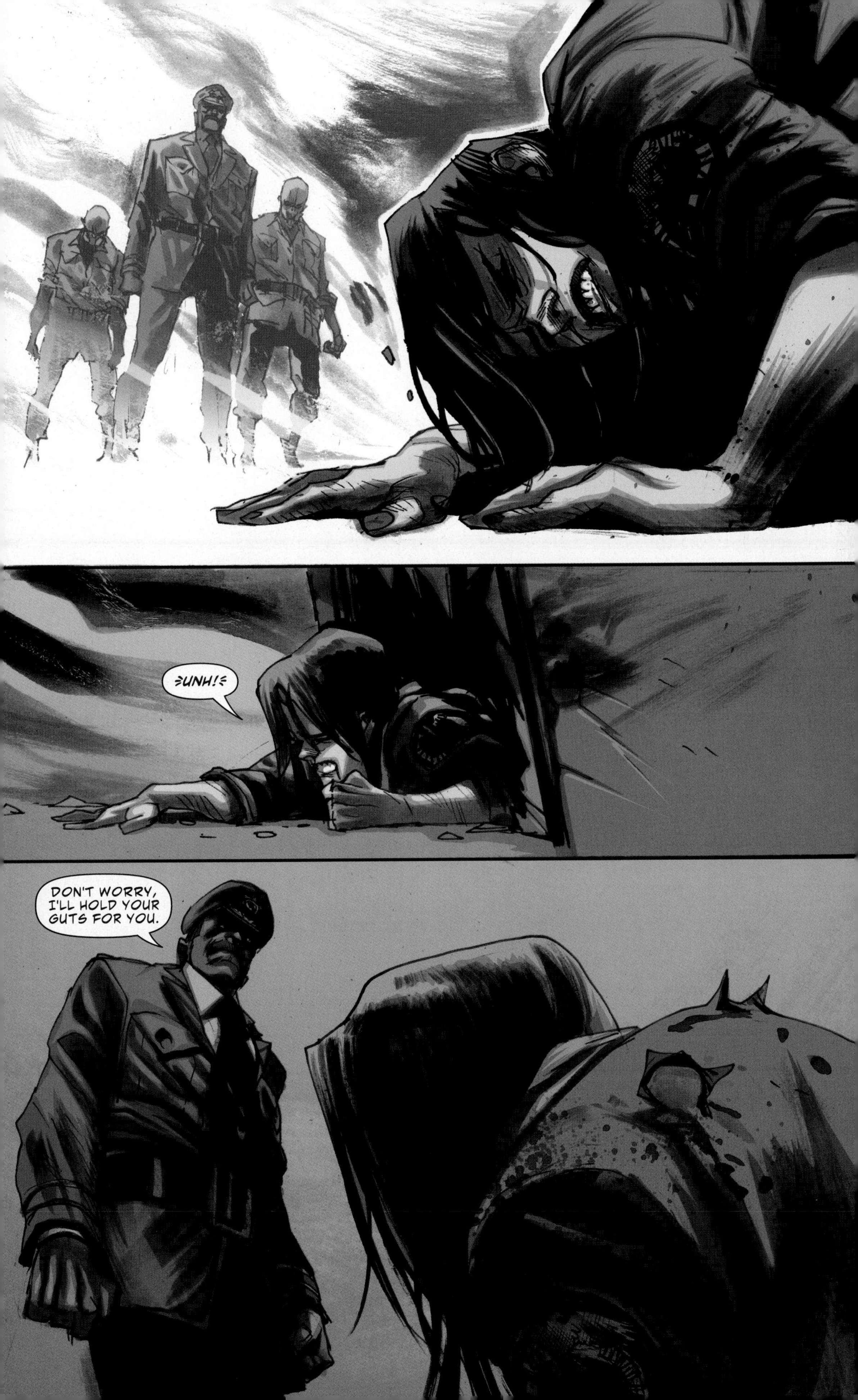
UNH!
DON'T WORRY, I'LL HOLD YOUR GUTS FOR YOU.

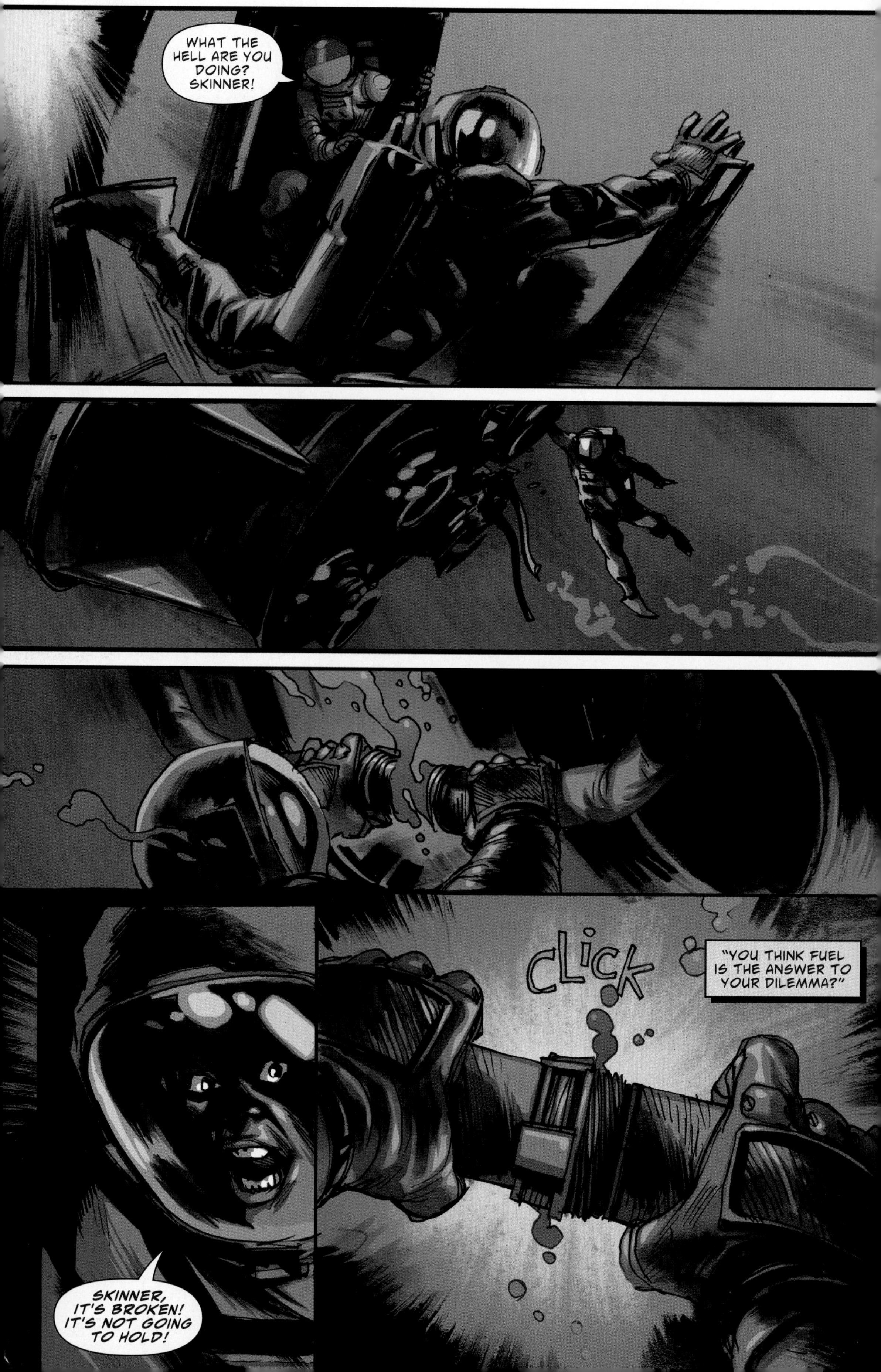
WHAT THE HELL ARE YOU DOING? SKINNER!
CLICK
"YOU THINK FUEL IS THE ANSWER TO YOUR DILEMMA?"
SKINNER, IT'S BROKEN! IT'S NOT GOING TO HOLD!

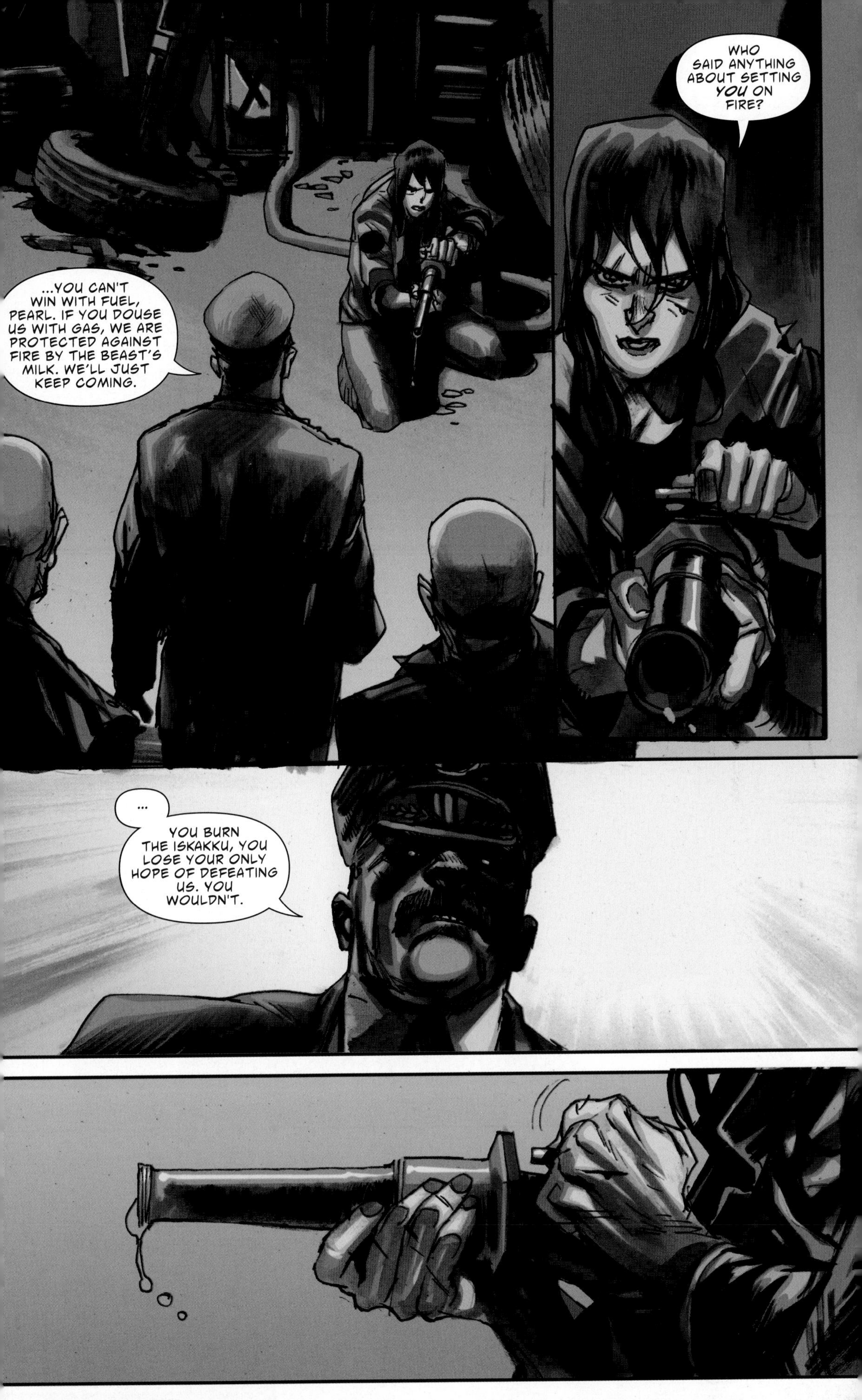
...YOU CAN'T WIN WITH FUEL, PEARL. IF YOU DOUSE US WITH GAS, WE ARE PROTECTED AGAINST FIRE BY THE BEAST'S MILK. WE'LL JUST KEEP COMING.
WHO SAID ANYTHING ABOUT SETTING *YOU* ON FIRE?
...
YOU BURN THE ISKAKKU, YOU LOSE YOUR ONLY HOPE OF DEFEATING US. YOU WOULDN'T.

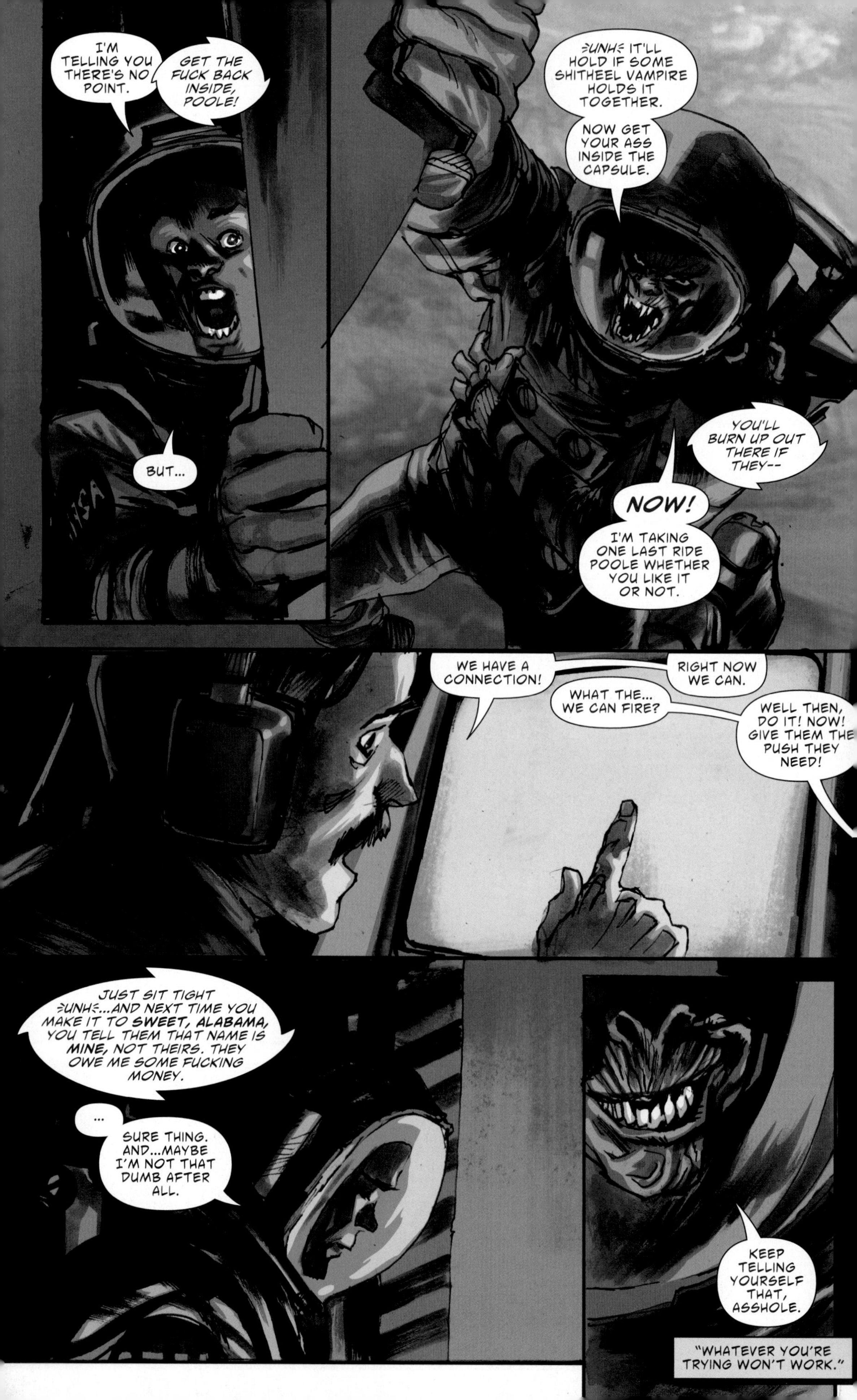
I'M TELLING YOU THERE'S NO POINT.
GET THE FUCK BACK INSIDE, POOLE!
BUT...
=UNH= IT'LL HOLD IF SOME SHITHEEL VAMPIRE HOLDS IT TOGETHER.
NOW GET YOUR ASS INSIDE THE CAPSULE.
YOU'LL BURN UP OUT THERE IF THEY--
NOW!
I'M TAKING ONE LAST RIDE POOLE WHETHER YOU LIKE IT OR NOT.
WE HAVE A CONNECTION!
RIGHT NOW WE CAN.
WHAT THE... WE CAN FIRE?
WELL THEN, DO IT! NOW! GIVE THEM THE PUSH THEY NEED!
JUST SIT TIGHT =UNH=...AND NEXT TIME YOU MAKE IT TO SWEET, ALABAMA, YOU TELL THEM THAT NAME IS MINE, NOT THEIRS. THEY OWE ME SOME FUCKING MONEY.
...
SURE THING. AND...MAYBE I'M NOT THAT DUMB AFTER ALL.
KEEP TELLING YOURSELF THAT, ASSHOLE.
"WHATEVER YOU'RE TRYING WON'T WORK."

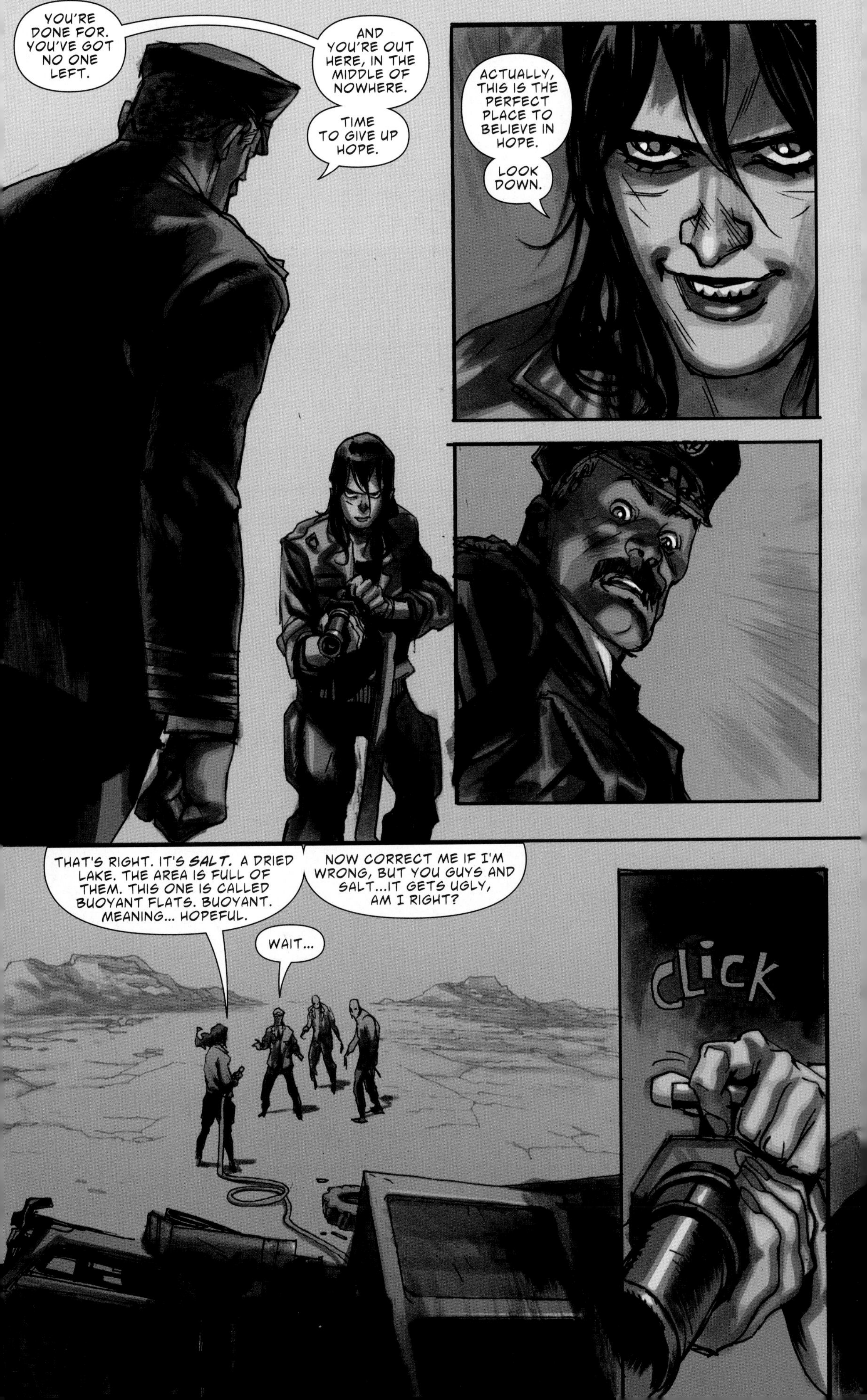
YOU'RE DONE FOR. YOU'VE GOT NO ONE LEFT.
AND YOU'RE OUT HERE, IN THE MIDDLE OF NOWHERE.
TIME TO GIVE UP HOPE.
ACTUALLY, THIS IS THE PERFECT PLACE TO BELIEVE IN HOPE.
LOOK DOWN.
THAT'S RIGHT. IT'S SALT. A DRIED LAKE. THE AREA IS FULL OF THEM. THIS ONE IS CALLED BUOYANT FLATS. BUOYANT. MEANING... HOPEFUL.
WAIT...
NOW CORRECT ME IF I'M WRONG, BUT YOU GUYS AND SALT...IT GETS UGLY, AM I RIGHT?
CLICK

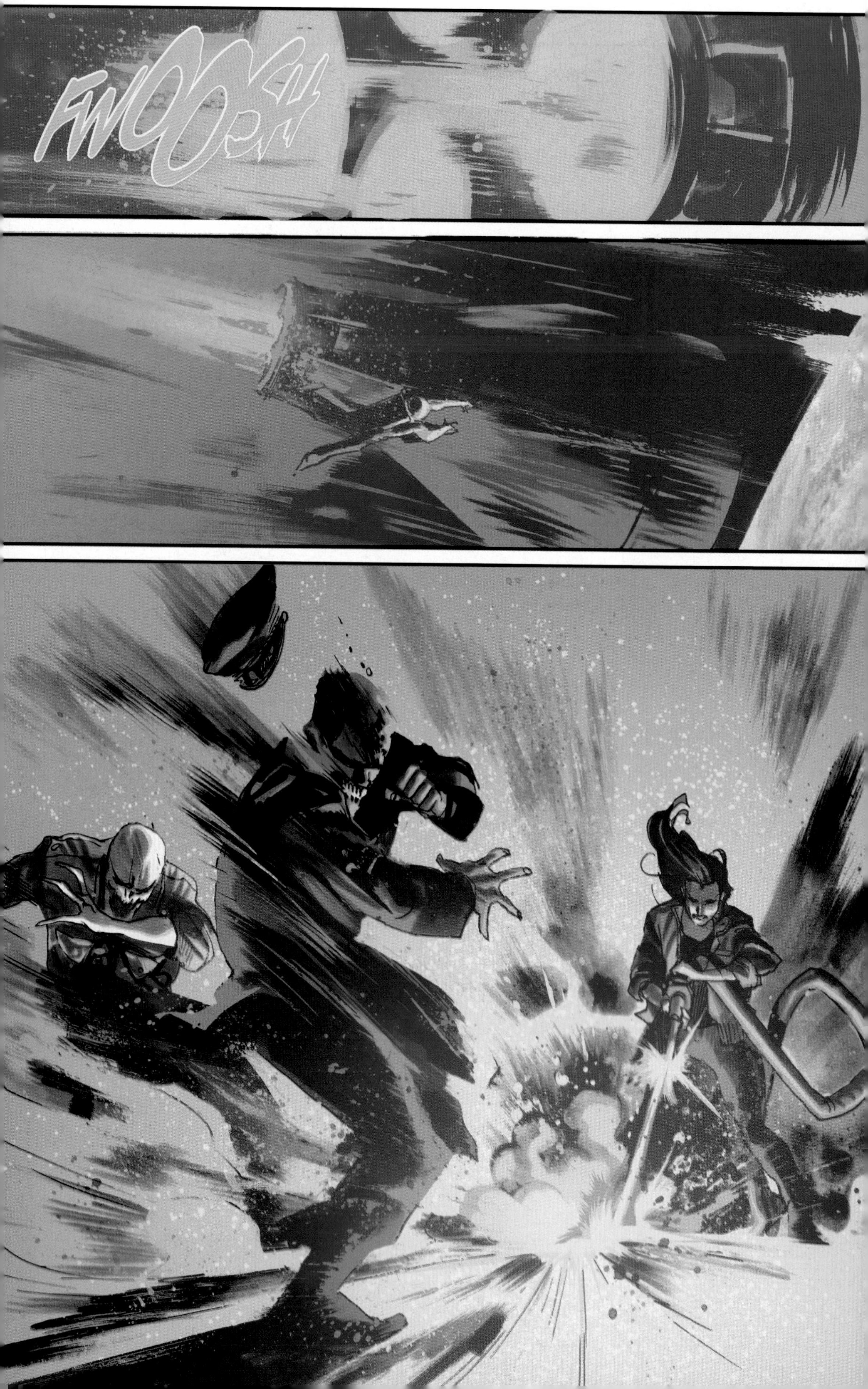
FWOOSH

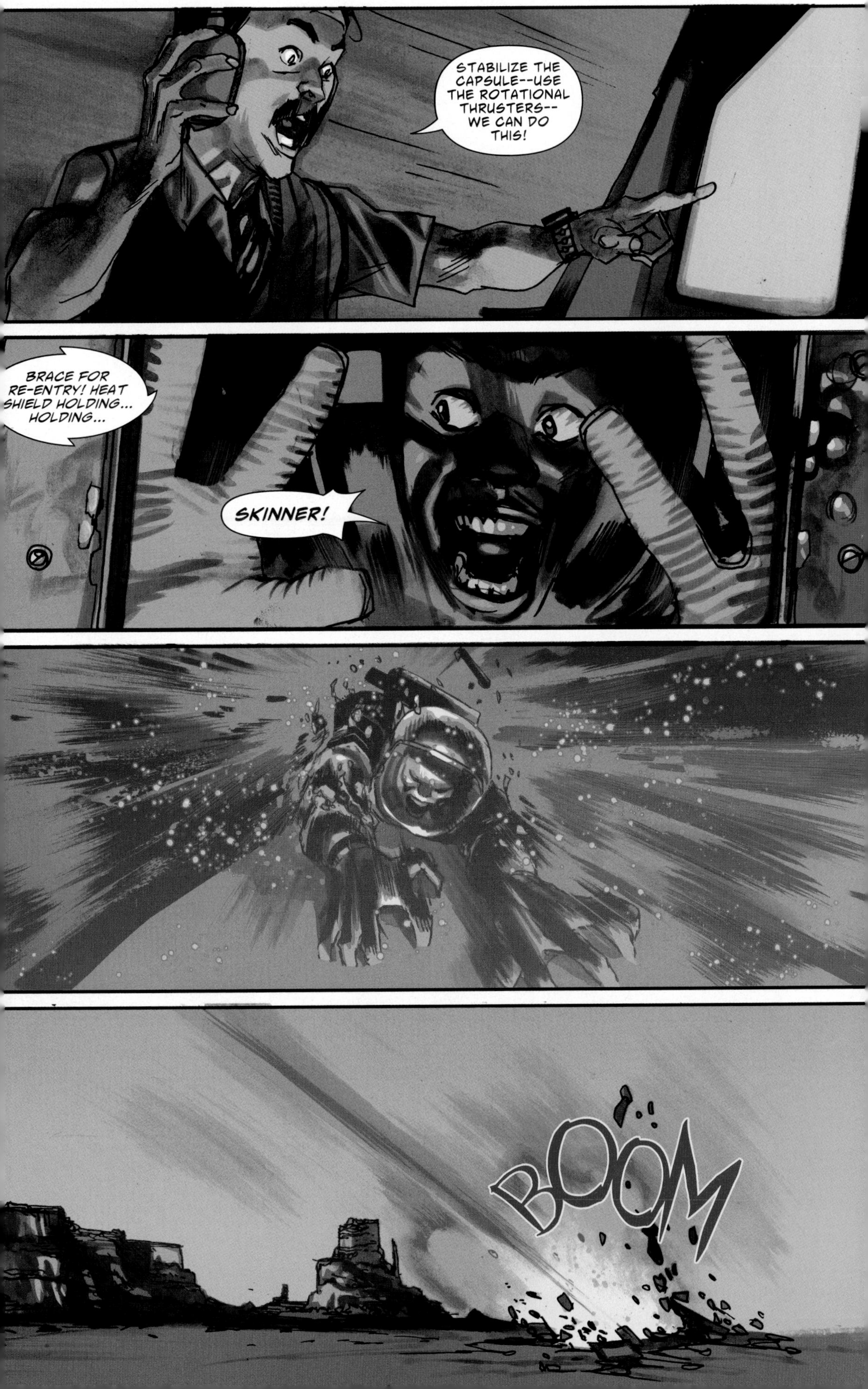

STABILIZE THE CAPSULE--USE THE ROTATIONAL THRUSTERS--WE CAN DO THIS!
BRACE FOR RE-ENTRY! HEAT SHIELD HOLDING... HOLDING...
SKINNER!
BOOM

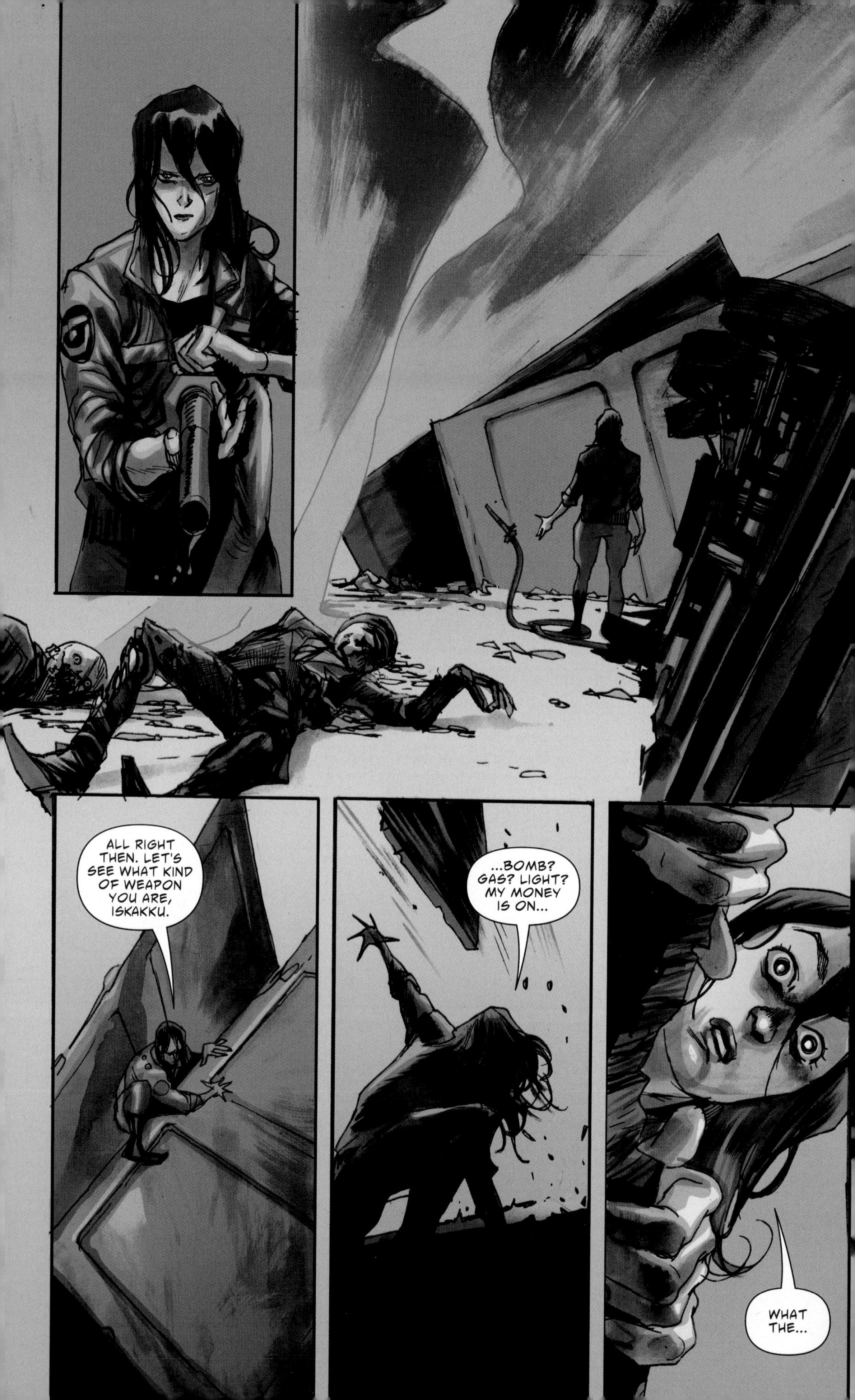

ALL RIGHT THEN. LET'S SEE WHAT KIND OF WEAPON YOU ARE, ISKAKKU.
...BOMB? GAS? LIGHT? MY MONEY IS ON...
WHAT THE...

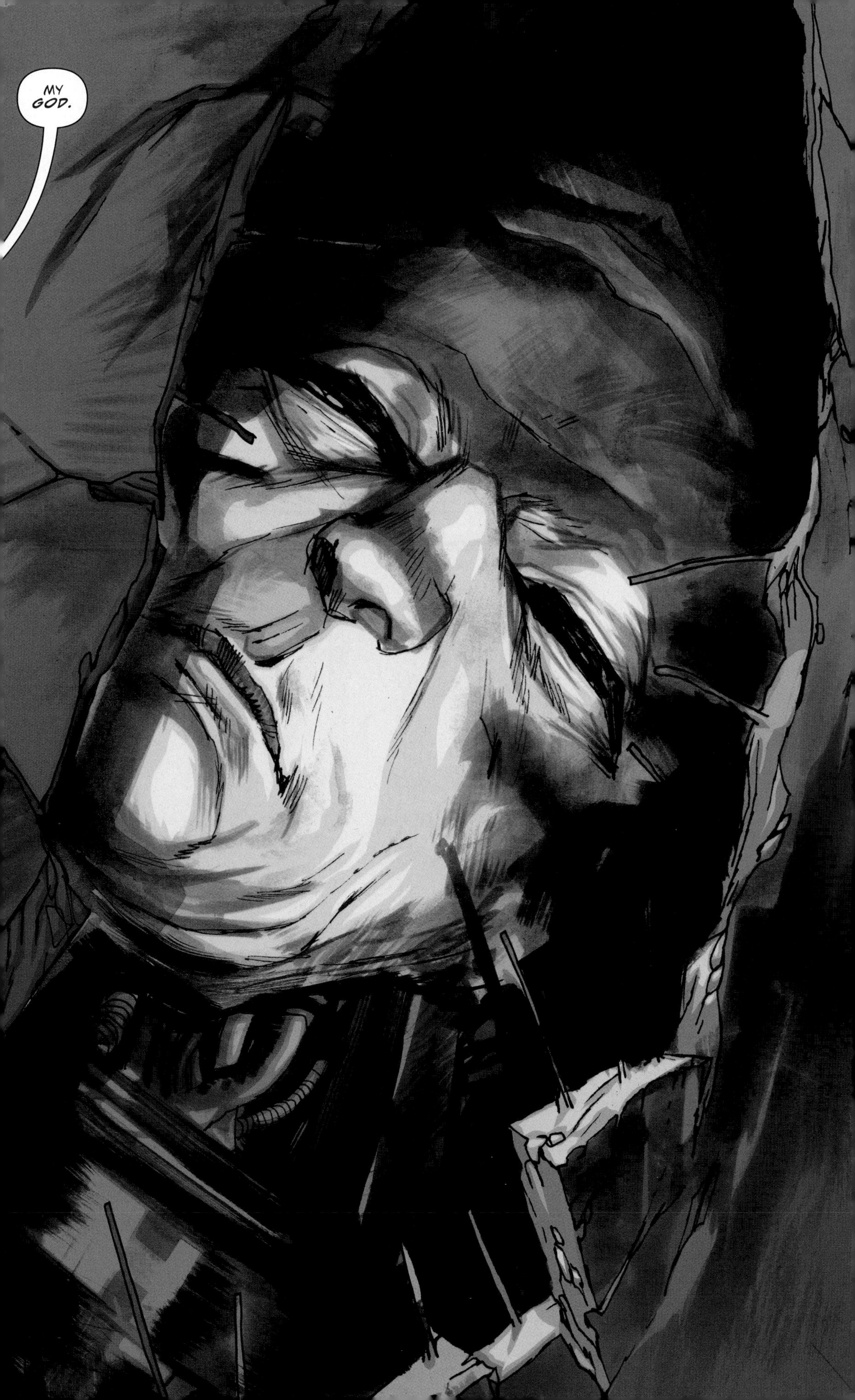
MY GOD.

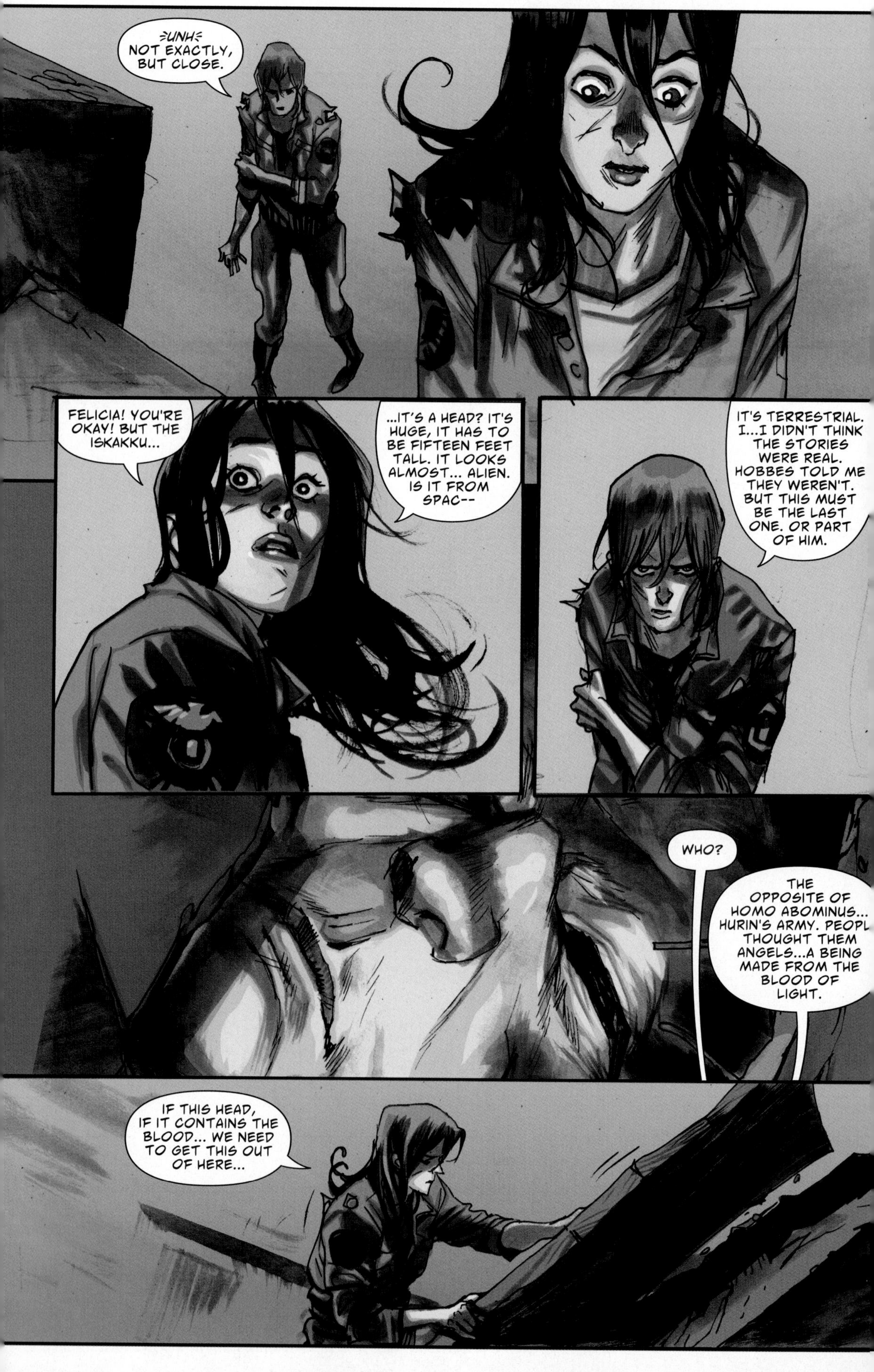

UNH
NOT EXACTLY, BUT CLOSE.
FELICIA! YOU'RE OKAY! BUT THE ISKAKKU...
...IT'S A HEAD? IT'S HUGE, IT HAS TO BE FIFTEEN FEET TALL. IT LOOKS ALMOST... ALIEN. IS IT FROM SPAC--
IT'S TERRESTRIAL. I...I DIDN'T THINK THE STORIES WERE REAL. HOBBES TOLD ME THEY WEREN'T. BUT THIS MUST BE THE LAST ONE. OR PART OF HIM.
WHO?
THE OPPOSITE OF HOMO ABOMINUS... HURIN'S ARMY. PEOPL THOUGHT THEM ANGELS...A BEING MADE FROM THE BLOOD OF LIGHT.
IF THIS HEAD, IF IT CONTAINS THE BLOOD... WE NEED TO GET THIS OUT OF HERE...

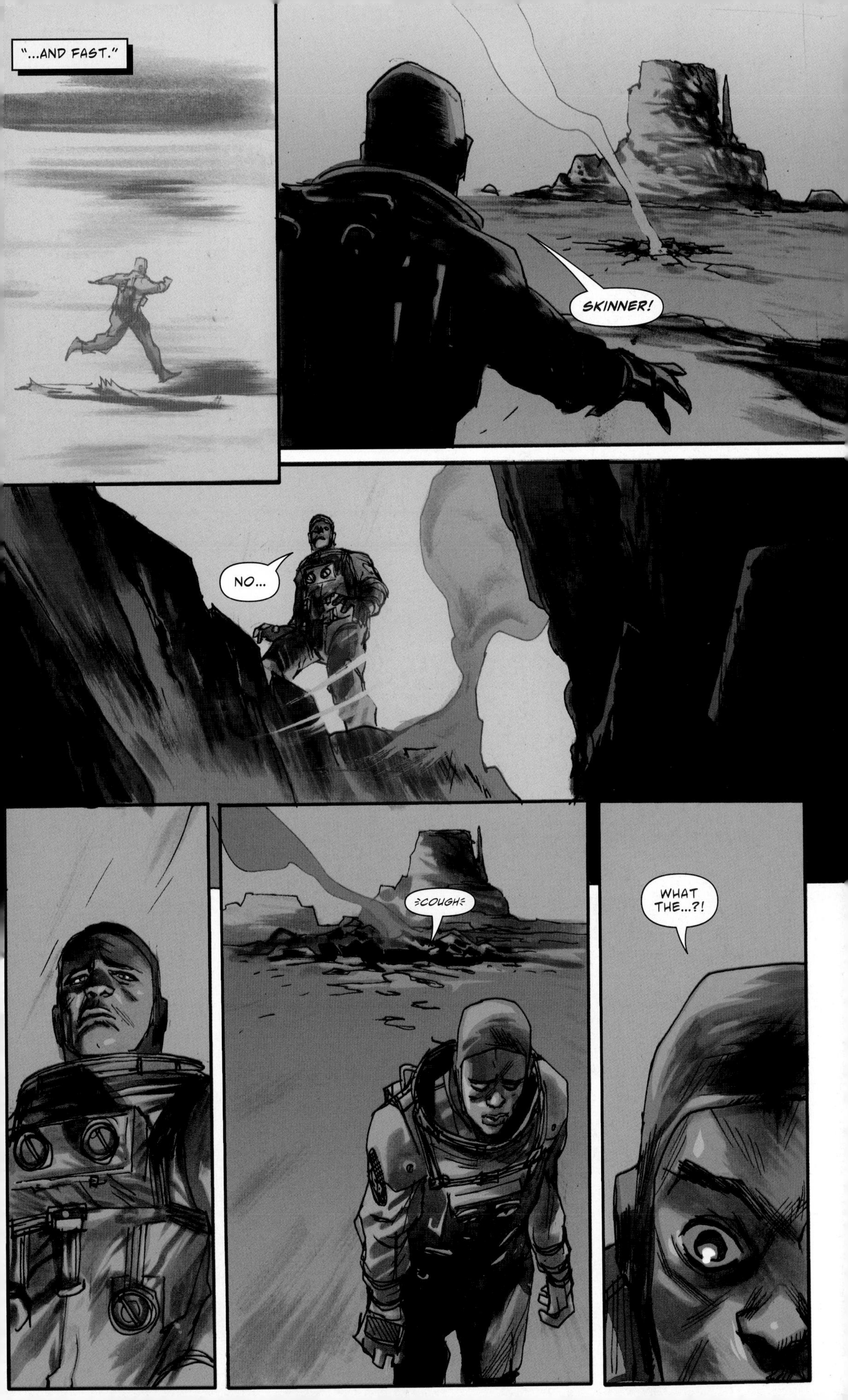
"...AND FAST."
SKINNER!
NO...
COUGH
WHAT THE...?!

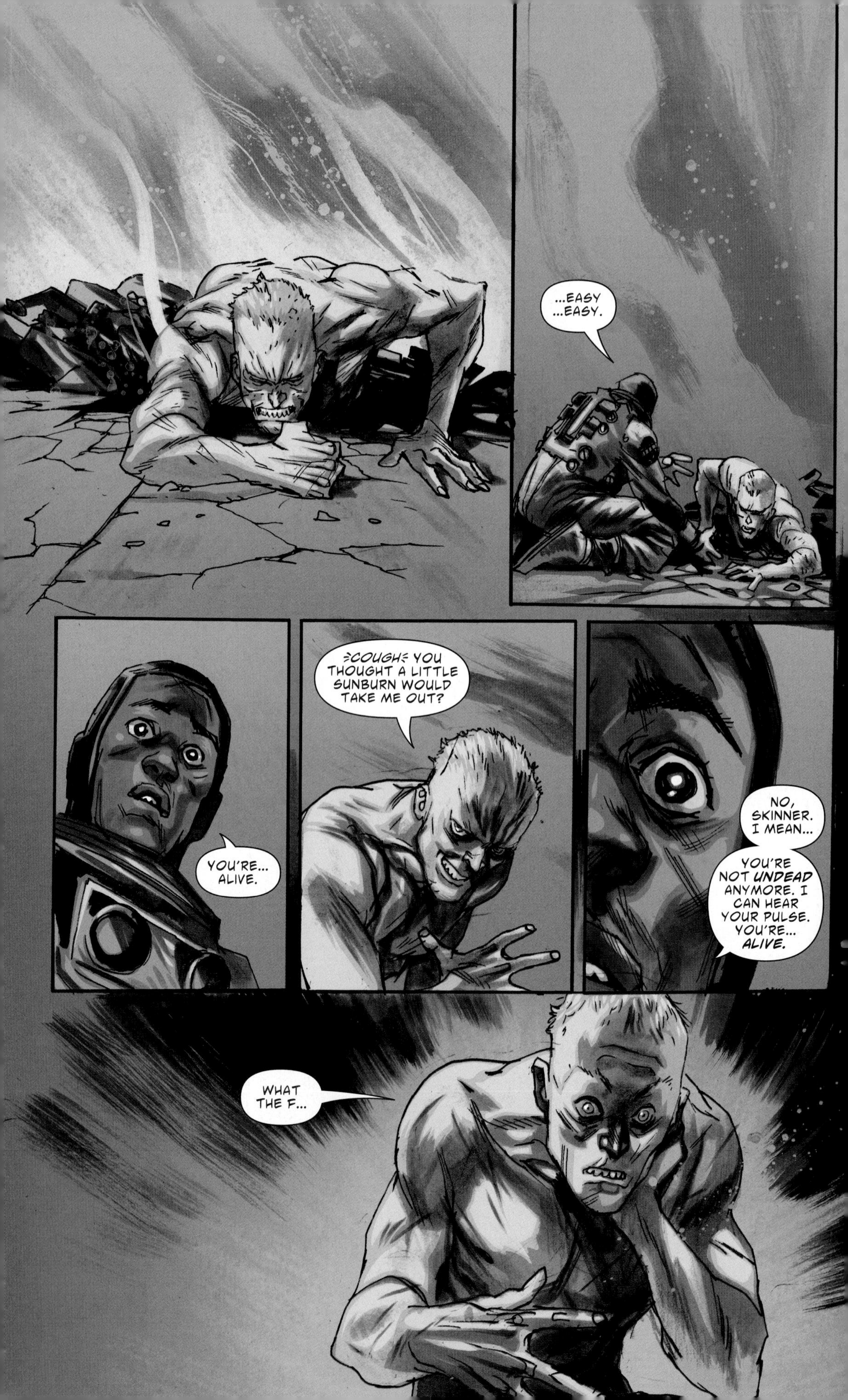
...EASY
...EASY.
YOU'RE... ALIVE.
=COUGH= YOU THOUGHT A LITTLE SUNBURN WOULD TAKE ME OUT?
NO, SKINNER. I MEAN...
YOU'RE NOT *UNDEAD* ANYMORE. I CAN HEAR YOUR PULSE. YOU'RE... ***ALIVE.***
WHAT THE F...

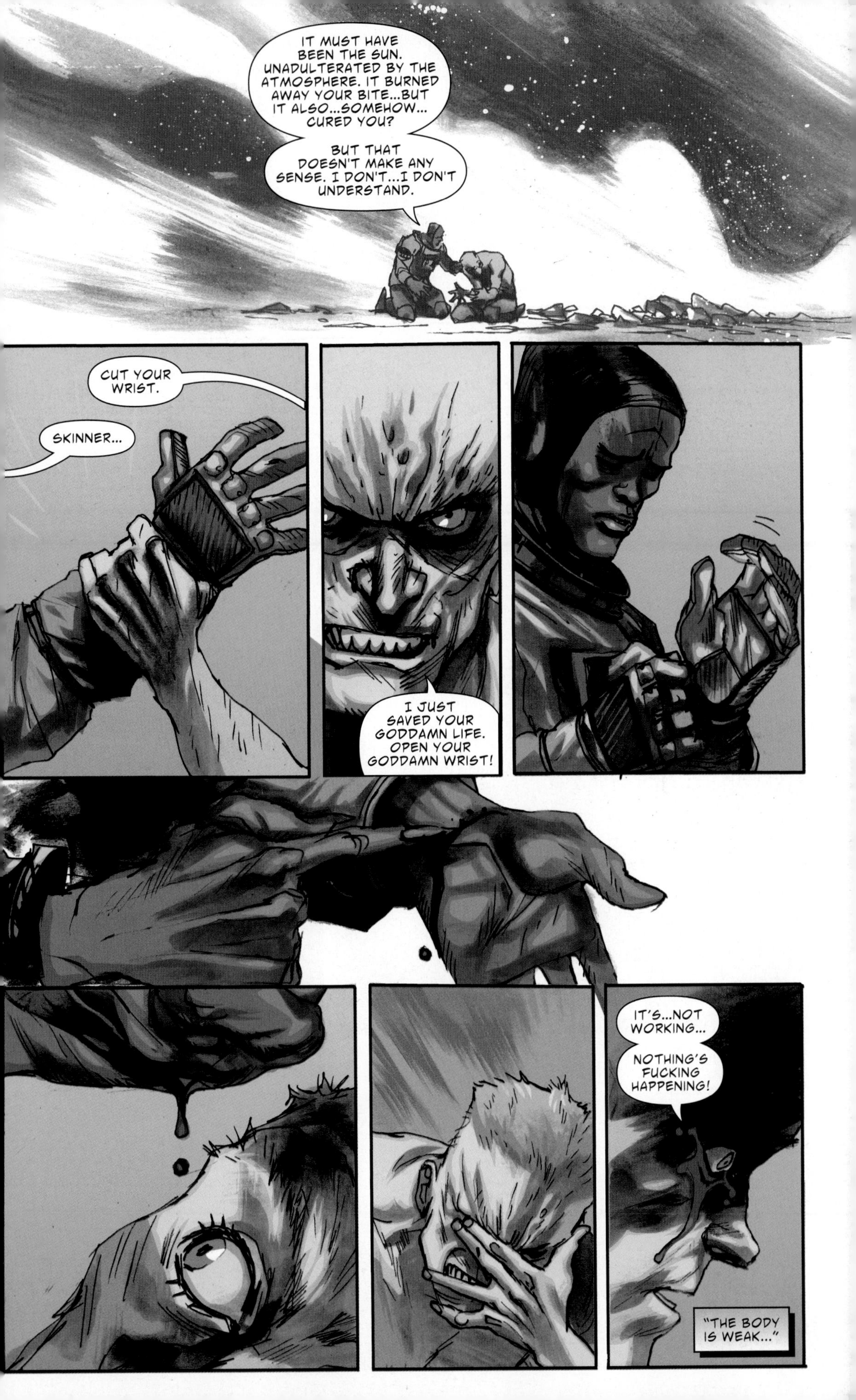
IT MUST HAVE BEEN THE SUN. UNADULTERATED BY THE ATMOSPHERE. IT BURNED AWAY YOUR BITE...BUT IT ALSO...SOMEHOW... CURED YOU?
BUT THAT DOESN'T MAKE ANY SENSE. I DON'T...I DON'T UNDERSTAND.
CUT YOUR WRIST.
SKINNER...
I JUST SAVED YOUR GODDAMN LIFE. OPEN YOUR GODDAMN WRIST!
IT'S...NOT WORKING...
NOTHING'S FUCKING HAPPENING!
"THE BODY IS WEAK..."

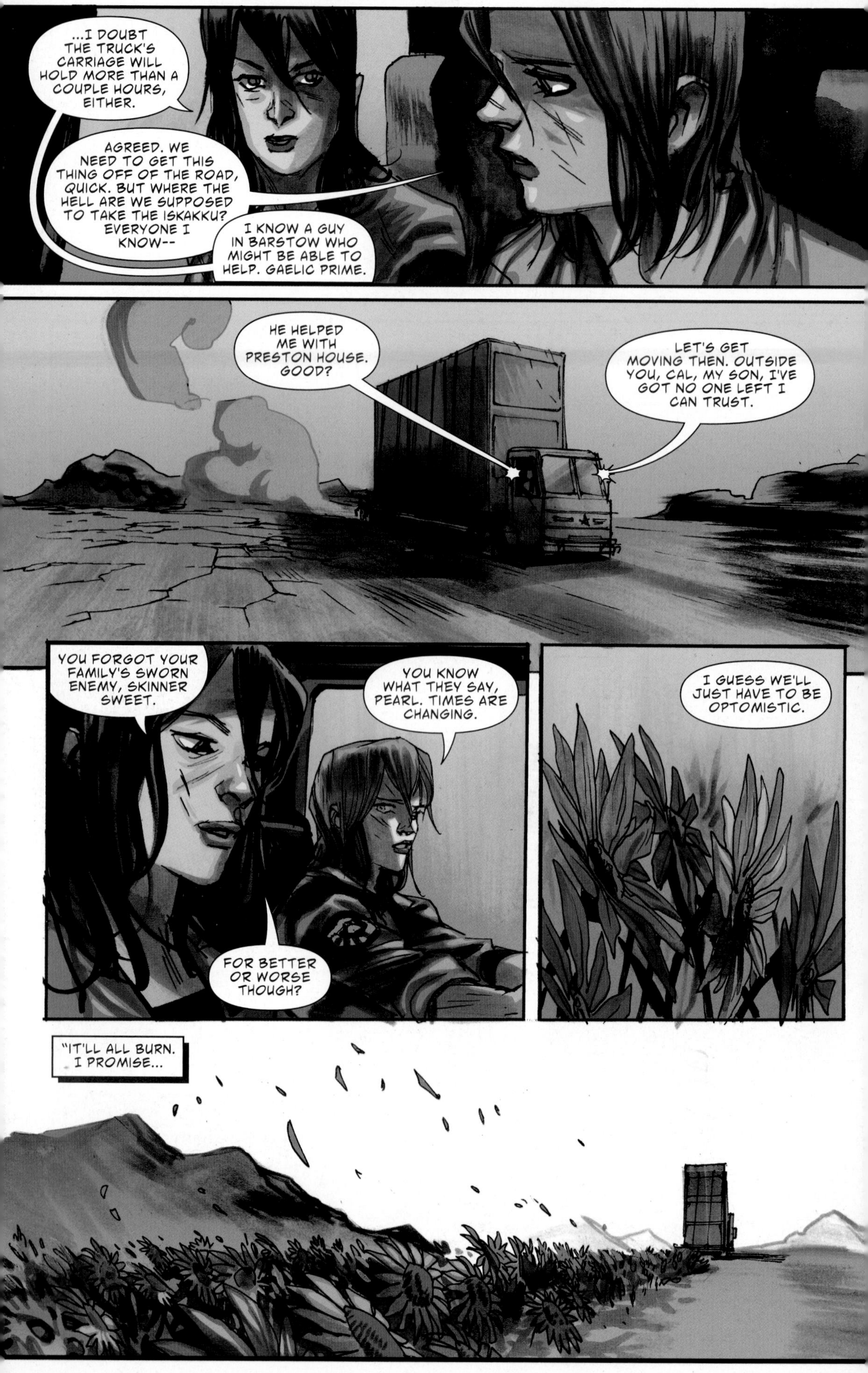
...I DOUBT THE TRUCK'S CARRIAGE WILL HOLD MORE THAN A COUPLE HOURS, EITHER.
AGREED. WE NEED TO GET THIS THING OFF OF THE ROAD, QUICK. BUT WHERE THE HELL ARE WE SUPPOSED TO TAKE THE ISKAKKU? EVERYONE I KNOW--
I KNOW A GUY IN BARSTOW WHO MIGHT BE ABLE TO HELP. GAELIC PRIME.
HE HELPED ME WITH PRESTON HOUSE. GOOD?
LET'S GET MOVING THEN. OUTSIDE YOU, CAL, MY SON, I'VE GOT NO ONE LEFT I CAN TRUST.
YOU FORGOT YOUR FAMILY'S SWORN ENEMY, SKINNER SWEET.
YOU KNOW WHAT THEY SAY, PEARL. TIMES ARE CHANGING.
FOR BETTER OR WORSE THOUGH?
I GUESS WE'LL JUST HAVE TO BE OPTOMISTIC.
"IT'LL ALL BURN. I PROMISE...

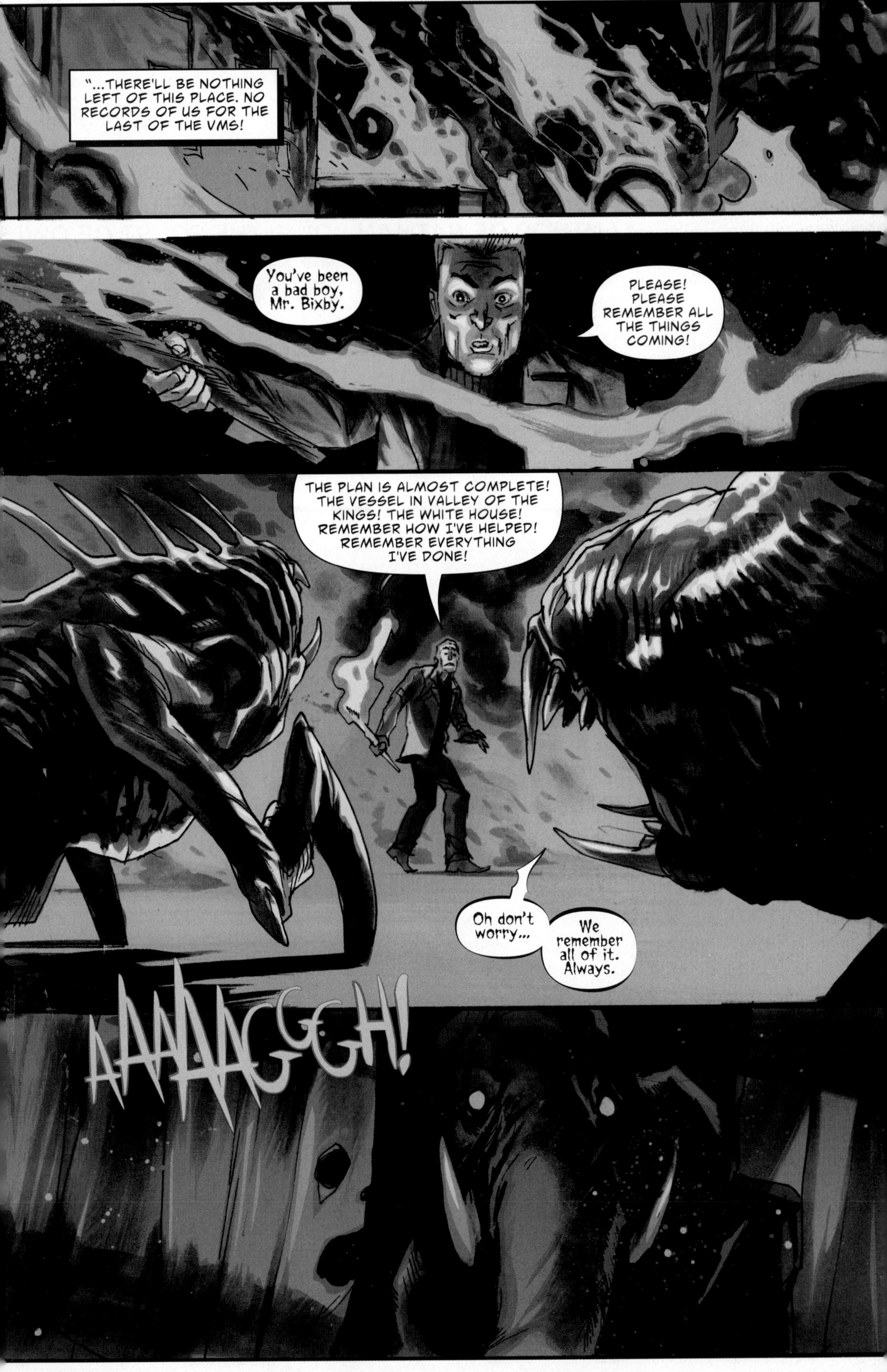
"...THERE'LL BE NOTHING LEFT OF THIS PLACE. NO RECORDS OF US FOR THE LAST OF THE VMS!
You've been a bad boy, Mr. Bixby.
PLEASE! PLEASE REMEMBER ALL THE THINGS COMING!
THE PLAN IS ALMOST COMPLETE! THE VESSEL IN VALLEY OF THE KINGS! THE WHITE HOUSE! REMEMBER HOW I'VE HELPED! REMEMBER EVERYTHING I'VE DONE!
Oh don't worry...
We remember all of it. Always.
AAAAAGGGH!